Economic Thought in Modern China

In this major new study, Margherita Zanasi argues that basic notions of a free-market economy emerged in China a century and half earlier than in Europe. In response to the commercial revolutions of the late 1500s, Chinese intellectuals and officials called for the end of state intervention in the market, recognizing its power to self-regulate. They also noted the elasticity of domestic demand and production, arguing in favor of ending long-standing rules against luxury consumption, an idea that emerged in Europe in the late seventeenth and early nineteenth centuries. Zanasi challenges Eurocentric theories of economic modernization as well as the assumption that European Enlightenment thought was unique in its ability to produce innovative economic ideas. She instead establishes a direct connection between observations of local economic conditions and the formulation of new theories, revealing the unexpected flexibility of the Confucian tradition and its accommodation of seemingly unorthodox ideas.

MARGHERITA ZANASI is Associate Professor of Chinese History at Louisiana State University.

Economic Thought in Modern China

Market and Consumption, c. 1500–1937

MARGHERITA ZANASI
Louisiana State University

CAMBRIDGE
UNIVERSITY PRESS

CAMBRIDGE
UNIVERSITY PRESS

University Printing House, Cambridge CB2 8BS, United Kingdom

One Liberty Plaza, 20th Floor, New York, NY 10006, USA

477 Williamstown Road, Port Melbourne, VIC 3207, Australia

314–321, 3rd Floor, Plot 3, Splendor Forum, Jasola District Centre, New Delhi – 110025, India

79 Anson Road, #06–04/06, Singapore 079906

Cambridge University Press is part of the University of Cambridge.

It furthers the University's mission by disseminating knowledge in the pursuit of education, learning, and research at the highest international levels of excellence.

www.cambridge.org
Information on this title: www.cambridge.org/9781108499934
DOI: 10.1017/9781108752787

First published 2020

Printed in the United Kingdom by TJ International Ltd, Padstow Cornwall

A catalogue record for this publication is available from the British Library.

ISBN 978-1-108-49993-4 Hardback

For Maria and Bob

Contents

Maps

Acknowledgments

No book is ever written in isolation and without the help of a number of colleagues and friends. This book is no exception. I could not have written it without the generous help of those who have advised and commented on this project since its inception. Among them are the members of a panel at a meeting of the Association for Asian Studies – Helen Dunstan, Peter Perdue, and Dai Yicong – who read an early paper related to the topic of this book and offered feedback that proved vital for pointing my research in the right direction. Other presentations of papers related to this book project generated further useful comments, including those offered by Philip Brown, Emma Rothschild, Christopher Reed, Paules Xavier, and Mark Metzler. I was also lucky to be able to rely on Ari Levine's expertise in Song history. He generously found time in his busy schedule to read the first chapter and help me better understand the Song philosophical and political environment. More support came from one of the always interesting and stimulating meetings of the writing group in my own department, the Department of History at Louisiana State University. It was in this context that my colleagues Aaron Sheehan-Dean, Cristine Kooi, Leslie Tuttle, Paul Paskoff, Paul Hoffman, and Meredith Veldman read sections of the book and offered insightful comments. I also wish to extend my thanks to Wu Jen-shu, who read and commented on an early version of an article that ended up forming a large portion of Chapter 2. I was fortunate to be able to draw on his expertise in the history of Ming–Qing consumption culture. Peter Carroll also read and commented on portions of the manuscript. I am also grateful to Wu Jingjie for his kind assistance with bibliographic matters during my research trip to Academia Sinica. A special mention goes to Parks Coble, who over the years has offered invaluable support and mentoring. On this occasion, too, he read my manuscript and shared his vast knowledge of the economic history of modern China. To this long list,

I need to add my longtime mentor and friend Madeleine Zelin, who has read and supported my work since I was a graduate student.

If no book could be written without the help of colleagues and friends, it could also never develop without the support of grants. I am, therefore, very grateful to the Center for Chinese Studies (National Central Library in Taipei), the National Endowment for the Humanities, the Institute of Advanced Studies in Princeton, the Fulbright Foundation, and the Atlas Foundation. They made research trips in both the People's Republic of China and Taiwan possible and gave me time free from teaching to process sources and to write.

My heartfelt thanks also go to the staff of Shanghai Library, the libraries of the Institute of Modern History and the Institute of History and Philosophy at Academia Sinica, and the East Asia Library at Columbia University, as well as to the indefatigable staff of LSU Interlibrary Loan Services (on which I rely heavily) for their patience and help.

I also consider myself very lucky to have been able to rely on the thoughtful and constructive comments of the two anonymous readers who reviewed my book manuscript for Cambridge University Press. My sincere gratitude also goes to Lucy Rymer, James Baker, and Natasha Whelan at Cambridge University Press, who guided me expertly through the review and production processes. Finally, I want to thank Gregory Epp for his careful copy-editing and for making my non-native English look good.

Chronology

Dynastic Timeline

Dynasty	Dates
Xia	c. 2100–1600 BCE
Shang	1600–1050 BCE
Western Zhou	1046–771 BCE
Eastern Zhou	
Spring and Autumn period	771–475 BCE
Warring States period	475–221 BCE
Qin	221–206 BCE
Former Han	206 BCE –9 CE
Xin	9–24 CE
Later Han	25–220 CE
Three Kingdoms period	220–280 CE
Western Jin	265–420 CE
Eastern Jin	317–420 CE
Southern and Northern Dynasties	420–588 CE
Sui	581–617 CE
Tang	618–907 CE
Five Dynasties	907–960 CE
Ten Kingdoms	907–979 CE
Song	
Northern Song	960–1127 CE
Southern Song	1127–1279 CE
Liao	916–1125 CE
Western Xia	1038–1227 CE
Yuan	1279–1368 CE
Ming	1368–1644 CE
Qing	1644–1911 CE
Republic of China (in Mainland China)	1911–1949 CE

Emperors of the Qing Dynasty

Reign Name	Dates of Reign
Shunzhi	1644–1661
Kangxi	1661–1722
Yongzheng	1722–1735
Qianlong	1735–1796
Jiaqing	1796–1820
Daoguang	1820–1850
Xianfeng	1850–1861
Tongzhi	1861–1875
Guangxu	1875–1908
Xuantong (Pu Yi)	1908–1912

Maps

Map 1 The maximum extent of the Qing Empire, c. 1780.

Map by Tracey Ellen Smith for Harold M. Tanner, China: A History, 2009. Reprinted here, with modifications, by permission of Hackett Publishing Company, Inc.

Map 2 The Jiangnan Region during the Qing Empire

Introduction

This book explores the evolution of Chinese economic thought from the late Ming and Qing periods (1500s–1911) through the first two decades of the Republic (1912–1930s). It focuses on the debates over the two closely related ideas of market and consumption in order to understand Chinese officials' and intellectuals' perceptions of their roles in the economy of the empire – or, after 1912, in that of the Republic. The results of this study challenge the chronological and spatial narrative of global economic modernization in two main ways. First, the study locates in China, rather than in Europe, the earliest formulations of the ideas of a self-regulating market and consumption-driven economy. This point is not intended to initiate a competition regarding who was first to generate theories that were to play a crucial role in the development of economic liberalism in eighteenth-century Europe, but to emphasize the ability of regions other than Western Europe to think about the economy in innovative ways in response to changing circumstances. Second, this study challenges the neoliberal narrative of economic modernization as a march toward increased reliance on an unregulated market. This highly ideologized narrative of developmental determinism mythologizes the power of the unregulated market as the main engine for economic development regardless of historical and geopolitical circumstances.[1] China offers a case against this form of determinism. As discussed in Chapter 3, starting from the 1800s China's particular geopolitical and historical circumstances appeared to most Chinese officials and intellectuals to require a retreat from earlier pro-market policies and inspired them to attempt the realization of a hybrid system that combined reliance on market forces with targeted state

[1] The term "developmental determinism" refers to the notion of a universally valid linear path to modernity based on the Western European countries' experience of industrialization.

intervention as the most efficient model for addressing China's specific needs.

This is a study of economic ideas, and not of China's economic conditions. I have chosen to focus on the intellectual discourse on the economy in order to highlight the importance of the complex relationship between, on the one hand, local circumstances and, on the other hand, how economic thinkers understood them and what solutions they proposed for perceived problems. Using this approach, this book reveals that in the mid-1500s, in response to changes in the economy triggered by a commercial revolution comparable to that which began in late seventeenth-century Europe, Chinese officials and philosophers developed the new notion that luxury consumption played a positive role in the economy. By this time, the idea that private interests acting in direct competition in the market could regulate prices efficiently and ensure a smooth flow of resources through the empire had also found a large number of supporters. In other words, in response to the onset of the commercial revolution, two notions central to the development of economic liberalism – the self-regulating market and the power of consumption to stimulate the economy – were already part of China's economic discourse more than a century before they emerged in the European intellectual landscape.

Different circumstances, however, determined the different development of pro-market and pro-consumption ideas in Europe and China. In the 1800s, when Europe was at the height of its commercial revolution, China witnessed the beginning of an economic decline that would plague the country right through the 1930s, bringing to an end the "prosperous age" (*shengshi*) that had characterized the first half of the Qing Dynasty (1644–1911). In response to this decline, Chinese officials and intellectuals reverted to favoring frugal consumption and state intervention in the market, motivated by their concerns about the impact of unprecedentedly fast population growth on dwindling economic resources and about the widening gap between the predominantly rural hinterland and highly commercialized areas such as Jiangnan (the area around the lower reaches of the Yangzi River and along the southern portion of the Grand Canal; see Map 2). It was, therefore, precisely at the time when pro-market and pro-consumption ideas began to merge into the new ideology of economic liberalism in Europe that China moved away from them.

The early nineteenth-century return to frugality and state intervention in China, however, should be seen not as a "failure" to take the next step in building a full-fledged liberal economic system and move toward a market-based model of modernization – as developmental determinism would have it – but as a response to economic circumstances that differed greatly from those of Western Europe. As European observers including the French economist François Quesnay (1694–1774) and the Scottish philosopher Adam Smith (1723–90) remarked, China's size and population were unmatched by any European country and its "home market" was "not much inferior to the market of all the different countries of Europe put together."[2] While these observations were intended to highlight positive aspects of China's economy and geopolitics, they overlapped remarkably with the features that Chinese officials and intellectuals perceived not as assets but as liabilities. Qing thinkers, in fact, saw the size of the population and of the country as, respectively, a severe drain on resources and an obstacle to the successful integration of the vast domestic economy. The question therefore arises as to whether, in China's particular situation, a system emphasizing the free market at the expense of institutional intervention would have halted the economic decline that began in 1800,[3] or whether more interventionist policies would have been a wiser response to China's specific circumstances. In the words of Tamara Chin, we should "de-parochialize Eurocentric histories of economic thought" and question the validity of their models when "divorced from their … historical contexts." We should also avoid thinking of early non-Western economic concepts "as immature 'proto' theories" of theories later developed in Europe.[4] Chinese pro-market and pro-consumption notions, in fact, were not proto-liberal ideas that should have matured into a Western-style liberal ideology; they were instead pragmatic policies employed ad hoc for solving targeted problems and were no longer

[2] Giovanni Arrighi, *Adam Smith in Beijing: Lineages of the Twenty-First Century* (London; New York, NY: Verso, 2008), 3–4.

[3] For an in-depth discussion of the difference in circumstances between Western Europe and China see Kenneth Pomeranz, *The Great Divergence: China, Europe, and the Making of the Modern World Economy* (Princeton, NJ: Princeton University Press, 2000).

[4] Tamara T. Chin, *Savage Exchange: Han Imperialism, Chinese Literary Style, and the Economic Imagination* (Cambridge, MA: Harvard-Yenching Institute, 2014), 33.

favored when new circumstances and problems appeared to require different solutions. China's experience, therefore, differs significantly from that of Europe, where economic liberalism became a powerful ideology and an all-encompassing system – at least in theory – that came to justify, if not completely inform, domestic policies and imperialist expansion.

Finally, the nineteenth-century debates on frugality and state intervention can help explain the Chinese government's reluctance to fully embrace a Western-style free-market system in the modern and contemporary period, a reluctance that goes beyond Communist ideology. Despite the sweeping changes that marked nineteenth- and twentieth-century China, basic geopolitical and economic features that emerged in the mid-Qing – such as population growth, economic scarcity, and the coastal–hinterland gap – continued to work against the full adoption of this model, even after it was introduced into China as the epitome of economic modernization with the arrival of Western imperialism in the mid-nineteenth century. We see, instead, the emergence of a hybrid market structure that attempted to synthesize "the global expansion of the Western system" with a variety of statist policies for pursuing China-centered goals and needs.[5]

I want to emphasize that by tracing the sources of China's difficult relations with the Western-style free market in the modern and contemporary period I am *not* arguing that China exhibited a long-term authoritarian tradition determined by its political heritage or by its economic or geopolitical structure. Late Qing and early Republican officials and intellectuals did not face a choice between two starkly opposed economic models: a liberal one and an authoritarian one marked by state control. Their choice of state intervention was not a precursor to the post-1935 Fascist military corporativism of the Nationalist Government (1927–49) or to the realization of a Communist economy attempted during the Mao period (1949–76). Instead, they were attempting to build a hybrid form of market economy with ad hoc government intervention, which more closely resembled forms of developmental state and was intended to solve the

[5] Giovanni Arrighi, *Adam Smith in Beijing*, 8, 9. According to Arrighi, the Chinese economy will become even more hybridized with the diminishing "relevance of the Western system of states" that will mark the end of the American century.

China-specific threats of scarcity and, after the mid-1800s, of imperialist interference.

The Debate on China's Economic Modernization: Eurocentrism and Problems with Comparison and Terminology

The last few decades have witnessed significant changes in the historical debate on economic modernization in China. Historians have focused their attention on reformulating the problem of "the great divergence," an expression historian Kenneth Pomeranz uses to indicate the different economic paths pursued by Europe and China during the nineteenth century. Historiography before the 1990s tended to characterize the path taken by the "advanced" Western European nations as one of "modernity" and that taken by "*all* other parts of the world" as one of "backwardness" and stagnation.[6] To counteract this Eurocentric and outdated interpretation of this "divergence," a wave of new studies on the economic history of Qing China has brought to light the vitality of the imperial Chinese economy as well as the creativity, pragmatism, and rationality of economic actors at the levels of both state and society, all of which are elements generally associated with Western economic modernity.[7]

Because it is generally believed that the decline of state intervention in the market played a crucial role in the emergence of economic modernity in Europe, several historians of China have tried to prove that Qing officials and emperors also came increasingly to rely on market networks to carry out important economic functions, including solving currency issues, distributing basic staples such as grains throughout the empire, and supplying and financing the imperial

[6] Kenneth Pomeranz, *The Great Divergence*, 4. For a discussion of these historiographical trends see Paul A. Cohen, *Discovering History in China: American Historical Writing on the Recent Chinese Past* (New York, NY: Columbia University Press, 2010).

[7] Among recent publications that have contributed to a more positive understanding of the economy in Qing China are Madeleine Zelin, *The Merchants of Zigong: Industrial Entrepreneurship in Early Modern China* (New York, NY: Columbia University Press, 2008); Jane Kate Leonard and John R. Watt, *To Achieve Security and Wealth: The Qing Imperial State and the Economy, 1644–1911* (Ithaca, NY: East Asia Program, Cornell University, 1993); William T. Rowe, *Saving the World: Chen Hongmou and Elite Consciousness in Eighteenth-Century China* (Stanford, CA: Stanford University Press, 2002).

army.[8] Other historical works have directly compared the supposedly stagnant late-imperial Chinese economy with that of Europe in the eighteenth and nineteenth centuries. Kenneth Pomeranz and Roy Bin Wong, among others, have argued that, on the eve of the Industrial Revolution, China enjoyed similar, if not better, standards of living and economic circumstances than England. Pomeranz's studies have also proved that the English developmental experience can be considered an exception, the product of extraordinary circumstances that allowed that country to break away from the constraints experienced by the rest of the world. This point is also clearly argued by the late historian Joyce Appleby, who, in taking a global approach to the history of industrialization, has stressed the almost accidental nature of the series of events that led to the English Industrial Revolution. In this context, Appleby has urged historians not to ask why other countries did not industrialize, but to ask why and how England was able to do so.[9]

These works have greatly eroded the Eurocentrism of previous historical approaches and have saved late-imperial China from negative representations that wrongly depicted the period as one of Confucian immobility, incompetent rule, and general decline. They have also revealed China's participation in and contribution to worldwide historical developments, avoiding a return to an excessive focus on domestic factors (China's exceptionality) and freeing Chinese history from the pigeonhole of Sinology, a highly specialized and isolated subfield. In general, these historians have contributed significantly to

[8] See, among some of the most recent publications in this area, Helen Dunstan, *State or Merchant: Political Economy and Political Process in 1740s China* (Cambridge, MA: Harvard University Press, 2006); Lillian M. Li, *Fighting Famine in North China: State, Market, and Environmental Decline, 1690s–1990s* (Stanford, CA: Stanford University Press, 2007); Lin Man-Houng, *China Upside Down: Currency, Society, and Ideologies, 1808–1856* (Cambridge, MA: Harvard University Asia Center, 2006); Pierre-Etienne Will and Roy Bin Wong, *Nourish the People: The State Civilian Granary System in China, 1650–1850* (Ann Arbor, MI: Center for Chinese Studies, University of Michigan, 1991); Dai Yingcong, "Yingyung Shengxi: Military Entrepreneurship in the High Qing Period, 1700–1800," *Late Imperial China* 2 (2005), 1–67, and "The Qing State, Merchants, and the Military Labor Force in the Jinchuan Campaigns," *Late Imperial China* 2 (2001), 35–90.

[9] Pomeranz, *The Great Divergence*; Roy Bin Wong, *China Transformed: Historical Change and the Limits of European Experience* (Ithaca, NY: Cornell University Press, 2000); Joyce Appleby, *The Relentless Revolution: A History of Capitalism* (New York, NY: W. W. Norton & Co., 2011).

the generation of a more accurate understanding of the characteristics and functioning of the Chinese economy in the Qing period.

"Provincializing Europe," however, has proved an arduous task, Eurocentrism being more resilient than expected.[10] As historian Lillian Li observes, in responding to earlier Western-centered negative interpretations of the Chinese economy, studies have counteracted each criticism one by one, proving, for example, that rationality or growth existed where it had not been detected before. In their point-by-point refutation of negative comparisons of China with the West, however, they have ultimately perpetuated a narrative of change that is based mostly on the Western experience.[11] Economic historian Richard von Glahn takes a position similar to Li's. He argues that the recent works challenging the linear, Western-centered modernization approach have focused almost exclusively on "particular institutions and quantitative measurement," thus "los[ing] sight of the Chinese economy as a whole" and of the specific context of Chinese economic history. Von Glahn thus questions the main tenet of the modernization paradigm, the notion, central to neoclassical economics, that "the market is *the* driving force in economic development and the creation of wealth." The excessive attention paid by recent studies to the market, he argues, "has obscured the impact of other institutions ... in promoting economic development."[12]

Persistent difficulties in approaching the issue of economic change in China without relying on the European experience are also in large part the result of a general lack of understanding of Chinese economic ideas and vocabulary. It is for this reason that we tend to turn automatically to the language, elements, and categories of modern Western economics. In this context, one of my main goals in this book is to excavate basic economic terminology, issues, and tropes that are crucial for understanding the late-imperial discourse on the economy. For example, the use of the term "consumption" – which is

[10] Dipesh Chakrabarty, *Provincializing Europe: Postcolonial Thought and Historical Difference* (Princeton, NJ, and Oxford: Princeton University Press, 2008).

[11] Li, *Fighting Famine in North China*, 9–10. Li refers specifically to Wong's *China Transformed*, Pomeranz's *Great Divergence*, and Andre Gunder Frank's *ReOrient: Global Economy in the Asian Age* (Berkeley, CA: University of California Press, 2008).

[12] Richard von Glahn, *The Economic History of China: From Antiquity to the Nineteenth Century* (Cambridge: Cambridge University Press, 2016), 6, 7–8.

loaded with conceptual implications strictly linked to the liberal market economy, especially regarding the relationship between "demand" and production – does not really help us to understand the Chinese historical discourse on this economic function. That discourse developed around different concepts, in particular, those of "frugality" (*jian*) and "luxury" (*shechi*). The two terms expressed different levels of consumption in relation to the availability and distribution of resources. Although these notions were closely entwined with the Confucian moral values of virtue and debauchery, respectively, their use did not prevent the formulation of pragmatic economic ideas. This was not a peculiarity of China. Across regional boundaries, notions of frugality became interwoven with dominant religious and ethical discourses while also responding to changes in the economy. In seventh-century Arabia, for example, in response to a rapidly urbanizing and commercializing society, the Qur'an used religious language to address problems of wealth distribution, the morality of wealth, and sociopolitical stability.[13] In the same vein, late-medieval European intellectuals articulated their debate on consumption in Christian terms. Like their Arab counterparts, they used religious language to consider the circulation of goods and hoarding as well as the relationships between wealth and morality and between the accumulation of wealth and the plight of the poor.[14] Analyzing these economic discourses through the lens of our contemporary economic vocabulary can be very misleading, blinding us to the fact that, despite their use of distinctive religious and cultural tropes and terminology – which today we tend to dismiss as unspecialized or unscientific – these economic debates addressed economic issues in a pragmatic and competent way.[15]

[13] Michael Bonner, "Poverty and Economics in the Qur'an," *Journal of Interdisciplinary History* 3 (2005), 391–406.

[14] Giacomo Todeschini, "Theological Roots of the Medieval/Modern Merchants' Self-Representation," in *The Self-Perception of Early Modern Capitalists*, ed. by Margaret C. Jacob and Catherine Secretan (New York, NY: Palgrave Macmillan, 2008), 17–48, and *Franciscan Wealth: From Voluntary Poverty to Market Society*, ed. by Michael F. Cusato, Jean François Godet-Calogeras, and Daria Mitchell (Saint Bonaventure, NY: Franciscan Institute, Saint Bonaventure University, 2009).

[15] Bonner, "Poverty and Economics in the Qur'an," 391–406; Faith Ermis, *A History of Ottoman Economic Thought: Developments before the Nineteenth Century* (Abingdon and New York, NY: Routledge, 2014).

Industrious Economies, New Luxury, and the Long Consumption Revolution

As argued earlier, new economic ideas generally emerge in response to evolving circumstances, as they both generate new problems and appear to create new solutions for old dilemmas. In China, for example, the mid-1500s commercial revolution challenged the notion of the empire's limited and finite economic resources and offered new solutions for maximizing production and distribution. The notion that a country's economic resources were fixed and finite was common among most premodern agricultural societies worldwide, being rooted in the idea that wealth rested on agricultural production and was thus limited by the amount and quality of the land.[16] This idea generated a perennial state of anxiety among both rulers and the people at large, as the dividing line between survival and death was very fine. One year of failing crops could usher in a devastating famine.[17] In this context, frugal consumption – with the twin aims of avoiding the exhaustion of resources and allowing for some degree of storage – appeared to be the best approach to preventing disaster.

In Europe, the idea of fixed and limited resources began to be challenged with the advent of what historian Jan de Vries in his study of European consumer culture between 1650 and 1850 defines as the "Industrious Revolution." In this period, he explains, the agricultural sector began to generate surplus through labor-intensive techniques adopted in an attempt to boost production in support of population growth. This surplus contributed to an increase in the amount of goods circulating on the market. The new material abundance, and the new market opportunities it generated, induced households "to relocate their productive resources ... in ways that increased *both* the supply of market-oriented, money-earning activities *and* the demand for goods offered in the marketplace. Increased production specialization in the household gave access to augmented consumption choices in the marketplace."[18] According to de Vries, this period was marked by the

[16] S. Todd Lowry, *Pre-Classical Economic Thought: From the Greeks to the Scottish Enlightenment* (Boston, MA: Kluwer, 1995), 3.

[17] Appleby, *Relentless Revolution*, 5–6.

[18] Jan de Vries, *The Industrious Revolution: Consumer Behavior and the Household Economy, 1650 to the Present* (Cambridge: Cambridge University Press, 2009), 10.

rise of the "New Luxury" form of consumption. The "Old Luxury" mode was generally confined to a small elite and was often a symbol of power, conveying a grandeur that could not be easily emulated. The New Luxury, on the other hand, "striving for more comfort and pleasure, lent itself to multiplication and diffusion" and thus came to involve a larger portion of the population. This new form of luxury came to be seen not as a drain on resources but as a stimulant to the increasingly commercialized economy.[19]

These changes in consumption practices did not amount to a "consumer revolution," a phrase coined to describe the exploding volume of purchased goods that jump-started the growth of production of the Industrial Revolution. Rather, de Vries argues, "an expanded range of goods, and more numerous venues for purchase and consumption, led to the more frequent exercise of individuated choice. Experience and exposure led to an accumulation of consumption capital, consolidating in time the practices of consumption recognizable to us today."[20] In other words, although they did not equal the extent and impact of the consumerist revolution of the industrial age, the industrious economies "should be seen as a jump from an old to a new state, requiring simultaneous changes in the productive organization of the household and its desired 'consumption bundles,'" which now came to include not only essential goods but also goods intended to improve the comfort of family life, which had previously been considered an extravagance.[21]

The notion of Industrious Revolution allows us to deconstruct the myth of the Industrial Revolution as a short-term "revolutionary" change in the modes of production and consumption and to recognize an intermediary moment of growth based on new labor-market relationships and new practices of consumption. It is only at the height of the Industrial Revolution, at the end of the nineteenth century, that we see the development of the notion of an "economy of plenty" that came to characterize consumerism in the post–Industrial Revolution period. In the industrialized world of the late nineteenth and early twentieth centuries, it was widely believed that industrialization had led to the unlimited production of goods, generating unlimited wealth. The

[19] De Vries, *The Industrious Revolution*, 44–45.
[20] De Vries, *The Industrious Revolution*, 122–123.
[21] De Vries, *The Industrious Revolution*, 177.

economy was, therefore, one of unlimited resources, and consistent expansion of consumption was crucial for supporting a corresponding expansion in industrial production. This understanding of economic growth, referred to as "growthism," differs from the ideas of increased production that characterized the Industrious Revolution. Growthism, in fact, identifies the "increase in the total size of the gross domestic product (GDP) of a national economy" as the most important sign of economic success.[22] In this context, consumption loses its more direct objective of meeting the needs of consumers and turns into "consumerism," i.e. the consumption of luxury goods for the primary goal of expanding production (GDP).

These views were accompanied by changes in popular culture and the identification, to use the words of historian Jackson Lears, of the "efficient factory" as the source of a country's wealth.[23] This redefinition equated "plentitude with mass production" while encouraging a materialist narrative of progress based on the acquisition of goods. These "fables of abundance" – popular imagination and expectation of "abundance" often being as important for consumerist culture as the reality on the ground – generated a widespread acceptance of an unprecedented level of consumption of luxury goods and services.[24] Support for consumerism was also rooted in its supposedly mass aspect and its ability to raise the standard of living for the population at large. Consumerism, in fact, rested on both industrial mass production and the development of a consumerist apparatus (from department stores

[22] Historian of Japan Scott O'Bryan uses the term "growthism" to refer to "conceptual frameworks, modes of economic imagination, and political programs" that originated in the late nineteenth and early twentieth centuries. In this period, he argues, the idea of "growth" came to be perceived as the "organizing principle of political economy" and "an analytical paradigm" influencing economic choices around the world in the postwar period and already discernable in the early twentieth century. Scott O'Bryan, *The Growth Idea: Purpose and Prosperity in Postwar Japan* (Honolulu, HI: University of Hawaii Press, 2009), 2.

[23] T. J. Jackson Lears, *Fables of Abundance: A Cultural History of Advertising in America* (New York, NY: Basic Books, 1994), 18. Lears, however, tends to describe the passage from "scarcity" to "abundance" as centered on the Industrial Revolution, ignoring the important role of the Industrious Revolution in redefining the relationship between resources and consumption.

[24] Lears, *Fables of Abundance*, 18; Andrew Gordon, "Consumption, Leisure and the Middle Class in Transwar Japan," *Social Science Japan Journal* 1 (2007), 1–21; Peter N. Stearns, *Consumerism in World History* (London: Routledge, 2006).

and movie theaters to the expansion of credit and of mail-order catalogs) designed to distribute goods widely and to cater to a new high volume of consumption, as well as to the commercialization of the standard of living and leisure time of a large section of the population.[25] Consumerism, therefore, brought consumption to a new level both in terms of what was defined as "luxury" and in terms of its ideological meaning linked to the ideas of progress and modernity. In studying consumption, therefore, it is important to adopt a terminology that reflects three different stages – Old Luxury, New Luxury, and Consumerism – in the long-term process of transformation of its practices presented by de Vries, rather than continuing the narrative of a sudden "revolutionary" shift from the era of scarcity and frugality to one of plenty and mature consumerism as presented by Lears. This distinction is particularly important for understanding market policies in Qing China, a period characterized by an industrious economy and New Luxury trends of consumption in the most commercialized regions of the empire.

As discussed in more detail in Chapter 2, China experienced an Industrious Revolution as early as the mid-1500s. At this time, the Chinese economy presented many traits similar to those discussed by de Vries for Western Europe between 1650 and 1850. Although distant from each other, both geographically and chronologically, these industrious economies shared some crucial factors, including increased productivity, increased availability of consumer goods on the market, the rise and marketization of the service industries (especially in relation to leisure and travel), the expansion of luxury consumption to include the "middle man," the inclusion in daily consumption of what had earlier been considered "superfluous things" (luxury items), and the ability of small businesses (especially manufacturers of luxury goods, shopkeepers, and providers of entertainment and other pleasure activities) to thrive while relying exclusively on expanded market demand.

These comparable circumstances generated comparable perceptions of the workings of the economy in China and in Europe. It was, in fact, in the context of their respective industrious economies that observers in each region began to challenge the notion of limited resources and to propose the idea that market-based luxury consumption could be

[25] Lears, *Fables of Abundance*, 18; Stearns, *Consumerism in World History*.

beneficial for the economy. As discussed in detail in Chapter 3, however, in China the idea that the country was trapped in an "economy of scarcity" proved very resilient and re-emerged with new vigor in the early nineteenth century. Although, by this time, the notion that resources were not naturally fixed and limited and that their production was to some extent elastic had become widely accepted, the fast pace of population growth appeared to place severe stress on the empire's economy, creating a new situation of scarcity. After the Opium War (1839–42), Western-imported liberal notions of market and consumption clashed with this persistent idea of scarce resources and endemic poverty. Although Adam Smith's writing gained widespread attention after the 1901 translation by the prominent scholar Yan Fu (1854–1921) of *The Wealth of Nations* (originally published in 1776), Chinese intellectuals and reformers ultimately rejected some of Smith's ideas for mostly the same reasons that had motivated their mid-Qing counterparts to revive policies of frugality and state intervention. China, they argued, was still fighting scarcity, and thus, its circumstances differed greatly from the economy of abundance of the Western industrialized world. Fully embracing the new Western economic theories, they believed, would not benefit China in its particular economic and political conditions. China had not yet stepped into the era of industrial plenty, they argued; consumerism was not a mass phenomenon raising the standard of living of the population at large but the wasteful practice of a small elite that was undermining nation building. To solve China's scarcity problem, they believed, it was important for the state to intervene to plan both the production and distribution of resources, focusing especially on daily-need items. Relying on an economic system based on market-driven consumerism and catering to luxury consumption would have dire consequences.

Organization of the Book

This book is organized into four chapters. Chapter 1 provides the background for a discussion of Chinese economic thought in the Qing period, introducing its most important ideas, terminology, and tropes. In this context, it stresses the unique centrality of economic issues in imperial politics. It also illustrates how dismissing imperial tropes related to the notion of "nurturing" and "pacifying the people" (*yangmin* and *anmin*) as mere empty rhetoric prevents historians from fully understanding important political and economic objectives of the Chinese imperial government. This chapter also examines the pro-market trends that accompanied the commercial growth of the Song Dynasty – the beginning of a process of commercialization that was to come to maturation in the late Ming and early Qing periods. Chapter 2 focuses on the further expansion in the late Ming and early Qing periods of pro-market trends and the rise of pro-luxury consumption ideas in response to the emerging industrious economy and the New Luxury mode of consumption. In addition to introducing fundamental concepts and developments in Chinese economic thought, these first two chapters illustrate the flexibility of the Confucian discourse on the economy and its ability to adapt to actual changes in the economy of the empire, thereby challenging the common notion that Chinese Confucian ideology led to intellectual immobility.

Chapter 3 examines the early nineteenth-century return of the notion of limited resources and the decline of the idea that market-based luxury consumption could have a positive effect on the economy. It was at this time that population growth, the pressure it exerted on resources, and the rural–coastal gap appeared to require the curbing of luxury consumption – and the market-driven mode of growth it entailed – and a return to state intervention in the production and distribution of resources. Chinese intellectuals and reformers continued to believe in the stimulating power of consumption, but they wanted to channel demand away from luxury goods and deploy it in support of the production of daily-need items as a solution to the poverty crisis. This chapter also discusses the early impact of Western ideas of economic liberalism in the late nineteenth and early twentieth centuries and how these ideas were received by Chinese intellectuals and reformers. The arrival of Western imperialism led to changes in the terminology used by Chinese economic thinkers, although the use of new terms cannot obscure significant continuities in themes and concerns from the earlier period. The most important change brought by Western imperialism was a shift in the main conceptual parameters of the economic discourse from dynastic stability (*anmin*) to defensive nation building (*jianguo*). Pro-frugality policies acquired a new popularity in the context of the confrontation with Western models of evolutionary modernity, the rise of defensive economic nationalism, and the return of the idea of economic scarcity (poverty).

Chapter 4 illustrates the continuing impact of the trends discussed in the previous chapter on the economic and political thought of the 1920s and 1930s and how they led to economic solutions that tended to marginalize the market, including Chiang Kai-shek's New Life Movement (*xinshenghuo yundong*) – a Fascist vision of frugal modernity as a tool for the mobilization of resources – and various projects of economic cooperation (the Cooperative Society Movement, *hezuo shehui yundong*).[26] This period witnessed an intensification of the tension between treaty port consumerist trends and economic decline in the rural hinterland, as well as that between the nation-building perspective of the state – which focused on developing the country as a whole – and the treaty-port-based view of consumerist modernity. In addition, an escalating sense of crisis and of the need for decisive action to save the nation led to particular admiration of Fascist models of a "controlled economy" (*tongzhi jingji*), such as those of Italy, Germany, and Japan.

[26] While I use *pinyin* to transliterate Chinese names, passages, and terminology, for Chiang Kai-shek I maintain the transliteration by which he is more commonly known.

1 *The Political and Intellectual Framework*

The *Minsheng* Mandate and China's Economy of Scarcity

This chapter offers a brief overview of important concepts and terminology related to notions of market and consumption in Chinese economic thought.[*] It also explores a few historical debates to provide a relevant background for understanding the transformation of these notions during the late Ming and Qing periods. These debates highlight the complexity and inherent pragmatism of generations of Chinese economic thinkers and their ability to respond to significant transformations in the economy of the empire. The complexity of Chinese economic thought should not come as a surprise if we consider the importance of economic issues for wider political goals of the imperial state. At the foundation of the imperial Chinese political discourse was the objective of "nurturing the people" (*yangmin*), which derived from the trope of the "Mandate of Heaven" (*tianming*) and its dictate that it was the emperor's paternalistic duty to foster the welfare of the population of the empire. *Yangmin* became a rhetorical pillar of dynastic legitimacy. It also came to constitute the foundation of the empire's stability. It, in fact, incorporated two main economic and political goals: ensuring the people's livelihood (*minsheng*) and promoting virtue among the people (*jiaomin*). The first goal, *minsheng*, was based on the idea that hungry and disgruntled peasants would inevitably stage rebellions and that economic prosperity ensured a stable tax base. In other words, the rhetoric of *minsheng* was tightly intertwined with the political imperatives of "pacifying the people" (*anmin*) and of ensuring fiscal stability. The second prong of the *yangmin* mandate was *jiaomin*, also aimed at social stability. *Jiaomin* – literally, "teaching the people" – mostly consisted of an ideological

[*] This chapter includes sections originally published in Margherita Zanasi, "Frugality and Luxury: Morality, Market, and Consumption in Late Imperial China," *Frontiers of History in China* 10(3) (2015), 457–485.

indoctrination of Confucian principles, such as Filial Piety (*xiao*), considered crucial for preserving social order by inspiring respect for hierarchies based on age, gender, and status.[1] The *yangmin* formula, therefore, indicated a political system focused on economic and social stability, with *minsheng* a prerequisite for the latter, since it assumed that hungry peasants would be less responsive to ideological indoctrination, as the philosopher Mencius (c. 372–c. 289 BCE) famously argued in his often-quoted dialogue with King Hui of Liang: "The people, lacking a constant means of livelihood, will lack constant minds, and when they lack constant minds there is no dissoluteness, depravity, deviance, or excess to which they will not succumb." For the ruler, Mencius continued, it was essential to prioritize food security by promoting among the population such economic activities as the planting of "mulberry-trees," the "raising of chickens, pigs, dogs, and swine," and agricultural "cultivation." Mencius concluded that when a sage governs so that "pulse and grain will be as plentiful as water . . . how could there be any among the people who are not humane."[2] In other words, the "virtuous" – not rebellious – behavior of the peasants relied on their having adequate access to basic food staples and a minimal standard of living.

Although written during the Warring States period (Zhanguo, c. 475–221 BCE), the passage quoted above – together with other similar passages from the Confucian classics – remained an important reference for generations of rulers and thinkers, who freely borrowed, adapted, and reinterpreted them to derive both inspiration and legitimacy. Within the imperial Confucian ideology – in its various philosophical and institutional reinterpretations – the priority of *minsheng* in the *yangmin* formula was rarely challenged. We can find an argument in favor of its demotion during the Song Dynasty (960–1279 BCE). At this time the Neo-Confucian philosopher Cheng Yi (1033–1107) famously stated: "dying of hunger is a trivial matter; losing moral integrity is a serious matter."[3] This statement mostly

[1] Filial Piety is one of the principles at the foundation of Confucius' idea of a harmonious and stable society. It bases social and political stability on the respect of five basic hierarchical relations in society. These are, in order of importance: father and son, older and younger brothers, emperor and minister, husband and wife, friend and friend.

[2] Mencius, Irene Bloom, and P. J. Ivanhoe, *Mencius* (New York, NY: Columbia University Press, 2011), 11–12; 148–149.

[3] Cheng Yi and Cheng Hao, *Ercheng yishu* (Shanghai: Shanghai guji chubanshe, 2000) 356.

addressed the specific issue of female chastity and did not necessarily assume canonical importance within the Song Neo-Confucian system.[4] It nevertheless had the potential to alter the established relationship between a full stomach and any kind of virtue, even that of respecting political and social hierarchies. It was only in the Nationalist period (1927–49), however, that Cheng Yi's statement came to be heavily reinterpreted and fully deployed by the state against the implementation of *minsheng* policies, as discussed in Chapter 4. Until then, this trope consistently expressed the importance of ensuring economic subsistence for the stability of the empire.

The persistent use of the trope of *minsheng* in philosophical texts, memorials written to the throne, and court documents should not be confused with an immutable or monolithic ideology. As this chapter illustrates, while *minsheng* remained a fairly consistent goal of the imperial state – at least at the rhetorical level if not always in practice – the ways to achieve this objective evolved. This mandate, in fact, accommodated diverse economic policies reflecting conflicting ideas of how to realize it. The Confucian rhetorical and philosophical tradition – from which most terms and tropes related to *minsheng* derived – did not prevent a pragmatic understanding of the functioning of the economy; nor did it imply intellectual rigidity. By the time the Qing adopted it, views of how to realize *minsheng* had undergone deep transformations.

Historically, the main challenge to the realization of the *minsheng* mandate was the empire's vulnerability to economic scarcity, an idea articulated through the notion that the resources (wealth, *cai*) of the empire were finite – "the wealth of Heaven and Earth is fixed in amount" (*tian di sheng cai zhi you ci shu*), to use an often-quoted expression of the famous Song Dynasty philosopher and official Sima Guang (1019–86).[5] In China, as in most agrarian economies, this situation of fixed and finite resources influenced government policies on food distribution and consumption. Most premodern European states, for example, acted to prevent extreme economic scarcity, aware

[4] Patricia Buckley Ebrey, *Women and the Family in Chinese History* (London: Routledge, 2005), 12.

[5] Quoted in Paul Jakov Smith, "Shen-Tsung's Reign and the New Policies of Wang An-Shih, 1067–1085," in *The Cambridge History of China*, Vol. 5, Pt. 1, *The Sung Dynasty and Its Precursors, 907–1279*, ed. by Denis Crispin Twitchett and Paul Jakov Smith (New York, NY: Cambridge University Press, 2008), 387.

that it had the potential to severely damage their tax base and generate widespread discontent and uprisings. To counteract the dire consequences of scarcity, they encouraged the storing of surplus for private benefit, regulated prices, attempted to prevent hoarding of basic staples, and limited consumption through sumptuary laws.[6]

Chinese rulers also feared the consequences of economic scarcity and engaged in policies very similar to those adopted by their European counterparts. As historian Lillian Li points out, however, they differed from them in paying particular attention to political economy. In her discussion of Qing famine prevention strategies, she argues that the idea of nurturing the people "played an important ideological role in the formation of state policy and shaping of state goals."[7]

Minsheng: Morality, Ideology, and Pragmatism

The importance of *minsheng* as an essential strategy for a successful ruler went beyond the *yangmin* formula and its implications of Confucian morality. Xunzi (c. 310–c. 235 BCE) – together with Mencius one of the most representative figures of the second generation of Confucian philosophers – while agreeing with Mencius on the importance of *minsheng* for preserving social order, de-emphasized its ability to foster virtue among the population and focused directly on the danger to the state posed by popular discontent. In his discussion of the difference between the Kingly Way (*wangdao*) and Hegemonic Rule (*ba*), for example, Xunzi remarked that those rulers who "in managing the people's livelihood … cause them to be pinched and destitute" will cause "the common folk [to] look down upon them as if they were witches and hate them as if they were ghosts. Every day the common folk desire to find an opening to cast down their rulers, trample them, and drive them out."[8] Mencius' and Xunzi's divergent approaches to *minsheng* were mostly rooted in their opposing views of human nature; for Mencius, human nature was intrinsically inclined to be potentially good, while, for Xunzi, it was inherently selfish. This philosophical disagreement was to become the source of the important dilemma of whether the emperor should rule by nurturing and exemplary virtue

6 Appleby, *The Relentless Revolution*, 5–6.
7 Li, *Fighting Famine in North China*, 2, 4.
8 Xunzi and Eric L. Hutton, *Xunzi: The Complete Text* (Princeton, NJ: Princeton University Press, 2014), 114.

(Mencius' humanist Confucianism) or by imposing laws and punishments on the people (Xunzi's authoritarian Confucianism).[9] Mencius' "virtuous" population – when adequately fed and well indoctrinated in virtue – could properly regulate their social and economic lives without much intervention from the state. This relaxed attitude has often been compared with liberal *laissez faire* policies, although it is more correctly described as a form of humanist paternalism, since the state still played a crucial role in setting the parameters and goals of the societal economy through its moral indoctrination efforts (*jiaomin*) and its focus on *minsheng* objectives. Xunzi's selfish population, on the other hand, was not as malleable and responsive to the teaching of moral principles even when well fed. For this reason, they formed a conflictual and unruly society and needed to be regulated closely by the state through intensive education and institutional restraints.

How deep and wide were the roots of the idea of *minsheng* – especially when detached from the moral ideology of *yangmin* – is illustrated by its appeal across philosophical and political borders. One of the texts that best represents the school of Legalism (*fajia*) and its rejection of Confucian morality, *Guanzi* (seventh century BCE), was also in agreement with the strategic aspects of this policy. In the section devoted to "ruling" (*zhiguo*), this text declares that "those skilled in ruling will first enrich the people, and thereafter impose their government on them."[10] The Legalist thinkers' rejection of the political function of morality as expressed by Mencius led them to further develop Xunzi's arguments. They, in fact, assigned the state the central role of directly managing the economy, presenting it as the best solution for both strengthening the state and ensuring the livelihood of the people (Legalist interventionism).[11] In other words, different classical schools of thought perceived *minsheng* as an important political

9 I adopt here the term "authoritarian Confucianism" used by Allyn Rickett in his discussion of Chapter 35, "On Extravagant Spending," in Guanzi, Liu Xiang, and W. Allyn Rickett, *Guanzi: Political, Economic, and Philosophical Essays from Early China*, 2 Vols. (Princeton, NJ: Princeton University Press, 1985–98), Vol. 2, 294–336.

10 Xiao Gongquan, *A History of Chinese Political Thought* (Princeton, NJ: Princeton University Press, 1978), 356.

11 For a more in-depth discussion of Legalist thought see William Theodore De Bary, Irene Bloom, Wing-tsit Chan, and Joseph Adler, *Sources of Chinese Tradition, Vol. 1* (New York, NY: Columbia University Press, 1999), Chapter 7, "Legalists and Militarists," 190–223.

objective, whether they framed it in terms of political morality or tactical pragmatism. Even the *Daodejing* (sixth century BCE), the foundational text of Daoism, famously declared: "Therefore in governing the people, the sage empties their minds but fills their bellies."[12]

The political problem of the relationship among morality, government imposition of restraints (laws), and *minsheng* was resolved through syncretic ideological solutions, as exemplified by the popularity, during the Warring States and early Han periods, of the Huang-Lao school of thought, which inspired the famous Legalist thinker Han Fei Zi (279–233 BCE) as well as Emperor Wen of Han (202–157 BCE). Huang-Lao thought supported a Legalist view of ruling through rewards and punishments, although it framed it within ideals of Daoist universal unity and non-deliberate action (*wu wei*), inspiring minimalist state intervention in the economy that deeply contradicted the interventionist impulse of Legalism.[13] Although Huang-Lao influence declined after the reign of Emperor Wen, ideological syncretism continued to characterize dynastic rule. Later administrations of the Han Dynasty, in fact, developed a hybrid Confucian–Legalist tradition that came to dominate state ideology through most of China's imperial period. While Han officials could have favored Legalist methods of governance, they were aware that doing so would have inevitably generated opposition from humanitarian Confucians. In the words of historian Michael Loewe, "such methods would again prove to be intolerable without the clemency that is traced to the humanitarian ideals of Confucius, Mencius, or Mo-ti." On the other hand, a "perfectly ordered hierarchical society which is described as Confucian could not withstand the grim realities of crime, dissidence, or invasion without some effective measure of legalist controls."[14] A working system needed to be based on a synthesis of the two schools of thought. In this syncretic tradition, laws were severely enforced and consistently administered but were also intended to support Confucian moral

12 Laozi and D. C. Lau, *Tao te ching* (Baltimore, MD: Penguin Books, 1963), 9.

13 For more information on Huang-Lao thought see Guanzi, Liu, and Rickett, *Guanzi*, 1:19–22.

14 Michael Loewe, "The Former Han Dynasty," in *The Cambridge History of China. Vol. 1, The Chin and Han Empires 221 BC–AD 220*, ed. by Denis Crispin Twitchett and Michael Loewe (Cambridge: Cambridge University Press, 2008) 106.

values such as Filial Piety and to be balanced with moral exhortations and exemplary rites (*li*).[15] Han syncretism also combined the Confucian mandate of *yangmin* and its moral implications with targeted Legalist-style interventionism and statism and aimed at correcting specific problems, as most famously illustrated by the imperial policies for regulating the price of grain discussed later in this chapter.

Building on this strong political, institutional, and philosophical legacy, the Qing emperors embraced the *minsheng* heritage with a determination that was unprecedented.[16] They accorded great importance to the objective of *minsheng* for its role in ensuring the political security of the empire and its fiscal health, an objective the Qing state summarized in the formula of "state finances and people's livelihood" (*guoji misheng*). This goal was clearly announced in 1665 by the Kangxi Emperor (r. 1661–1722): "The original reason for the establishment of government is in order to nurture the people. If the people have enough, then the state is rich."[17] In November 1735, a mere month after his ascension to the throne, Emperor Qianlong (r. 1735–96) clearly restated the dynasty's commitment to this policy: "The way in which the kings have nurtured China has always been through the two tasks of teaching and nourishing." After extensively quoting appropriate passages from the *Book of History* (*Shujing*) and other Confucian classics that stressed the importance of *minsheng*, Qianlong

[15] For the introduction of the principle of Filial Piety into the Chinese legal code see Geoffrey MacCormack, "Filial Piety and the Pre-T'ang Law," *Fundamina: A Journal of Legal History* 8 (2002), 137–164. In Confucianism, the term "rites" (*li*) refers to a system of rituals that regulated the conduct of an individual within the family and society at large. Specific rites, for example, were used to reinforce the principle of Filial Piety (*xiao*). Burial ceremonials for a father were more complex and lengthier than those for a mother, in order to emphasize the primary importance of the father–son relationship. For a brief examination of the role of rites in ordering society see Richard J. Smith, *China's Cultural Heritage: The Qing Dynasty, 1644–1912* (Boulder, CO: Westview Press, 1994), 157–162.

[16] Sun E-tu Zen, "The Finance Ministry (Hubu) and Its Relationship to the Private Economy in Qing Times," and Jane Kate Leonard, "The State's Resources and the People's Livelihood (*Guoji Minsheng*): The Daoguang Emperor's Dilemmas about the Grand Canal Restoration, 1825," in *To Achieve Security and Wealth: The Qing Imperial State and the Economy, 1644–1911*, ed. by Jane Kate Leonard and John R. Watt (Ithaca, NY: East Asia Program, Cornell University, 1992), 10–11, 49–50, 53.

[17] "Shengzu shilu," (March 6, 1665) *Qingshilu* (Beijing: Zhonghuashuju 1985), Vol. 2, juan 14, 216.

continued: "if the granaries are full, then the people will know rites and righteousness." Consequently, he concluded, "the way to teach the people must be through first nourishing them." If the common people ate their fill and wore warm clothes, they would naturally be docile and abide by the teachings.[18]

These assertions cannot be taken as empty rhetorical statements, although they were certainly part of a performance of imperial virtue based on a well-established practice of recycling standard rhetorical tropes. At the head of a conquest dynasty, Qing rulers certainly felt that they particularly needed the trappings of Confucian tropes to overshadow the memory of their foreign Manchu ethnicity and consolidate their political legitimacy among the Chinese gentry and elites. The notion of "state finances and the people's livelihood" (*guoji minsheng*), however, deeply affected their actual policies. Historian Jane Kate Leonard argues that the Qing rulers and officials' ubiquitous use of this trope illustrates their acknowledgment that "the logistical network that sustained the empire depended on the wealth generated in the grain-producing regions of China" and that "the uninterrupted flow of revenue and food grains to the capital depended on peace and security in the grain-producing heartland." According to Leonard, the Qing rulers' intention in promoting "prosperity and growth in the private economy ... was, of course, to generate reliable tax revenue, but it did so in ways that strengthened and enhanced economic stability in the agricultural heartland." As Leonard concludes, nurturing the people "went to the very heart of Qing strategic views of empire and the intimate connection between economic and strategic power."[19]

The *minsheng* mandate inherited by the Qing, however, came with unresolved controversies that had inspired debates for centuries. Among them was the issue of the role of the state in the economy of the empire, which formed a point of confrontation between humanist Confucians and Legalists in the *Debate on Salt and Iron*. The great ideological and political synthesis that followed it did not solve this

[18] "Gaozong shilu" (January 5, 1723) *Qingshilu* (Beijing: Zhonghuashuju 1985), Vol. 9(3), 194–196.

[19] Leonard, "The State's Resources and the People's Livelihood," 50, 53. On this issue see also Roy Bin Wong, "Chinese Traditions of Grain Storage," in *Nourish the People: The State Civilian Granary System in China, 1650–1850*, ed. by Pierre-Etienne Will, Roy Bin Wong, and James Z. Lee (Ann Arbor, MI: Center for Chinese Studies, University of Michigan, 1991), 1–16.

issue, which, in the Song Dynasty, was to reignite a famous controversy triggered by the reforms launched by Wang Anshi, discussed later in this chapter.

The Debate on Salt and Iron: An Early Debate on the Role of the State in the Economy

From its earliest formulations, the idea of *minsheng* generated controversies about what constituted the proper relationship between the state and the private economy. Already in the Warring States period the question of whether the state should use taxation to monopolize the empire's resources or allow them to be channeled into the private economy engendered heated debates. The prevailing notion among Confucians was that, the wealth of the empire being limited, it could be stored "either with the government or with the people" (*bu zai guan ze zai min*), as Sima Guang was later to succinctly phrase it in the eleventh century CE. The early Confucian classics tended to favor the latter solution in their discussion of taxation. In an often-quoted passage from the *Analects* (*Lunyu*), when asked by the Duke of Ai (Ai gong) how best to manage finances in a year of scarcity, You Rou, one of Confucius' disciples, answered: "If the people have plenty, their prince will not be left to want alone. If the people are in want, their prince cannot enjoy plenty alone."[20]

Debates over the relationship between the state and the societal economy went beyond problems of taxation and also involved the issue of the extent and mode of state intervention. The question of whether a state-managed market was better suited than private economic forces to maximize the distribution of China's finite resources had, in fact, already arisen in the early stages of the Chinese empire, as exemplified by the Western Han Dynasty (206 BCE–9 CE) *Debate on Salt and Iron* (*Yantie lun*, 81 BCE). This text, compiled retrospectively during the reign of Emperor Xuandi (r. 74–49), records a discussion among court officials on the system of equitable marketing that had been adopted by Emperor Wu (r. 156–87 BCE) in his effort to centralize the empire's finances and check "aggrandizement" (*jianbing*) – concentration of wealth – by local nobles and wealthy merchants by

[20] Confucius and D. C. Lau, *The Analects [of] Confucius* (Harmondsworth: Penguin Books, 1979), 114.

preventing the first from engaging in trade and moneylending and the latter from acquiring landholdings. In general, Emperor Wu reorganized the fiscal and trade administrations, reversing the economic policies of Emperor Wen (202–57 BCE), which had been inspired by the Huang-Lao school's emphasis on frugal governance and light taxation. Emperor Wu brought under government control the lucrative trade in salt, iron, and alcohol by establishing state-led monopolies. He also established ad hoc trading agencies in charge of implementing the policy of "equitable delivery" (*junshu*), further developed into the "balanced standard" (*pingzhun*) system. This system focused on stabilizing prices and avoiding fluctuations by allowing the state to use public funds – including the revenues from monopolies – to trade in goods, acquiring them "when prices were low and selling them when prices were high."[21]

The *Debate on Salt and Iron* is structured as a confrontation between two parties: the "learned men" – mostly middle-level Confucian officials – and the Grand Secretary, Sang Hongyang (152–80 BCE), who had served as fiscal advisor to Emperor Wu.[22] This text is certainly "an idealized and dramatized description of the debate" rather than an exact record, but, according to Loewe, it adequately reflects the ideas presented by the two parties involved.[23] Sang's ideas closely echoed the arguments developed in the chapters of *Guanzi* devoted to "ratios and exchanges" (*qingzhong*). This section of the Legalist text argued that merchants' pursuit of private interests (*li*) exploited the people through unfair and corrupt market practices, mostly hoarding goods and speculating on prices. The state, therefore, had a duty to protect the population by equalizing distribution, preventing great disparities, and stabilizing the empire. The *qingzhong* chapters, therefore, denied the ability of market forces to ensure a smooth circulation of resources – or in today's economic terminology, to self-regulate. Only the state, through careful "manipulation of money and the relative prices (*qingzhong*) of all goods," could ensure an equalized distribution. "If money is highly valued (*zhong*), all goods are cheap (*qing*); money is devalued (*qing*), all goods will become expensive (*zhong*) … If the leader of the people controls the balance

21 Von Glahn, *The Economic History of China*, 85, 107, 113–116.
22 Von Glahn, *The Economic History of China*, 125.
23 Loewe, "The Former Han Dynasty," 187.

between grain, money, and gold, he will stabilize the empire. These are calculations for protecting the empire."[24] During the debate, Sang did not invoke *Guanzi* directly as the inspiration of the "balanced standard" policies, but his arguments closely reflected its basic principles, above all the idea that the state had the duty to manage the economy for the good of the commonwealth.[25]

In response to Sang's defense of Emperor Wu's policies, the "learned men" advanced two main criticisms. The first was that agriculture was the empire's foundational (*ben*, "roots") economic activity – i.e. it contributed directly to *minsheng* and was the main source of the empire's wealth. Other economic activities, such as trade, were non-fundamental (*mo*, "branches") – i.e. they did not directly contribute to *minsheng* since they did not produce resources directly linked to supporting the livelihood of the people. The attention of the state should therefore be focused on strengthening the *ben* sector, rather than on promoting the trade and manufacture of all goods, whether or not they were important for *minsheng*.[26]

The Confucians also criticized the "balanced standard" policies on the grounds that they were intended to generate profits (*li*) for the state, thus turning the ruler into an amoral merchant who put his own interests before those of the people. This image evoked long-standing notions of political corruption most famously enshrined in Confucian thought with the very first passage of *Mencius*. This text, in fact, begins with King Hui of Liang asking Mencius to suggest ways to "profit (*li*)" his kingdom. Mencius' response was famously fierce, as he urged the King to completely eliminate the notion of *li* when thinking in terms of state and society. If people, the King and high officials included, thought in terms of *li*, corruption would reign and social stability would collapse.[27] In this vein, the "learned men" condemned the

24 Quoted in Chin, *Savage Exchange*, 36.

25 Chin, *Savage Exchange*, 36, 48; von Glahn, *The Economic History of China*, 120–126.

26 Confucian philosophers did not identify agriculture as the only *ben* economic activity. They also included forms of artisan production that were in general carried out within the rural household and were integrated within the *minsheng* economy. For example, weaving was considered essential to *minsheng* because it fulfilled the second element of the "clothing and food" formula (*yi shi*) used to represent the basic needs of the people. Weaving was related to clothing and, therefore, essential for *minsheng*.

27 Mencius, Bloom, and Ivanhoe, *Mencius*, 1.

immorality of the "balanced standard" system, because it sought commercial profits for the state at the expenses of the *minsheng* economy of the empire. The state, they argued, should not compete with the people for profits and economic resources in general and should not abuse its power over the economy at the expense of the people.[28]

The *Debate on Salt and Iron* highlights two different views on how to achieve the same goal, i.e. the prosperity of the empire, and what constituted its foundations. Sang did not deny that he wanted to strengthen state finances in order to support Emperor Wu's military enterprises, as he was attempting to create stability in Central Asia and keep at bay the Xiongnu, a confederation of nomadic tribes at the northern border of the empire.[29] Although he had admitted this much, Sang based his argument primarily on the idea of maximizing the production and distribution of resources to sustain the people's livelihood. This goal, he believed, could not be entrusted to private merchants and their greed. This was, instead, the first duty of the state, which needed to manage trade directly, equalizing the distribution of resources and ensuring the welfare of all the people. The Confucian "learned men" distrusted the merchants' pursuit of private profits as much as the Legalists did. They did not believe, however, that greed was a systemic and unsolvable problem.[30] They declared their belief that "the principle of ruling men lies in nipping in the bud wantonness and frivolity." This could be done by promoting virtue, discouraging the pursuit of *li*, and not providing examples of dissoluteness, while always displaying disregard for personal profit.[31] The greed of the merchants, therefore, did not justify the structural changes brought about by Emperor Wu's reforms, which, they argued, disrupted the economy and threatened *minsheng* by valuing non-*ben* peripheral (*mo*) activities and turning the state into an immoral profit-seeking merchant. In other words, although the pursuit of *li* was always amoral

28 Von Glahn, *The Economic History of China*, 125.
29 Loewe, "The Former Han Dynasty," 189.
30 Michael Loewe, "The Former Han Dynasty," 162.
31 Esson M. Gale. *Discourses on Salt and Iron: A Debate on State Control of Commerce and Industry in Ancient China* (Taipei: Ch'eng Wen, 1973), 1–2. In his translation of this passage from the debate, Gale translates *li* as "commercial interests." This is a reductionist interpretation of this term, which had more flexible and nuanced implications, as discussed later in this chapter. A better translation of "material interest" is offered by William Theodore in "The Debate on Salt and Iron," in *Sources of Chinese Tradition, Vol. 1*, 360–363.

and negatively impacted the *minsheng* economy, it was a manageable problem when it arose among the general population but a much more serious one when it developed within the government.

The *Debate on Salt and Iron* is generally considered to have ended with a defeat of Sang Hongyang and the Legalist faction, marking, in the words of Tamara Chin, a restoration of "the concrete historical template and moral idiom" of the scholars "as the expert on political economy," replacing a more specialized approach "focus[ed] on quantitative calculations of *qingzhong*."[32] This idea that the *Debate* resulted in a return to Confucian moral rhetoric at the expense of the Legalists' more pragmatic approach, however, is somewhat misleading. The victory of the Confucians did not mark a return to unpragmatic and moralist theorizations of the management of the resources of the empire. Rather, it signified a return to a more holistic model that integrated economic objectives within a wider framework of social stability based on paternalistic relationships between state and society and among societal groups (humanist Confucianism).

Despite their heavily moralizing language, the Confucian scholars of the *Debate* proved capable of remarkable pragmatism, offering a very precise example of why they considered that state regulation of trade worked against the interests of the people and the societal economy at large. They pointed out that

> recently in some provinces and demesnes [the officials] ordered the people to make woven goods. The officers then caused the producers various embarrassments and bargained with them ... Goods manufactured by the people ... were mischievously sold at a standard price. Thus the farmers suffer twice over while the weaving women are doubly taxed ... the government officers swarm out to close the door, gain control of the market and corner commodities. With commodities cornered, prices soar, with price rising, the merchants make private deals by way of speculation.[33]

For the Confucians, therefore, Emperor Wu's equalization system was primarily a way of buying cheaply from the people, forcing the price of the goods to soar, and then selling them for significant profits. Thus, they complained: "Nimble traders and unscrupulous officials buy in cheap to get high returns. We have not yet seen that your standard is 'balanced.' For it seems that in ancient times equalizing distribution ...

[32] Chin, *Savage Exchange*, 67. [33] Gale, *Discourses on Salt and Iron*, 10–11.

was surely not for profit or to make trade in commodities."[34] The main drift of the debate, in fact, was not just ideological, as the language of the text would suggest, but developed within the larger confrontation between supporters of conflicting economic views and interests that went beyond economic and political morality. As Richard von Glahn argues, the Confucian scholars very likely supported the power of the big landowners – Sang's "aggrandizers" – who resisted the Han state's centralization efforts. During the *Debate*, Sang stated that equalizing the distribution system was a means of both "holding the balance of natural wealth and controlling the principalities."[35] On the other hand, as the Confucians implied, the equitable-market system offered plenty of opportunities for corruption, and the officials in charge probably benefited personally from it. After the *Debate*, the Eastern Han government ended up flexibly combining the Confucian and Legalist approaches. Although the "learned men" appeared to have won the debate, only some of Emperor Wu's reforms were actually dismantled. Emperor Zhao (94–74 BCE) abolished the equitable-trade agencies and eliminated the wine monopoly but retained those for salt and iron. He also did not cut taxes to the extent and in the areas proposed by the Confucians.[36] As the ideas presented by Sang Hongyang continued to lose favor, support for Confucian ideology gained momentum, reinforcing the Confucian legitimacy of the state – a move particularly important for the Han emperors, who built the fragile unity of the empire on their opposition to the ideology of its predecessor, the short-lived Qin Dynasty (221–206 BCE), which had embraced Legalism and persecuted Confucian scholars. The outcome of the *Debate*, however, highlights the staying power of Legalist economic notions and the hybridity of the economic policies adopted by the Han administration and by most of the dynasties that followed. Monopolies for a few specific items, such as salt and wine, remained a consistent practice. While the imperial government tended to give significant autonomy to market forces, it intervened in Legalist fashion in cases of real or perceived challenges to the smooth circulation of resources. The hybrid system established during the Han period became an established tradition and the boundaries of the two schools were

[34] Gale, *Discourses on Salt and Iron*, 11.
[35] Gale, *Discourses on Salt and Iron*, 14.
[36] Von Glahn, *The Economic History of China*, 125–126.

increasingly blurred. During the Song Dynasty, in fact, arguments in favor of reasserting state control over the economy came to be articulated entirely in Confucian terms.

Revisiting Circulation, Equalization, and Profits in Song China

The Song Dynasty (960–1279) witnessed a dramatic expansion of commercial networks, mostly as a result of the establishment in the eleventh century of a canal-based transportation system which allowed faster and cheaper movement of goods through the empire. The Song decided not to return to the historical capital of Chang'an and remained in the Late Zhou Dynasty (951–960) capital of Kaifeng, located at the center of the water transportation networks linking the Yellow and Yangtze rivers. The Song capital, therefore, stood at the very center of the canal system, contributing to the integration of north and south within the imperial market system and "fueling an unprecedented period of development in Song long-distance trade."[37] Testifying to the unprecedented growth of this commercial economy is the dramatic change in the composition of revenue. As historian William Guanglin Liu points out, the Song state in Kaifeng "derive[d] more than two-thirds of its tax revenues from indirect taxes ... Commercial taxes collected in 1077, for instance, amounted to 7.7 million strings of cash, about one-third of the amount levied in land taxes."[38]

The Northern Song economy also experienced unprecedented growth in the agricultural sector. In this period, significant technological innovations in the cultivation of rice – including terraced fields, deep tilling, frequent weeding, and irrigation ponds, as well as the introduction of a new strain of fast-growing and drought-resistant rice (the Champa variety) – triggered what von Glahn calls "the Great Leap Forward in economic productivity."[39] This "Great Leap" was not limited to agriculture. Manufacturing also experienced significant growth, sustained by expanding cash crops (tea, sugar, sericulture-related mulberry, and

[37] Chang'an, located in the area of today's Xi'an (Shaanxi Province) had been the capital of the earlier dynasties of Han, Sui, and Tang; William Guanglin Liu, *The Chinese Market Economy, 1000–1500* (Albany, NY: State University of New York Press, 2015), 94.

[38] Liu, *The Chinese Market Economy*, 94.

[39] Von Glahn, *The Economic History of China*, 223, 242.

indigo) as well as new technologies (such as the invention of true ceramic) and the expansion of overseas markets.[40]

The remarkable economic growth enjoyed by the Northern Song Dynasty inspired new understandings of the workings of the market as well as renewed discussions on the relationship between the state and societal economy and how to ensure efficient circulation of resources through the empire, as illustrated by the debate surrounding the reform program launched by Wang Anshi (1021–86). Again, this controversy seemed to pit against each other the humanist Confucian tradition and the statist views associated with Legalist *qingzhong* theories, echoing arguments presented in the *Debates on Salt and Iron*. The terms of this controversy, however, differed significantly from those of the Former Han court debate. In the Song intellectual and economic environment, arguments in favor of state intervention were presented as being rooted in the Confucian classics, highlighting the ever-evolving nature of this philosophical tradition and its ability to integrate statist notions previously identified with Legalism. In addition, the idea that the empire's resources were fixed came to be challenged, and new treatises on famine relief strategies reflected a new confidence in the market's capacity to independently maximize the distribution of resources as well as new positive perceptions of the effect of personal profits (*li*) on the flow of goods in the market, ending centuries of negative evaluations.

The Debate on Wang Anshi's New Policies

Wang Anshi was, in the words of historian John Keay, "an unkempt, combative but highly regarded Confucianist," who had served for almost two decades as a local official before he was called to court by Emperor Shenzong (r. 1067–85) in 1096.[41] Wang had long been concerned with the difficult situation the dynasty was facing at that time and in 1058 had submitted to an earlier emperor (Emperor

[40] Von Glahn, *The Economic History of China*, 242. For an in-depth discussion of the political and economic views of Wang and Sima also see Peter K. Bol, "Government, Society, and State: On the Political Vision of Ssu-Ma Kuang and Wang An-Shih," in *Ordering the World: Approaches to State and Society in Sung Dynasty China*, ed. by Robert P. Hymes and Schirokauer Conrad (Berkeley, CA: University of California Press, 1993), 128–192.

[41] John Keay, *China: A History* (London: Harper Press, 2009), 317; Smith, "Shen-Tsung's Reign and the New Policies of Wang an-Shih," 350.

Renzong, r. 1022–63) his "Myriad Word Memorial" in which he proposed a series of economic and social reforms aimed at strengthening the empire. Wang's reformist fervor developed against a background of military trouble at the northern border, a situation very similar to that which had inspired Emperor Wu's controversial economic policies. During the Northern Song period (960–1127) the imperial army could hardly contain the military forces of the two states at its northern borders, Khitan Liao and Tangut Western Xia. Other prominent scholars and officials were also concerned with strengthening the faltering empire, and several pleas for reform reached the throne at this difficult time, including a set of memorials by Sima Guang, another prominent scholar and vocal critic of Wang's reform plan.

Emperor Shenzong ultimately favored Wang and appointed him chief minister in 1069. In this new capacity, Wang launched the New Policies (*xinfa*), one of the most ambitious reform plans attempted in imperial China, which aimed to reorganize not just the financial and economic structures of the empire but also those of the administrative bureaucracy and of society at large.[42] All aspects of the New Policies had the overall goal of strengthening state finances in support of the Song's military effort against the Tanguts and the Liao on the northern border.[43] Wang intended to reach this goal by reducing or eliminating in-kind tax payments and labor service, taking advantage of the unprecedented level of monetization of the Song economy. Other measures included in the reform plan were also supposed to ensure the smooth flow of resources to the state, which was then supposed to redistribute them among the population. Wang explained that wealth should "flow to all from a single source [the state]." Political and economic affairs would be in disarray if left to "churlish people in the villages and towns," who would amass wealth in competition with the state. Reflecting long-term preoccupations with circulation and hoarding, Wang distrusted the same groups targeted by Sang Hongyang – rapacious landowners and big merchants – and blamed them for

[42] Smith, "Shen-Tsung's Reign and the New Policies of Wang An-Shih," 350. For an extensive discussion of all aspects of the New Policies reforms, in addition to this article see also Paul J. Smith, *Taxing Heaven's Storehouse: Horses, Bureaucrats, and the Destruction of the Sichuan Tea Industry, 1074– 1224* (Cambridge, MA: Council on East Asian Studies, Harvard University, 1992).

[43] Smith, "Shen-Tsung's Reign and the New Policies of Wang An-Shih," 392.

damaging the economy by unfairly absorbing the land of small farmers and the businesses of small competitors. These "engrosser" families (*jianbing zhi jia*) wasted their wealth on luxuries at the expense of the people and did not contribute to strengthening the country.[44] Wang, therefore, called for "smashing the engrossers" and for state control over the market to ensure the proper flow of resources into the state's coffers.[45] To achieve this goal and to fight economic "engrossers," in von Glahn's words, "Wang created state agencies to manage wholesale trade at the capital and provide credit for retail businesses, turn private brokers into government agents, tighten the state's control of foreign trade, and extend the existing monopoly on salt production to include much tea cultivation as well."[46]

Part of the plan for "smashing the engrossers" relied on the "Green Sprouts" (*qingmiao*) loan program. This program provided low-interest monetary loans to farmers, the primary goal being to "revitalize the agrarian base of society through state investments ... and expanding the reach of public relief in rural areas." This program was intended above all to check the rise of the large landholders. The landed elite was, in fact, generally the only source of loans in rural villages. Because the landholders imposed high interest rates, peasants soon found themselves heavily indebted and, unable to repay what they owed, were forced to surrender their fields to the lenders as a form of repayment, a process that contributed greatly to the concentration of land ownership in the hands of a few.[47]

Wang's reforms and the steep rise in taxation they entailed were met with the staunch opposition of some state officials and reformist scholars, causing the emperor to fire Wang as chief minister (1075) and disband the New Policies.[48] Sima was among the fiercest

44 The Chinese term, *jianbing*, is translated differently by Gale and Smith, respectively, as "aggrandizers" and "engrossers." I maintain the two different translations when quoting directly from these sources.

45 Smith, "Shen-Tsung's Reign and the New Policies of Wang An-Shih," 439.

46 Von Glahn, *The Economic History of China*, 236–237.

47 Von Glahn, *The Economic History of China*, 236–237.

48 For a detailed discussion of Sima Guang's opposition to the New Policies and the factional struggle surrounding the dismissal of Wang Anshi as prime minister and the eventual appointment of Sima Guang to that position see Ari Levine, "Che-tsung's Reign (1085–1100) and the Age of Faction," in *The Cambridge History of China, The Sung Dynasty and its Precursors, 907–1279, Part 1*, ed. by Denis Crispin Twitchett and Paul Jakov Smith (Cambridge: Cambridge University Press, 2009), 556–643.

opponents of Wang's New Policies. Wealth, he argued, should be "stored among the people" (*cang fu yu min*). The state should not regulate trade and should leave the circulation of goods in the hands of private merchants. Because the empire's resources were fixed, Sima argued, increasing state revenue could only lead to a decrease in the wealth of the people. The way to enrich the empire was to limit excessive burdens imposed by the state in order to allow the societal economy to prosper. Referring directly to the economic reforms of Emperor Wu and to what Sima believed to have been their dire consequences, Sima concluded that extracting resources from the people would lead to a situation in which "bandits swarm like wasps," referring to the traditional notion that impoverished peasants would be forced into banditry for survival.[49]

In his discussion of the controversy over Wang Anshi's New Policies, historian Paul Smith correctly points out that Wang had a vision of the economy "as dynamic and expanding," thus challenging the notion of the empire's finite resources. Wang's ambitious plan, in fact, aimed at improving state "institutions so as to make the [productive] base grow strong" and "so great that no matter how much the state uses it cannot possibly exhaust all of it."[50] While Wang's reforms certainly reflected a new confidence in the potential of the economy in response to the recent exceptional growth, they mostly signaled a return to a statist approach to the management of the imperial economy. On the other hand, Sima perceived the economy of the empire as more static, as testified by his famous statement, quoted earlier, that "the wealth of Heaven and Earth is fixed in amount." His opposition to the New Policies, however, was not primarily rooted in this notion, but was mostly motivated by the idea that state management would ultimately hurt the societal economy (a situation that would also hinder any possible growth) and that a clear distinction between the realms of the public and the private should be maintained.[51] As with the *Debate on Salt and Iron*, the disagreement between non-interventionists and interventionists was mostly rooted in different views of society, although, this time, the confrontation between Sima

[49] Smith, "Shen-Tsung's Reign and the New Policies of Wang An-Shih," 388–389.

[50] Smith, "Shen-Tsung's Reign and the New Policies of Wang An-Shih"; William T. Rowe, *Saving the World*, 386–387.

[51] Bol, "Government, Society, and State: On the Political Vision of Ssu-Ma Kuang and Wang An-Shih," 136, 177.

and Wang was articulated entirely within the Confucian tradition. Even Wang's statist views were based on his commentary on the *Rites of Zhou* (*Zhou li*).[52] According to Smith, Sima Guang saw the market as "benign" and ultimately "mutually beneficial" for different groups in society. He believed that, in case of need, the wealth of the rich elites could be mobilized to equalize the economy by measures such as opening the doors of their granaries. Wang Anshi, on the other hand, "saw the economic landscape as dominated by coercive and predatory 'engrossers,' magnates who preyed on the poor and usurped the fiscal prerogative of the state."[53] Echoing their counterparts in the *Debate on Salt and Iron*, the non-interventionist Confucians refused to see the problem as systemic and as necessitating direct state management over the economy. They also held steadfast to a holistic view of the economy as part of an orderly system characterized by mutually beneficial relationships among social groups and a clear separation between state and society.

The Sima–Wang controversy over the role of the state in the economy, although still contraposing statist and societal models in a way similar to the *Debate on Salt and Iron*, reflected a deeply changed economy. Wang Anshi's program reflected emerging views of an economy able to grow, while its Green Sprouts program relied on the commercialization of the economy and the rise of wealthy local elites. During the Song Dynasty, more innovative ideas emerged in debates on the issue of grain circulation and storage in the context of famine prevention strategies. It was in this area that new positive interpretations of the effects of personal interests (*li*) on the flow of grain in the market ended centuries of negative assessments.

Master of Destiny: The Grain Market and Personal Profits

The Song re-evaluation of the potential of the new commercial economy of the empire also generated conflicting views on policies related to famine relief and grain storage. Storing grain had been a strategy for fighting famines since the early imperial period. Arguments stressing the vital importance of the smooth distribution of grain for the

52 Jaeyoon Song, *Traces of Grand Peace: Classics and State Activism in Imperial China* (Cambridge, MA: Harvard University Asia Center, 2015).
53 Smith, "Shen-Tsung's Reign and the New Policies of Wang An-Shih," 387–392.

stability of the empire can already be found in *Guanzi*. This text argued that grain was "the master of destiny" for the welfare of the people and that the state should pay particular attention to its smooth circulation. The price of grain, *Guanzi* explains, is particularly volatile because it responds regularly to supply and demand, much more so than that of salt or iron. It, in fact, could fluctuate widely, as the supply was at the mercy of unpredictable weather and other natural phenomena. It was for this reason, *Guanzi* continues, that the state should keep private merchants in check and manipulate this specific trade by building its own reserves of grain to be released onto the market in times of crisis.[54]

In the early imperial period, three kinds of granaries were established: "ever-normal" (*changpingcang*) granaries, which operated under state control and funding, "charity" (*yicang*) granaries, and "community" (*shecang*) granaries, which relied on private funding and management. The ever-normal granary system dated back to the Han Dynasty and mostly worked to ensure provisions for military bases at the borders of the empire. The functions of this kind of granary expanded during the Jin Dynasty (265–429). At this time, they were also used to regulate the flow of grain on the market by releasing stored grain in times of scarcity. The Tang Dynasty (618–907 CE) adopted the Jin ever-normal system but integrated it with charity granaries initiated during the Sui Dynasty (581–618). These granaries were specifically intended to store grain for local famine relief, although their functions came to be increasingly combined with those of the ever-normal granaries.[55]

The Song administration continued to rely on the Sui ever-normal and charity models. In its Southern period, prompted by economic, social, and political factors, it also introduced community granaries. This kind of granary relied on new levels of commercialization of the economy and the emergence of unprecedentedly wealthy and influential local merchant elites expected to directly contribute to the restocking and managing of the stored grain. Community granaries, therefore, were supposed to relieve the state by shifting onto local elites the burden and expenses of grain storage. They were also a product of prominent Neo-Confucian philosopher Zhu Xi's (1126–1271) attempt

[54] Von Glahn, *The Economic History of China*, 120–126.
[55] Wong, "Chinese Traditions of Grain Storage," 8–12.

to replace Wang Anshi's Green Sprouts loan program by creating a society-based alternative.[56] In theory, the charity and community granaries were to constitute a more direct form of relief for the destitute in times of severe scarcity, since their main function was to loan grain at reduced prices.[57] In the late imperial period, however, despite the public or private nature of their management and funding and the theoretical differentiation of tasks, it was difficult to find a coherent pattern in the political and economic goals of each type of granary, since, at times, local granaries were used to stabilize the flow of grain on the market and to regulate prices, while the ever-normal granaries occasionally issued low-interest loans.[58]

The granary system testifies to the imperial officials' understanding of the relation between supply and demand and its effects on both the circulation and the prices of goods traded on the market, further highlighting Confucian thought's ability to flexibly combine the moralist notion of *minsheng* with basic *qingzhong* principles. Following established practice, in regular times, the government instructed the ever-normal granaries to sell a portion of their grain, which was to be replaced with new acquisitions. This practice was mostly intended to ensure the rotation of stored product, preventing spoilage and rotting, rather than to stabilize prices (*pingtiao*). Sales during normal times were not to interfere too heavily with the market, and state grain was sold at only nominally reduced prices. This was not the case in situations of crop failure, when scarcity led prices to rise above levels that the government considered acceptable. In these cases, a wider portion, or the entirety, of the stored grain was sold at prices greatly below the market rate to generate a downward trend in prices.[59]

The growth and commercialization of the economy in the Song period triggered a re-evaluation of granary policies in two main ways. Community granaries reflected increased confidence in the local commercial economy and a diminishing need for state intervention. At the

56 Richard von Glahn, "Community and Welfare: Chu Hsi's Community Granaries in Theory and Practice," in *Ordering the World*, ed. by Robert P. Hymes and Schirokauer Conrad, 225–279.

57 Wong, "Chinese Traditions of Grain Storage," 3.

58 Wong, "Chinese Traditions of Grain Storage," 12; Li, *Fighting Famine in North China*, 172.

59 Li, *Fighting Famine in North China*, 172, especially Chapter 6. Also see Will and Wong, *Nourish the People* for a detailed explanation of the operation of ever-normal granaries during the Qing.

same time, a new interpretation emerged of the role of private interests (*li*) in the economy and how they affected the circulation of grain. Reflecting the Southern Song's reliance on local elites and resources, officials, such as Huang Zhen (1213–80), the administrator of Fuzhou Prefecture, tended to favor plans for famine relief that relied on the actions of the gentry. Local officials were to "urge [the elite] to share" their surplus grain with the famine-stricken population by reminding them of their moral duties toward the community. Moral considerations were also supposed to incentivize merchants to sell grain in the stricken regions and to inspire the local wealthy to make their stocks available on the market.[60] Departing from this strategy, Dong Wei (?–1217) – holder of a *jinshi* degree and author of the influential treatise on disaster relief, *A Treatise on Saving People Afflicted by Disaster* (*Jiuhuang huomin shu*)[61] – opposed the state's deployment of moral arguments, deeming them both ineffectual and dangerous. Rather than arguing, as in similar earlier discussions, to replace this humanist corrective approach with direct government intervention, Dong presented a new alternative that relied on a positive view of the effects of material interests (*li*) when they competed in the market.[62]

Dong was a strong believer in the ability of private trade to circulate grain efficiently and was a vocal opponent of practices that might hinder its circulation (*liu*). He was particularly critical of officials who placed embargos on exporting grain outside of their jurisdiction with

[60] Bol, "Government, Society, and State: On the Political Vision of Ssu-Ma Kuang and Wang An-Shih," 128–192.

[61] The *jinshi* was the highest degree in the imperial examination system – a series of examinations administered by the state and based on the Confucian classics – through which officials for the government administration were selected. The *jinshi* was granted to those who had already passed lower-level examinations – held at the county (*shengyuan*), provincial (*juren*), and imperial capital (*gongshi*) levels – and had succeeded in the final examination held in the imperial palace (the palace examination). A *jinshi* degree not only bestowed high status among the Chinese scholarly intelligentsia but also opened the door to the most prestigious positions in the imperial administration. For an in-depth discussion of the imperial examination system see Benjamin A. Elman, *Civil Examinations and Meritocracy in Late Imperial China* (Cambridge, MA: Harvard University Press, 2013) and John W. Chaffee, *The Thorny Gates of Learning in Sung China: A Social History of Examinations* (Albany, NY: State University of New York Press, 1995).

[62] Robert P. Hymes, "Moral Duty and Self-Regulating Process in Southern Sung Views of Famine Relief," in *Ordering the World*, ed. by Robert P. Hymes and Conrad Schirokauer Conrad, 280–309.

the intent of keeping it in local granaries and avoiding local scarcity. Dong accused these officials of "favoring their own" and lacking compassion for people outside their areas.[63] Dong's criticism of this practice, however, was not just rooted in moral considerations. He firmly believed that they actually hurt the economy of the empire as a whole by interfering with the market-based distribution of grain. If allowed to compete freely, he believed, private interests would ensure the efficient circulation of this vital resource. Dong, in fact, maintained that merchants were naturally inclined to bring their grain to the areas afflicted by famine because the high local demand presented an opportunity to sell at higher prices, thus maximizing their profits. Opening up the interregional market to merchants from other regions, Dong continued, would certainly lead to higher prices, as the incoming merchants would take advantage of the local situation of scarcity. Prices, however, would eventually adjust spontaneously, as local gentry would also rush to sell their own grain, increasing competition among sellers and consequently driving down prices.[64] Keeping the flow of grain unhindered, therefore, constituted the best solution for preventing famine.

Dong Wei's views of the market reflected a wider trend that emerged in response to the first wave of the commercial revolution initiated in the Tang–Song transition period. As historian Helen Dunstan points out, Dong Wei's treatise on famine relief reproduced a story, probably apocryphal, of an earlier successful adoption of his strategy. The story focused on Fan Zhongyan (989–1052), a prefect in Hangzhou, and his strategy for solving a crisis of scarcity that had generated a local famine. Despite the fact that the price of grain was rising fast, in Dunstan's words, "Fan baffled everyone by raising the market price of 120 coins per peck by 60 coins. He then had notices posted 'along the rivers' announcing the size of the price rise. The result was merchants 'vying' to bring their grain to Hangzhou. Once the imports had flooded in, Fan restored the price of 120 coins per peck."[65] In his *Zizhi tongjian*

[63] Zoe Shan Lin, "'Favoring Their Own': Grain Embargoes in Southern Song China," *Journal of Song-Yuan Studies* 46 (2016), 207, 174–175, 177.

[64] Robert P. Hymes, "Moral Duty and Self-Regulating Process in Southern Sung Views of Famine Relief," 280–309.

[65] Helen Dunstan, "A Different Trajectory: Market-Consciousness in Chinese Political Economy, 800–1800," *Journal of Chinese History*, n.d., 1–29, doi:10.1017/jch.2019.21, 22.

(*Comprehensive Mirror Aiding Governance*) Sima Guang also produced a precedent of earlier market-based strategies for fighting famines. Sima's story centered on Lu Tan, a surveillance commissioner in today's southern Anhui. Lu Tan refused to abide by an order to lower prices of grain in response to a crop failure that was due to a protracted drought in the region. Lu Tan chose instead to rely on the naturally rising prices to attract merchants from outside the afflicted region to sell their grain on the local market. As Dunstan argues, Sima actually simplified the Lu Tan story, emphasizing Lu's reliance on the market and omitting any mention of other supporting measures that Lu had adopted.[66]

To strengthen his case, therefore, Dong Wei could rely on narratives of the earlier uses of market-based anti-famine strategies – even if their historical accuracy was somewhat shaky. These new anti-famine strategies reflected changes in the nature and scope of Chinese markets, especially the expansion of long-distance and interregional trade networks fueled by the water transportation-based commercial economy, which allowed private merchants to move resources across an increasingly wide portion of the empire.[67] At the same time, as Dong's arguments illustrate, the commercial growth of the Song period weakened scholars' and officials' diffidence toward merchants and private interests. Despite the persistence of official anti-profit rhetoric – an integral part of the imperial *jiaomin* didactic approach to social stability – some officials came to perceive profits as proper stimulants for keeping goods flowing smoothly through the empire and suggested limiting the state's attempts to manage the grain trade. In the Southern Song period, after the demise of Wang Anshi's New Policies, officials also began to experiment with using private merchants to carry out functions generally managed by the state. This was the case, for example, with the attempt to cut military expenses through market mechanisms. These embryonic experiments with market-based strategies came to be expanded and systematized during the Qing period, as discussed in Chapter 2.[68]

66 Dunstan, "A Different Trajectory," 22–23.

67 Hymes, "Moral Duty and Self-Regulating Process in Southern Sung Views of Famine Relief"; Pierre-Etienne Will, *Bureaucracy and Famine in Eighteenth-Century China* (Stanford, CA: Stanford University Press, 1990), 280–309.

68 Dai, "The Qing State, Merchants, and the Military Labor Force in the Jinchuan Campaigns" and "Yingyung Shengxi: Military Entrepreneurship in the High Qing Period, 1700–1800."

Regulating Consumption: "Revering Frugality and Eliminating Luxury" (*Chong jian chu she*)

In addition to attempting to regulate the circulation of basic staples through the market, a traditional strategy for managing the empire's finite resources and its chronic vulnerability to scarcity was to limit consumption by advocating frugality (*jian*) and implementing sumptuary laws. These strategies were common among all regions in the premodern period, including Europe and the Middle East, where sumptuary laws were intended to discourage luxury and preserve vital resources as well as reinforce social hierarchies and religious virtues.

In Chinese culture, frugality and morality were also closely associated. The term *jian* (frugality) was generally combined with *jie*, a term indicating moderation as a moral virtue. Most Chinese philosophical and religious schools, from Confucianism and Mohism to Buddhism and Daoism, advocated this virtue. According to the *Analects*, Confucius himself was not a supporter of thrift per se but had stated: "Extravagance (*she*) leads to presumption, while frugality (*jian*) leads to shabbiness. Compared to presumption, though, shabbiness is to be preferred." Frugality, especially the avoidance of extravagance and of ostentatious behavior, became a crucial aspect of the main virtues of a gentleman (*junzi*): self-cultivation, honesty, and righteousness.[69] Frugality was also advocated in Daoism. The *Daodejing*, Daoism's foundational text, included it among its three treasures (*sanbao*): frugality (*jian*), compassion (*ci*), and "not daring to take the lead in the empire" (*bu gan wei tianxia xian*).[70]

The idea of frugality, however, had equally important practical objectives in both the economic and the political spheres. Confucius placed the parsimonious expenditure of resources among the basic strategies for successful rule, arguing that extravagance generally led to insubordination and exhaustion of resources. He also ranked frugality as high as rites (*li*), arguing that, when in doubt, it was better to give priority to simplicity over the literal execution of prescribed rituals.[71] In Mencius, rites and frugality emerged, in fact, not as contradictory but as mutually

[69] Quoted in Chin, *Savage Exchange*, 78, 79.
[70] Laozi and Lau, *Tao te ching*, 129.
[71] Confucius, "Analects. Xue Er," in Legge, *Chinese Classics* 1:1861; Wang Xueping, "Rujia de jiejian zhizu xiaofeiguan ji qi xiandai jiazhi," *Shehui kexuejia* 2(154) (2010), 32–35.

supportive. Mencius advocated the parsimonious use of resources, arguing that consumption should be regulated according to seasons and rites to prevent their exhaustion: "Let their foods be seasonable and their consumption according to ritual, so that their resources cannot be exhausted."[72] Mencius especially advocated the regulation of consumption through rites related to Filial Piety (*xiao*) for establishing the proper level of consumption, not just in burial ceremonies, but also in other rituals intended to celebrate parents, the elderly, and ancestors. For example, he wanted to see that the "black-haired [i.e. young] people are neither hungry nor cold" – ensuring basic livelihood being an essential goal of the *minsheng* mandate – while "people of seventy wear silk and eat meat," a luxury the young should postpone until old age.[73] Rites of Filial Piety, therefore, were to regulate daily consumption within the household by reserving for the elderly the consumption of goods that went beyond subsistence, such as meat and silk.

Xunzi also supported frugality, arguing that strengthening production and regulating consumption were essential for prosperity: "Strengthen the fundamental ... and consume sparingly, then All Under Heaven cannot experience poverty." He also believed that consumption should be regulated through rites: "the way to make the country prosperous is to consume sparingly and to enrich the people by carefully storing surplus. Use the rites to consume sparingly and enrich the people to govern. He who enriches the people therefore has much surplus."[74] These early, embryonic regulations for limiting consumption inspired by Confucian rites developed into the most complex system of sumptuary laws in world history. Chinese sumptuary laws grew into a body of extremely detailed regulations governing all aspects of everyday life, including buildings, clothing, food, and means of transportation, according to hierarchies of status, age, and gender.[75] According to legal historian Wallace Johnson, during the Tang Dynasty there were sixty-six statutes devoted just to clothing.[76]

[72] Mencius, Bloom, and Ivanhoe, *Mencius*, 148.
[73] Mencius, Bloom, and Ivanhoe, *Mencius*, 149.
[74] Quoted in Wang, "Rujia de jiejian zhizu xiaofeiguan ji qi xiandai jiazhi," 33.
[75] Wallace S. Johnson, "Sumptuary Laws in Chinese Law," in *The Oxford International Encyclopedia of Legal History*, ed. by Stanley Nider Katz (Oxford: Oxford University Press, 2009), 409–410.
[76] Chusei Suzuki, *Shinchō chūkishi kenkyū* (Tokyo: Ryogenshobo, 1971), 37–39; Johnson, "Sumptuary Laws in Chinese Law."

Limiting consumption in the attempt not to exhaust the empire's wealth, however, was not the only strategy for achieving the ever-important goal of maximizing the circulation of resources among the population. Condemnations of luxury, in fact, were accompanied by warnings against thriftiness and encouragement of spending. For example, in a discussion of burial rites, Xunzi stated the importance of "understanding that freely spending money is [a way] to nourish wealth," indicating that unspent wealth, removed from circulation, contributed to scarcity.[77] In *Guanzi* we also find statements that seem to conflict with this text's general support for frugality, an inconsistency that at times reflects its mixed authorship. Although the entire collection of essays that constitute this text is supposed to express the ideas of Guan Zhong (720–645 BCE), an official of the State of Qi during the Warring States period – each essay being presented as a conversation between Master Guan (Guanzi) and some important personality in a position of power – in fact, it expresses the different voices of a multiplicity of authors. In apparent contradiction of the pro-frugality arguments that dominate the "ratios and exchanges" chapters, generally attributed to a different author, in the seventh chapter, "*Ban fa*," we find Master Guan warning that "parsimony causes sheer waste."[78] The meaning of this statement is clarified in the fifth chapter, "On Military Taxes" (*Cheng ma*), where *Guanzi* declares that "too much thrift restricts business; extravagance wastes goods."[79] In these two chapters, therefore, *Guanzi*'s promotion of spending constitutes a condemnation of thrift as a form of hoarding. The problem, therefore, was to find the right balance between thriftiness and waste in order to maximize the ever-important function of circulation of wealth. We can find a similar notion in the *Debate on Salt and Iron*, in which Sang Hongyang argued that "the true gentleman, while checking extravagance, would disapprove of parsimoniousness because over-thriftiness tends to narrowness. When Sun-shu Ao was

[77] Yang Lien-sheng, "Economic Justification for Spending—An Uncommon Idea in Traditional China," *Harvard Journal of Asiatic Studies* 1–2 (1957), 43.

[78] Yang, "Economic Justification for Spending," 44. The title of this chapter, "*Ban fa*," is difficult to translate. In his preface to his translation, Allyn Rickett (*Guanzi* [Vol. 1], 136–147) states: "*Ban* probably refers to a tablet made of wood or bronze on which a document had been inscribed. *Fa* usually refers to laws, but, in this chapter, it primarily means a 'model' or 'guideline,' or as a verb 'to model.'"

[79] Yang, "Economic Justification for Spending," 44.

the prime minister of Ch'u and his wife did not wear silk or his horse feed on grain, Confucius said: 'One should not be too thrifty so as to be hard on one's inferiors.'" Here Sang referred to Guanzi's contention that, without embroidered ceremonial robes, there will be no work for seamstresses and, "without the hankering for profit, the fundamental occupation will have no outlet."[80]

The thirty-fifth chapter of *Guanzi*, "On Extravagance in Spending" (*Chi mi*) presents a stronger early case in favor of luxury consumption. This complex text articulates two main lines of thought: a pro-spending theory for sustaining production and advocacy of status-regulated levels of extravagance to ensure wealth redistribution and "equalization" (*ping*).[81] According to this Master Guan, in fact, the rich should spend extravagantly, circulating resources through the market and helping to stimulate the economy. For example, when the Duke of Huan asks Master Guan what to do to "bring about the transformation of the time," the Master Guan speaking in this chapter responds: "Nothing is better than a policy of extravagance in spending. If the prince treats the necessities of life as having little value but useless things with great respect, men can be shaped at will. Accordingly, the prince should treat grain as having little value but pearls and jade with respect. Likewise, he should express his liking for ceremony and music but belittle productive enterprises. Such a policy is the beginning of essential production."[82] The quite opaque meaning of this piece is clarified by the statement that follows, which argues that the ruler

> should maintain stores of pearls and jade, his feudal lords should maintain stores of musical instruments made of metal and stone, great officers should raise dogs and horses, and the hundred surnames should maintain stores of cloth of hemp and silk ... otherwise, the strong will be able to gain control of these things, while the clever will be able to acquire them through trickery. The cheap will become expensive and the expensive cheap, but the widower

[80] Yang, "Economic Justification for Spending," 45–46. Yang points out that this quotation of Guanzi does not appear in the current text.

[81] For in-depth discussion of authorship accreditation see Yang, "Economic Justification for Spending"; Guanzi, Liu, and Rickett, *Guanzi*, 2:292–336.

[82] Guanzi, Liu, and Rickett, *Guanzi*, 2:306–307. I have adopted Rickett's translations of *Guanzi*. In this and the following translations from *Guanzi*. I have, however, omitted some of the Chinese characters and suggested pronunciation and have not maintained Rickett's format of one sentence per line.

and widow, those who are alone and old will gain nothing. Such a policy is the beginning of equalization.[83]

These two passages articulate the idea of prescribing levels of consumption according to status as a means for ensuring the livelihood of the people. If the elites stored goods that were necessary to meet the daily needs of the people, their prices would go up and there would be fewer goods available to the common people. "Equalization" (*ping*) in the distribution of resources should rely on hierarchically regulated consumption.

In his dialogue with the Duke, Master Guan further clarifies the practical implementation of his plan:

Lengthen the mourning period to reduce the time [a family may be rich]. See that the funeral escort is very lavish so the rich will spend their money ... This is called having much but being poor ... Have the rich build grandiose tombs to employ the poor, construct elaborate grave sites to employ engravers and sculptors, use large coffins to provide work for carpenters, and prepare numerous sets of funerary clothing and coverlets to provide work for seamstresses.

This, Guanzi concluded, was the way to provide everyone with a source of income.[84] Extravagant expenses, Guanzi continued, contributed to the circulation and "equalization" of resources.:

let those who have accumulated wealth dress and eat in lavish fashion; use highly decorated carriages and horses in an extravagant way; and consume large quantities of sweet wine in a luxurious manner; then no one, even in a thousand years, will ever lack for food; this is because there will have been the promotion of essential production.[85]

The pro-luxury arguments presented in this chapter have created some controversy among economic historians who have pondered whether they are signs of early liberal consumerist "modernity."[86] Historian Yang Lien-sheng, weighing in on this debate, argues that this cannot be the case, since these calls for spending were not aimed at

[83] Guanzi, Liu, and Rickett, *Guanzi*, 307.
[84] Guanzi, Liu, and Rickett, *Guanzi*, 319.
[85] Guanzi, Liu, and Rickett, *Guanzi*, 315.
[86] Among these historians are Hu Jichuang, Chen Hengli, Sun Yin and Tao Li, Zhuang Chunbo, and Zhou Qianrong (Guanzi, Liu, and Rickett, *Guanzi*, 284, n. 9, and Yang, "Economic Justification for Spending," 37).

economic growth or prosperity. In China, instead, "one finds fragments of economic thought that recognize the importance of spending in the whole circulating process of flow of the economy."[87] To Yang's observation we should add that these texts do reveal a pragmatic understanding of the function of demand, in relation not only to circulation but also to production, since, for example, Guanzi argued that without demand for robes, there would be no production of these items and no work for seamstresses. These passages, however, reflect an economy with very limited elasticity in production and demand as well as one characterized by an Old Luxury mode of consumption. In this context, Chinese intellectuals could not have envisioned roles for demand and consumption – such as the stimulation of growth – that they could only assume during the commercial revolution of the late Ming period (discussed in Chapter 2).

Faced with an economy of fixed resources and a constant threat of scarcity, the imperial state mostly adhered to the formula of "honoring frugality and eliminating extravagance" (*chong jian chu she*). Frugality remained a constant policy until the late Ming period when Chinese philosophers and official faced deeply changed economic circumstances. The idea of frugality was not challenged even during the Song first wave of the commercial revolution and of expansion of agricultural production, when the notion of finite resources began to wane and that of a self-regulating market began to emerge. Even Wang Anshi, who envisioned a measure of economic growth, declared that strengthening state finances ultimately still required a significant reduction in consumption by the people – in Wang's words, while "the [productive] base grow[s] strong, the [consumer] end diminish[es]."[88] In his vision, production of resources could increase but they would not yet be enough to create a situation of plenty for both the state and the people. Even during the Song period, positive views of extravagant spending remained confined to strategies for circulating wealth among the people during times of famine.[89]

The warnings of the ancient texts against unregulated consumption continued to resonate with rulers and officials as long as the idea of

87 Yang, "Economic Justification for Spending," 37; on this issue see also 48.
88 Smith, "Shen-Tsung's Reign and the New Policies of Wang An-Shih"; William T. Rowe, *Saving the World*, 386–387.
89 See, for example, the case described in Luo Dajing, *Helin yulu* (thirteenth-century edition of Wang Ruilai, Beijing: Zhonghua shuju, 1983), juan 3, 52.

the empire's vulnerability to economic scarcity and famine persisted. The basic rationale was that, because resources were finite or largely inelastic, luxury consumption by some people would inevitably result in scarcity for others, or – as summarized by the late-Ming philosopher Lu Ji (1515–52), who, as discussed in Chapter 2, came to criticize this view – "if someone has less, then someone else has more" (*bi you suo sun, ze ci you suo yi*).[90] In this context, luxury consumption was perceived as generating the same problems as hoarding. By removing from circulation an excessive amount of crucial resources, it impeded their even distribution among the general population. It was only with the late-Ming "maturation of the market economy," as von Glahn described it,[91] and the rise of New Luxury consumption that the formula of "honoring frugality and eliminating extravagance" came to be challenged (Chapter 2). This formula was pursued through imperial edicts and local bans and a complicated set of sumptuary laws.

Already in the Song period, however, despite the government's attempt to promote frugality, luxury consumption had assumed an increasingly important role in constructing informal and alternative relationships between elites and the government administration, fueled by the exchange of gifts linking literati and merchant elites with representatives of the local government. Literati and commercial elites generated alternative aesthetics of consumption and rationales for standards of living, following practices that had become integral to social rituals, political networking, and the construction of social and cultural identities.[92] For most of the imperial period, therefore, social consumption trends were generally in direct conflict with the goals of the state.

[90] Lu Ji, "Jinshebian," *Jianjiatang gao* in *Jilu huibian, Vol. 204* (Taipei: Taiwan shangwu yinsuguan, 1969), 2-4. The full text of *Jinshebian* is also reprinted in Lin Liyue, 'Jianjiatang gao' yu Lu Ji 'Fan jinshe' sixiang zhi chuanyan," 134.

[91] Von Glahn, *The Economic History of China*, Chapter 8.

[92] Wu Jen-shu, *Pinwei shehua: WanMing de xiaofei shehui yu shidaifu* (Beijing: Zhonghua, 2008); Timothy Brook, *The Confusions of Pleasure:* Commerce and Culture in Ming China (Berkeley and Los Angeles, CA: University of California Press, 2011); Cynthia Joanne Brokaw, *The Ledgers of Merit and Demerit: Social Change and Moral Order in Late Imperial China* (Princeton, NJ: Princeton University Press, 1991); Craig Clunas, *Superfluous Things:* Material Culture and Social Status in Early Modern China (Honolulu, HI: University of Hawaii Press, 2016); Tobie S. Meyer-Fong, *Building Culture in Early Qing Yangzhou* (Stanford, CA: Stanford University Press, 2003).

Conclusion

Three main ideas framed Chinese economic thought throughout the late imperial period. *Minsheng* constituted the overall political-economic objective. Scarce and fixed resources were the main obstacles to achieving this ever-important goal. Maximization of the distribution of resources through the market (mostly by discouraging all forms of hoarding, from those linked to merchant speculation to extravagant lifestyles) and regulation of consumption were the primary strategies to overcome the scarcity obstacle and achieve *minsheng*. The tension among different views about how to solve this economic conundrum characterized much of Chinese economic thought, engendering debates on such issues as the role of the state in the economy. The idea that the market was the basic channel for the circulation of resources remained mostly unchallenged, but two issues remained the focus of contentious debate. The first issue concerned who was more likely to hinder the proper flow of goods in the market: the state or the merchants. The second concerned whether the flow of resources should be directed toward the state, to be managed centrally, or toward the societal economy, to ensure socioeconomic stability and a strong tax base.

The problems of the circulation of resources and the direction of its flow raised a closely related question: Was greedy pursuit of private interests (*li*) an unchangeable and systemic problem requiring the state to manage trade directly, or could it be "nipped in the bud," making it possible for the people to manage their own resources? The problem of circulation also involved conflicting views about the relationship between the rich and the poor. Was their relationship mutually beneficial because morality (paternalistic humanism) would, in case of need, induce the former to open the doors of their granaries for the latter, or were the rich basically predatory, needing to be restrained by the government? In response to the expansion of the commercial economy in the Song period, a third option emerged within the context of this debate. Private interests began to be perceived as capable of exercising a regulatory function when allowed to compete freely without state intervention or calls of morality.

This chapter also questions the general tendency to present a sharp opposition between the Legalists and the Confucians. Mostly based on the *Debate on Salt and Iron* and on the "Qingzhong" chapters of *Guanzi*, a general view has emerged that Legalism was the more pragmatic and rational of the two philosophies because it tended to disregard the distinction between *ben* and *mo* economic functions and to value trade equally with agriculture. This pragmatism is generally perceived as a proof that the Legalist approach to the economy was more "modern" than that of Confucianism. Confucian scholars are portrayed as relying to a greater extent on moral, rather than practical, considerations and therefore as being more conservative than the "modern" Legalists.[93] While openly pragmatic in their formulation of economic policies, in fact, Sang Hongyang's views are fundamentally anti-market. Sang implied that only the state can ensure a smooth and "equalized" distribution of resources, and he assumed that the pursuit of private profits (*li*) by the individual always has negative effects on the economy. This view was strikingly different from the humanist pro-market attitude of the Confucians. In general, the moral rhetoric deployed by the Confucians cannot obscure their respect for the private market and the role it played in supporting the economic and social order, the foundations of the *minsheng* mandate. It was this economic mandate that defined the morality of economic activity. Merchants, for example, would become traitors (*jianshang*) if they placed *li* over their assigned task of circulating resources (*liu*). Consumers, on their part, were supposed to follow sumptuary laws, which restrained their purchasing goals, saving resources and reinforcing social hierarchies. The state would take corrective action when economic actors strayed from their assigned roles. As the Former Han Confucian "learned men" argued, however, these problems could be solved and did not jeopardize the entire system. The Confucians, therefore, respected the public–private divide as well as the existence of different interest groups in society.[94] Their adherence to the rhetoric of *minsheng* signifies a commitment to a view of the economy as an integral part of a paternalistic and humanist system aimed at social and political stability. In this model, the state intervened in didactic ways, to teach and encourage moral values among the people (*jiaomin*), and in corrective ways, to remedy situations of crisis, such as famines,

[93] This is the position taken by Tamara Chin, who defines the Qingzhong chapters of *Guanzi* as presenting "modern" economic theories (Chin, *Savage Exchange*, 32–33). Michael Loewe also supports this idea. In his discussion of the *Debate on Salt and Iron*, he defines the group of officials led by Sang Hongyang as the "modernists" ("The Former Han Dynasty," 162–163).

[94] Gale, *Discourses on Salt and Iron*, 10–11.

paying particular attention to problems in the smooth distribution of grain, "the master of destiny" of the people.

The hybridity of the economic systems established since the Han Dynasty testifies to the ability of the Legalist and Confucian schools of thought to coexist comfortably, often in a complementary manner, as Legalist-inspired polices came to be integrated into an ever-evolving Confucian tradition. The Legalist legacy of statism tended to find favor in periods of military emergencies. Legalism had, in fact, long been associated with the rise during the Warring States period of the state of Qin – which culminated in the establishment of the first unified Chinese empire, the Qin Dynasty (221–206 BCE) – as well as with the consolidation of state power in the first century of the Former Han and its successful expansionist drive.[95] The Legalist statist legacy, therefore, is more closely associated with war exigencies, focusing more directly than humanist Confucian ideology on mobilizing resources and empowering the state. It is not a surprise, therefore, that it gained strength at times of intense military activity, when the Confucian tendency to "store the wealth with the people" appeared to run contrary to the security of the empire. The reforms realized by Sang Hongyang and Wang Anshi were, in fact, intended to strengthen the resources and capabilities of the state in its effort to fight the Xiongnu and the forces of the Khitan Liao and Tangut Xi Xia states. Military crises appear to have sorely tested the Confucian idea that a humanist paternalistic relationship between the state and the people was the foundation of the strength of the empire. Differences between Legalist and Confucian thought, however, went beyond the exigencies of war. The reformist visions of Sang Hongyang and Wan Anshi addressed wider issues, including how to ensure suitable production of resources, the role to be played by private interests, and the position of the local elites *vis-à-vis* the state and the people at large.

[95] Loewe, "The Former Han Dynasty," 104–105.

2 *Efficient Markets, Jiangnan's Luxury, and Productive Consumption (1500–1800)*

The idea that competition among private interests was more efficient in regulating the market than state intervention gained popularity in the late Ming and early Qing periods, supported by the revival of the commercial revolution, which, beginning in the late Song, had met significant challenges in the turbulent years of the Mongol domination (Yuan Dynasty, 1279–1368) and the restoration of Han rule with the establishment of the Ming Dynasty (1368–1644).* In this period, the notion that competition of private interests could efficiently regulate prices and improve circulation of resources was shared by most officials and intellectuals. It also came to influence the economic strategies adopted by the Qing state, expanding practices initiated in the Southern Song in the fields of grain storage and famine relief.

The late Ming and early Qing periods also witnessed two more momentous developments in the Chinese perception of the economy. At this time, the notion of consumption, which had remained mostly unchanged, underwent an important transformation. Luxury consumption (*shechi*) came to be viewed as generating wealth, going beyond issues of circulation and equalization of resources. This innovative understanding of luxury was possible because of a redefinition of what constituted the wealth (*cai*) of the empire and how it was produced. By this time, in fact, intellectuals and officials had come to perceive trade as contributing to the generation of wealth – not just to its circulation – and had abandoned the notion of finite agricultural resources. These new views reflected two main developments in the economy. The consumer base had expanded considerably, as had the amount and types of commodities available to consumers because of the growing number of small traders and artisans who had come to rely on the market for their livelihood.

* This chapter includes sections originally published in Zanasi, "Frugality and Luxury."

This expansion contributed to the increased monetization of the economy – by this time, 40 percent of the grain consumed in China was acquired through the market.

Most pro-luxury views came from intellectuals and officials linked to the Jiangnan region, which had emerged as the center of the empire's commercial economy since the Song, despite the negative effects in the region of the Public Land Law.[1] After the loss of the northern regions to the Mongols, the Song had moved the capital from Kaifeng to Hangzhou, a town in Zhejiang Province, at the southern end of the Grand Canal. During this period (Southern Song, 1127–1279), this area also witnessed a large influx of refugees escaping the Mongol invasion, leading to a significant growth in population. As agricultural output increased, it also became more specialized in response to growing levels of consumption from the booming urban centers, which energized local and long-distance market networks.[2]

Influenced by the lifestyle of the new rich elite families who had followed the Song court south, the nature of the local demand also changed, transforming Jiangnan into the wealthiest and most elegant region in the empire. As art historian Craig Clunas argues, the passion for "superfluous things" (luxury goods) seems to have been a cultural development concentrated in this area and especially in Suzhou, which set the standard of fashion for other regions of the empire.[3] Jiangnan, in fact, dominated the "fashion circuit" from the mid-sixteenth century. It was also here that treatises setting the rules of taste and guides to leisure travel were printed and circulated.[4] Although Jiangnan's

1 After the loss of the North to the Mongols, the Song state launched a series of reforms in a last desperate attempt to strengthen the empire and stop their advance to the South. As part of this wider set of reforms, the state enacted a Public Land Law (*gongtianfa*) forcing Jiangnan landowners to sell to the state a significant portion of their holdings (one-third of their land beyond 200 *mu*). This policy was supposed to guarantee a rental revenue for the state, strengthening the state finances. Although applied only to six prefectures in Jiangnan, this law still transferred approximately 20 percent of the total arable land in the region to state ownership. While this reform did strengthen state finances, it affected the local private economy negatively, and ultimately it was reversed on the eve of the Mongol conquest of the South. Von Glahn, *The Economic History of China*, 255, 277–278.

2 Von Glahn, *The Economic History of China*, 255–256.

3 Clunas, *Superfluous Things*, 173.

4 Pomeranz, *The Great Divergence*, 150; Brook, *The Confusion of Pleasure*, 220–221.

trends did spread in both North and South China, this region remained the unrivaled center of fashion, taste, and leisure lifestyle.

One more element contributed to making Jiangnan the cradle of pro-luxury consumption theories. The new *kaozheng* school of thought – generally translated into English as Evidential Studies – thrived in the region as local scholars developed an impressive network for the circulation of writings and the sharing of ideas.[5] This new intellectual trend, in combination with the social and cultural environment of the region, greatly contributed to the formulation of innovative conceptualizations of pro-luxury ideas.

The rise of anti-frugality arguments in this period further highlights the pliability of the conceptual framework of *minsheng*. New pro-luxury arguments were easily deployed within the same syncretic ideology that had supported frugality. For example, most pro-luxury writers referred to Mencius' famous statement advocating "circulation of products or exchange of services, allowing what one person has in excess to compensate for the deficiency of another" (*tong gong yi shi, xian bu zu*).[6] This, and other similar quotes from the classics, bestowed an aura of Confucian legitimacy to new pro-luxury arguments, despite the fact that they were deployed in support of expanding the production of commercial wealth, a goal which significantly departed from their original context of "circulation" (*liutong*) and "equalization" (*ping*) of finite resources.

The idea of luxury, however, proved difficult to dissociate from the problem of the ingrained corruption that plagued the imperial administration. Arguments against market-based luxury consumption also came from some prominent officials and scholars who articulated anti-luxury critiques based on moralist considerations or nostalgia for some idealized golden age of the past. In this chapter, my discussion of anti-luxury criticism focuses primarily on those writers who developed their arguments in economic terms, including scholars such as the pioneer of Evidential Studies and Ming loyalist Wang Fuzhi (1619–92) and pursuers of Practical Studies (*shixue*) Li Gong (1659–1733)

5 Benjamin A. Elman, *From Philosophy to Philology: Intellectual and Social Aspects of Change in Late Imperial China* (Cambridge, MA: Harvard University Press, 1984), Chapter 6, 209–267.

6 Lin Liyue, "'Jianjiatang gao' yu Lu Ji 'Fan jinshe' sixiang zhi chuanyan," *Mingren wenji yu Mingdai yanjiu* (Taipei: Zhongguo Mingdai yanjiu xuehui, 2001), 121–134; Mencius, Bloom, and Ivanhoe, *Mencius*, 64.

and Wang Yuan (1648–1710). Their criticisms were mostly motivated by a wish to protect the declining rural economy from both state intervention and the silver-based interregional market, which they perceived as, respectively, hindering the workings of the local economy and drawing resources away from the copper-based agricultural economy. This divergence in views of consumption, in fact, reflected a growing gap between, on the one hand, the economies of the coastal areas which operated on silver and connected China's domestic long-distance and overseas trade networks and, on the other hand, the rural hinterland economy which relied mostly on locally minted copper coins.

The Market

The dramatic political changes that followed the fall of the Southern Song and the establishment of the Mongol Yuan Dynasty did not fundamentally threaten Jiangnan's prominence in the economy of the empire, despite the Mongols' anti-Han bias. The Mongol rulers encouraged trade, especially maritime trade, but they did so through state monopolies or special trade licenses granted mostly to Uighurs and Muslim merchants, opening up maritime trade opportunities for private Chinese merchants only in the late years of the dynasty. The Yuan state also heavily taxed the Jiangnan region, which they expected to contribute 37 percent of the empire's grain tax quota. The imposition of this high revenue quota did indeed pose a significant burden on the local economy, but it did not fundamentally hinder the vitality and growing prosperity of the region. The Mongols' unwillingness to intervene in the local economy of southern China, in fact, generated an environment that ultimately proved beneficial. Their lack of interference, together with the end of the Song Public Land Law, allowed the local great landlords to reconstitute and actually widen their landholdings.[7] The local wealthy families were also able to amass fortunes in commercial and manufacturing enterprises because of the absence of a Confucian state that discouraged the "immoral" pursuit of personal interests (*li*) and engagement in peripheral (*mo*) commercial activities. In addition, the Mongols' general reliance on non-Han officials for the higher ranks of the imperial administration left the local elite – deprived of the traditional prospects of prestigious administrative

[7] Von Glahn, *The Economic History of China*, 255, 278–284.

careers – free to devote their attention to amassing wealth. In this new environment, in the words of von Glahn, the initiative of "these wealthy magnates … gave further impetus to commercial growth."[8] Jiangnan's agricultural and commercial growth, however, met with real challenges with the restoration of a Chinese dynasty, the Ming. The first Ming emperor, Hongwu (r. 1368–98), wishing to counteract the impact of Mongol rule over China, adopted anti-commercial policies and attempted to revive agriculture while promoting the development of a rural society that adhered to the traditional Confucian principles of frugality and morality, free from the venality and exploitation which, he believed, accompanied the trade economy. Hongwu, in fact, attempted to restore the self-sufficient rural village as idealized by classic Confucian philosophers, while significantly limiting the market economy.[9] For this reason, he banned the thriving private maritime trade, which Chinese merchants had once again come to control in the later years of the Yuan Dynasty, bringing maritime expeditions under state control and intending them to function primarily as diplomatic missions rather than commercial enterprises.

As for Jiangnan, Hongwu's goal was to mobilize its wealth to rebuild the empire after a century of war devastation. Initially, he attempted to gain the support and cooperation of the local elites, but he soon came to believe that this group was actually conspiring to hinder the realization of his plan. For this reason, echoing Southern Song policies, he confiscated almost half of the Jiangnan arable land in an attempt to weaken the great landowners, whom he blamed, together with corrupt officials, for exploiting the peasants and damaging the agricultural foundations of the empire's economy. These expropriations were also part of his attempt to realize his vision of a society based on small, self-sufficient, agricultural communities with minimal connection to trade networks. His decree that tax payments should be made in kind also contributed to the demonetization of the economy.[10]

According to Liu, the anti-market policies of the early-Ming state "caused a shift from a market-based economic system in the Song era to a command economy system that prevailed in the first century of the

[8] Von Glahn, *The Economic History of China*, 282.
[9] Von Glahn, *The Economic History of China*, 285–287.
[10] Von Glahn, *The Economic History of China*, 284–286.

Ming Dynasty (1368–1450)."[11] Liu takes the maritime expeditions of the Muslim admiral Zheng He (1371–1433 or 1435) as an example. Between 1405 and 1433, Zheng He traveled through the Southeast Asian and the Indian trade networks, reaching as far as the coast of East Africa and the Arabian Peninsula. His treasure ships (*baochuan*) became legendary, as they brought to court exotic animals and goods while successfully establishing strategic alliances for the Chinese empire.[12] Zheng He's expeditions, being state-sponsored, brought under the control of the state a vast array of manufacturing, mobilized to produce goods to supply the fleet or to serve as items for commercial or diplomatic exchange during the voyages. A large portion of handicraft production, therefore, was removed from the market. Even the riches brought back to China by Zheng He were not distributed through the market, but were offered as tribute to the emperor, who in turn would donate the surplus to soldiers and commanders as part of their salaries. According to Liu, therefore, the early-Ming policies were "devastating events that led to the lasting deterioration of her [China's] market economy until the mid-1500s." While in 1077 "the size of long-distance trade and urban markets reached 100 million taels of silver and above … the estimated gross value of trade in 1381 plunged to 5.3 to 8.58 million taels," signaling a dramatic demonetization of the economy and a sharp decline of the market economy.[13]

By the late sixteenth century, however, most of Hongwu's reforms had been reversed. By this time, tax payments were again converted into silver with the Single Whip Reform (*yitiao bianfa*). The ban on private maritime trade, if not removed, was hardly enforced, allowing merchants from the southern coast to resume their overseas trade activities.[14] By this time, China's trade network in Asia extended from Japan to Persia, and it continued to expand through the eighteenth and early nineteenth centuries, reaching a volume of trade "comparable to the whole of the English East India Company trade." The domestic long-distance trade also grew significantly as the newly conquered

[11] Liu, *The Chinese Market Economy, 1000–1500*, 4.

[12] For a detailed description of Zheng He's voyages see Edward L. Dreyer, *Zheng He: China and the Oceans in the Early Ming Dynasty, 1405–1433* (New York, NY: Pearson Longman, 2010).

[13] Liu, *The Chinese Market Economy, 1000–1500*, 1, 74. For a detailed description of early-Ming policies see Liu, Part III, "The Ming Era," 97–137.

[14] Von Glahn, *The Economic History of China*, 284–286.

northwestern regions – roughly today's Xinjiang Province – were incorporated within the market network of the empire. In addition, "Coastal trade linked Northeast farmers with the consumer of the Yangzi delta, and agricultural goods produced in Taiwan flowed across the strait into Fujian."[15]

In other words, despite the early-Ming state's anti-commerce polices, by the sixteenth century, China's commercial economy was recovering and growing. This economic revival was not fueled only by the return of private maritime trade and the expansion of the domestic interregional trade; other important contributing factors were improved agricultural production, increased specialization – due to the expansion of interregional market networks for such goods as cotton, silk, and porcelain – and a new influx of silver, first from Japan and then from the Americas. As von Glahn states: "Massive infusion of foreign silver stoked the fires of a commercial and industrial growth during the last century of Ming . . . The expansion of the money economy, the growth of rural industries, the increasing spatial range of markets, and the ascendancy of private enterprise over state economic management all contributed to what some scholars have referred to as a 'second economic revolution' (after the first 'economic revolution' of the Tang–Song transition) beginning c. 1550."[16]

This dramatic commercial growth was accompanied by the state's increased reliance on the market, consolidating and expanding views of wealth production and distribution, profits, and the workings of the market that had been brewing since the early stages of the commercial revolution during the Song Dynasty. By the mid-Ming period, despite the government's anti-profit rhetoric, the positive role of profits in smoothing the circulation of goods and in regulating prices was widely recognized. The Ming scholar Qiu Jun (1420–95) – a policy advisor in the Hanlin Academy[17] – made the case very cogently. Qiu believed that, in the words of historian Timothy Brook, "community,

[15] Evelyn S. Rawski, "The Qing Formation and the Early-Modern Period," in *The Qing Formation in World-Historical Time*, ed. by Lynn A. Struve (Cambridge, MA: Harvard University Asia Center: Distributed by Harvard University Press, 2004), 207–241, at 213.

[16] Von Glahn, *The Economic History of China*, 285, 292–293, and 295–296.

[17] The Hanlin Academy (*Hanlin yuan*) was the highest imperial academic and administrative institution, which housed distinguished scholars who often acted as secretaries or advisors to the emperor.

commerce, and state remain separate spheres," although he recognized that, in reality, they did influence each other. He believed that the market should be left to the merchants and the state should intervene only in case of crisis. In general, however, the more the state intervened, the more the gap between rich and poor would grow. On this issue, Qiu wrote: "they can readily negotiate quality and price to determine whether or not to buy something. When officials operate the markets for people, quality and prices are invariably fixed, yet self-interest and hidden dealings crop up all over the place. To operate [a state market] that produces profit and avoids corruption is difficult. The better course is for the state administration not to get involved."[18] As a consequence, Qiu concluded that the state should not operate handicraft industries, but should leave this task to the merchants themselves, who should regulate their own production.[19] Qu's statement reflected the long-standing idea held by humanist Confucians that the state could be more predatory than private merchants and that state and society should remain distinct, although in a harmonious relation. This position was to develop as a fierce argument against the Qing state during the period of the Ming–Qing transition.

The Market as a Political Arena and China's "Natural" Economy

Since antiquity, the debate on the relationship between state and private economies and the extent of state intervention had carried strong political implications, placing in contrast two economic models: a state-managed option and one that gave wider autonomy to economic forces in society (humanist Confucianism). The political implications of this issue had already been highlighted by the first century BCE. *Debate on Salt and Iron* and the eleventh-century controversy over Wang Anshi's New Policies that were discussed in the previous chapter. They were, however, to become even more politicized during the period of the Ming–Qing transition (1570–1670), when they developed into a full-fledged theorization of political despotism. In the early years of the Qing Dynasty, in fact, most of the intellectuals loyal to the Ming deployed the notion of "storing wealth among the people" (*cang fu*

[18] Quoted in Brook, *The Confusions of Pleasure*, 102.
[19] Brook, *The Confusions of Pleasure*, 101–103.

yu min) – in Sima Guang's popular expression – to denounce what they perceived to be the Manchu rulers' authoritarian economic policies and their oppression of China's "natural" (*ziran*) economic order. Echoing Sima's earlier arguments, these writers saw the danger to prosperity and economic stability coming not from the merchants' pursuit of personal interests, but from a system of state monopolies, special licenses, and brokerages that could hinder free competition and create dangerous collusion between merchants and an overreaching state.

The most representative voices of anti-Manchu economics were those of the "three giants" of the Ming–Qing transition, Huang Zongxi (1610–95), Gu Yanwu (1613–82), and Wang Fuzhi. Huang, Gu, and Wang were early pioneers of the emerging *kaozheng* school of thought that was to dominate the Qing intellectual discourse. *Kaozheng* scholars strongly opposed Neo-Confucianism, which had been adopted by the Ming state as its official ideology. They blamed it for the fall of the Ming, emphasizing especially its stress on moral cultivation and the abstract, "frivolous" debates it generated. Neo-Confucianism, critics explained, had ultimately undermined the intellectual and practical abilities of the literati class by disregarding practical issues and generating extreme factional fragmentation in the intellectual discourse. *Kaozheng* scholars disputed Neo-Confucianism by "search[ing] for truth in actual facts" (*shishi qiushi*).[20] In the words of historian Benjamin Elman, they "stressed exacting research, rigorous analysis, and the collection of impartial evidence" through a philological analysis of ancient texts.[21] This approach aimed at exposing what *kaozheng* scholars considered to be Neo-Confucianism's misinterpretation of the classics and especially its stress on morality and loyalty over knowledge, an interpretation, *kaozheng* scholars argued, that went against the original meaning of Confucian thought. The *kaozheng* philological approach brought about a re-evaluation of the meaning of concepts that were central to Confucian philosophy, including moral principles (*li*), nature (*xing*), energy (*qi*), and human emotions (*qing*), as well as others more directly linked to the economy, such as foundational (*ben*) and peripheral (*mo*) activities and material interests (*li*).[22] The *kaozheng* approach also inspired literati to focus on "concrete facts,

[20] Elman, *From Philosophy to Philology*, 86–87 and 80, respectively.
[21] Elman, *From Philosophy to Philology*, 4.
[22] Elman, *From Philosophy to Philology*, 19, 20–21.

documented institutions, and historical events" rather than "abstract ideas and emphasis on moral values,"[23] generating renewed interests in technical studies as a way to solve practical problems. *Kaozheng* scholars studied "astronomy for calendrical reform, hydraulics for flood control, cartography for military purposes," developing a branch of learning that came to be known as Statecraft (*jingshi*). Huang, for example, was well versed in astronomy and mathematics, while Gu studied military geography.[24]

Two of the main concerns of these Ming loyalists were how to understand the causes of the demise of the Ming Dynasty and how to bring back good governance, as best exemplified by Huang Zongxi's treatise *Waiting for the Dawn* (*Mingyi daifang lu*), which reads as a guide to help a ruler navigate difficult times.[25] These philosophers' efforts to retrieve the true meaning of ancient texts was not an exercise in nostalgia aimed at reviving past forms of political and social order. Wang Fuzhi, for example, was "committed to an evolutionary perspective." His objective was to find a model for renewal, rather than a model for a return to ancient forms of government. Wang, in fact, argued that "ancient institutions were used to govern the ancient world, but they cannot be applied across the board to the present day. Hence, these exemplary authors did not attempt to base policy on them. One applies what is appropriate today to govern the present world."[26]

In addition to identifying the causes of the Ming demise and restoring good governance, a third element that influenced the economic views of these scholars was their deep-rooted anti-Manchu sentiments. Huang, Gu, and Wang shared a similar background, their lives having unfolded in the complicated and turbulent period of the Ming–Qing transition. They and their families had been deeply involved in the late-Ming administration and had actively participated in the Ming

23 Elman, *From Philosophy to Philology*, 4.

24 Elman, *From Philosophy to Philology*, 4, 15, 89–90. For a discussion of the impact of the fall of the Ming Dynasty on the literati see Elman, *From Philosophy to Philology*, 85–89.

25 In translating this treatise, the Neo-Confucian specialist Theodore de Bary added the subtitle *A Plan for the Prince*, evoking Machiavelli's book, *The Prince*, which was intended to offer practical instructions for ruling successfully. William Theodore de Bary and Huang Zongxi, *Waiting for the Dawn: A Plan for the Prince: Huang Tsung-hsi's Ming-i-tai-fang lu* (New York, NY: Columbia University Press, 1993).

26 Quoted in Elman, *From Philosophy to Philology*, 36.

resistance against the Manchu invasion. Once they had given up hope of restoring the Ming, they retreated to private and secluded lives, hiding from the new dynasty, which had designated them as traitors, unwilling to serve it.[27] Their anti-Manchu sentiments were mostly reflected in their notion of China's "natural economy" (*ziran*) a notion that had traditionally referred to the foundational (*ben*) rural economy of the empire. These three Ming loyalists expanded this idea to include trade and industry among its crucial elements. They conceived China's "natural" economy as a locally based, small-scale trade system or, in Huang Zongxi's words, a "societal market system" (*minjian shiyi*).[28] Wang, for example, argued that "trade cannot be restricted. In that unfortunate case, people would have no means to exchange goods and to support their livelihoods. Although through trade people pursue excessive profits, they also rely on it for their lives." Trade thus ensured the proper "circulation of money and grains to eliminate scarcity among the poor and weak."[29] Huang, however, went beyond supporting trade for circulation and equalization of resources; he also revisited the boundaries between fundamental (*ben*) and peripheral (*mo*). He agreed with the idea that the sage kings "valued the fundamentals and restricted the peripherals" (*zhong ben yi mo*), but he disagreed with the standard interpretation that claimed that all commerce and industries were inevitably peripheral. He explained that "industry was certainly something the sage kings wanted to develop. They also wanted merchants to be plying the roads, because both industry and commerce are essential."[30] Huang, therefore, valued manufacturing and trade as much as agriculture because it directly contributed to the objective of social welfare (*minsheng*), which remained a crucial goal for restoring good governance. Forms of production and trading that did not support the people's basic needs, however, remained peripheral (*mo*).[31] Although Huang's views of industry and trade did not accommodate

27 Hummel, *Eminent Chinese of the Ch'ing Period*, 227–228; 351–354; 421–426.

28 Huang Zongxi and Shen Shanhong, "Ming yi dai fang lu," in *Huang Zongxi quanji* (Hangzhou: Zhejian guji chubanshe, 1965), 1–47, at 36.

29 Quoted in Ye Shichang, *Gudai Zhongguo jingji sixiangshi* (Shanghai: Fudan daxue chubanshe, 2003), 401; Wang Fuzhi and Shiquan Nie, *Huang shu* (Beijing: Beijing daxue chubanshe, 2014), 16.

30 De Bary and Huang, *Waiting for the Dawn*, 160.

31 De Bary and Huang, *Waiting for the Dawn*, 160; Richard von Glahn, *Fountain of Fortune: Money and Monetary Policy in China, 1000–1700* (Berkeley, CA: University of California Press, 1996), 223; Mio Kishimoto-Nakayama,

luxury consumption, they redefined the "natural" economy as not just based on agriculture but also complemented by "trade and industry," which also contributed to the production of wealth.

These Ming loyalists also revisited the meaning of *li* (material profits). In discussing its traditional contraposition to *yi* (righteousness), for example, Wang assigned a positive or negative value to economic functions motivated by *li* depending on whether they directly contributed to sustaining the livelihood of the people. The two principles of *yi* and *li*, he argued, were actually closely connected. Only when a political system declined did they become separate. Rulers should understand that they need to "use righteousness to generate profits" (*yi we li*), meaning that profits should not be pursued for the sake of the individual but for that of society as a whole and for long-lasting goals.[32] Wang believed that during the crisis of his time, profits were not pursued from the premises of righteousness, but rather righteousness and profits had become separated. This split, he explained, was caused by the influence of the "barbarian" Manchu rulers of the new Qing Dynasty. While righteousness was a virtue innate to the Chinese – a mark of their civilized ways – the "barbarian" Manchus crassly pursued profits in a corrupt manner, seeking only personal gains. The cooperation between some merchants and the Manchus had created a situation in which "barbarians assist merchants in gaining profits, and merchants rely on barbarians to flourish. As a result, the way of humaneness is almost obliterated."[33] In these passages, Wang merged a *kaozheng*-style reinterpretation of Confucian principles and an interest in problems of good governance with anti-Manchu sentiments. In this vein, he focused on the utilitarian aspects of "profits" but did not dismiss issues of morality, which he recast in terms of ethnic characteristics, portraying the Manchus as inherently lacking righteousness and the Han Chinese people as naturally possessing it.

This disjunction between *yi* and *li* was embodied, according to Wang, in the Qing's heavy-handed economic policies, including not only its heavy taxation, but also its corrupt practices of monopoly and collusion between state and economic elites, in which "corrupt

"The Kangxi Depression and Early Qing Local Markets," *Modern China* 2 (1984), 227–256, at 236.

32 Ye, *Gudai Zhongguo jingji sixiangshi*, 392–93.

33 Ye, *Guodai Zhongguo jingji sixiangshi*, 400.

merchants" (*jianshang*) cooperated with the state for the purpose of controlling trade and manipulating prices. Wang, for example, condemned the restriction of the areas in which salt merchants could sell their salt. Because each could only sell in a specific region, preventing competition, he argued, these unscrupulous merchants could hurt the people by "swinging [prices] up and down and creating abundance or scarcity."[34]

Ming loyalists, therefore, complicate the notion of "natural" economy not just by including trade and manufacturing, but also by defining it as free from state intervention and relying on private economic interests (*li*), which were innately righteous (*yi*) to the Chinese. The Chinese "natural" economy, therefore, was inherently market-based, self-regulating, and moral because it was oriented toward *minsheng*. *Yi* and *li* came to be detached only during periods of bad governance – marked by state intervention and disregard for *minsheng* – which they believed to be an essential trait of the rule of the ethnic Manchus. The image of Manchu economic policies as extracting wealth from the people and undermining the mandate of *minsheng* reinforced the notion of the Qing as an illegitimate conquest dynasty.

The criticisms of Qing economic policies offered by the three early representatives of the *kaozheng* school were certainly in large part motivated by their deep-rooted anti-Manchu feelings. They were, however, also a response to a poverty crisis that, according to the contemporary observer Wei Jirui (1620–77) – advisor to the inspector general of Zhejiang, Fang Chengmo (1635–76) – "afflicted the whole population" with a severity "unprecedented in the history of China."[35] Despite the recovery of productivity that had followed the serious scarcity of basic staples during the Manchu war of conquest, in the early Kangxi period China experienced a depression characterized no longer by scarcity but by the decline of prices of basic goods, such as grain and raw cotton. As historian Mio Kishimoto-Nakayama observes, "goods were cheap and abundant," but the people lacked

34 Ian McMorran, *The Passionate Realist: An Introduction to the Life and Political Thought of Wang Fuzhi (1619–1692)* (Hong Kong: Sunshine Book Co., 1992), 161, 167; Ye, *Gudai Zhongguo jingji sixiang*, 389–394, 401; Wang Fuzhi, *Du tong jian lun* (Taipei: Shijie shuju, 1962), Vol. 24, Dezong, 6; and Wang and Nie Shiquan, *Huang shu*.

35 Wei Jirui, "Preface," *Sichang gao*, quoted in Kishimoto-Nakayama, "The Kangxi Depression and Early Qing Local Markets," 229.

the money to buy them. Wei and other contemporary observers believed that the depression was caused by the decreasing amount of silver in circulation at the time and made worse by the Qing prohibition on mining and the blockade against the Zheng family in Taiwan.[36]

The Ming loyalists shared this view and blamed the poverty crisis not only on the Qing control over the market but also on its silver policies. Gu, Huang, and Wang all opposed the use of silver and advocated a return to copper cash. Their anti-silver stand was not motivated simply by the heavy burden that the collection of taxes in silver created for the people after the value of the copper currency used at the local level had dramatically decreased in comparison to that of silver.[37] They also decried the use of silver for commercial exchange, because the unfavorable copper–silver ratio of exchange would penalize the local economy. The anti-silverists were, in fact, "intent on preventing money from flowing out of the local markets" by advocating a return to "copper cash, an inconvenient medium of exchange that would certainly make the market less open and, consequently, less fragile."[38]

These three Ming loyalists, therefore, while recognizing trade as an integral part of the empire's *ben* economy, opposed the predominance of the silver-based long-distance and interregional trade networks, which they saw as dominated by state-licensed trade brokers and extractive of rural resources. Their criticisms of the Qing economic and monetary policies reflected the new tension between these two economic faces of the empire. On one side was the commercialized coastal economy that relied predominantly on silver, dominating and connecting the domestic interregional and global markets. On the other was the economy of the rural hinterland that relied on copper coins and was penalized by the unfavorable ratio of exchange with silver, especially in periods of crisis such as the Kangxi depression. It was in the context of this gap between two currencies and two economic systems that many scholars and officials questioned whether it was advisable to abandon the use of silver and pondered the nature of the Chinese economy and the role the market played in it.

[36] Kishimoto-Nakayama, "The Kangxi Depression and Early Qing Local Markets," 230–233.

[37] For an in-depth discussion of the interactions between China's silver and copper economies see Lin, *China Upside Down*, Chapter 3, 203–227.

[38] Kishimoto-Nakayama, "The Kangxi Depression and Early Qing Local Markets," 236–238, 244.

The Qing State and the Market

The Ming loyalists' denunciation of Qing economic policies as extractive and autocratic appears to contradict the view, prevalent among historians, of its "provisionist" nature – prioritizing the management of food resources for improving social welfare – and its increasing reliance on market forces. These accusations, however, were not just motivated by anti-Manchu sentiments or a reaction to the hardships suffered by the people during the Kangxi depression. They also responded to market policies adopted by the Qing. Above all, they reflected the Qing state's reliance on a system based on special licensing and brokerage. Going beyond salt monopolies, this system granted unprecedented power and autonomy to state-licensed trade brokers (*yahang*) – a common target of Ming loyalist criticism – who were supposed to facilitate contacts and commercial transactions between local merchants and long-distance traders. Some forms of brokerage had been in place since the Song Dynasty, but during the Qing period the brokers had increasingly assumed power in local communities, often taking over functions generally assigned to the magistrate, such as recording transactions, adjudicating disputes, and collecting taxes. It appears that often these brokers developed predatory tactics at the expenses of local small merchants.[39] The monopoly and brokerage systems were both prone to corruption and created what Wang Fuzhi described as corrupt collusion between the state and big merchants at the expense of the people's economy.

This system of special licenses created other unintended problems. The Qing administration, continuing earlier Song experiments, engaged private merchants to carry out tasks generally performed by the state, believing that, by doing so, they could transfer to them some administrative costs and that merchants could carry out those tasks in a more efficient manner.[40] As historian Dai Yingcong argues, this reliance on

[39] For more details on the Qing brokerage system see von Glahn, *The Economic History of China*, 328, and Susan Mann, *Local Merchants and the Chinese Bureaucracy, 1750–1950* (Stanford, CA: Stanford University Press, 1987), "Chapter 4: The State and Local Markets in Eighteenth Century Shandong."

[40] This trend had already begun in the Song Dynasty, which experimented with cutting military expenses through market mechanisms, especially in the Southern Song period after the demise of Wang Anshi's New Policies. The Qing expanded and systematized these policies. Dai, "The Qing State, Merchants, and the

merchants was part of a wider attempt to use the market to "mobilize societal forces to serve its public projects." Trying to "remedy the inadequacy of its bureaucracy," the Qing state, for example, turned to private merchants for the transport of military provisions. These practices started informally with Kangxi's campaign against the Zunghars (1690–7) – an inner-Asia group that threatened stability in the newly acquired area of Mongolia – and were later also adopted by the Yongzheng Emperor (r. 1722–35). Under Qianlong, the commercialization of military logistics was vastly expanded in support of the two Jinchuan campaigns (1747–9 and 1771–6) against local rebellions that challenged the Qing's control over Tibet. By the end of the second campaign, however, Qianlong was shocked to learn the full extent of corrupt practices that plagued the system. One of these practices was the *shanghao* (materials for reward). Military officials used state silver – intended for paying merchants for providing military supplies – to acquire non-military goods such as silk, satin, tobacco, and wine to reward soldiers. Many officials also used military silver to buy luxury goods and line their pockets. As Dai points out, the *shanghao* practice turned "campaign troops into an enormous consuming force."[41]

Another attempt to commercialize functions previously administered by the imperial bureaucracy was initiated by the Yongzheng Emperor and later expanded under Qianlong. In 1728 the Yongzheng Emperor officially established the system of *yingyung shengxi* (procuring profits through entrepreneurial operations) which provided for large sums of money to be entrusted to military units (both Manchu and Chinese) for investment in commercial enterprises. The profit thus obtained would contribute to supporting the soldiers' livelihood. With Yongzheng's agreement, many garrisons commissioned private merchants to invest their funds. Recognizing the fact that most garrison officials were not very adept at investment, Yongzheng had at first concentrated that function in the hands of provincial officials, but he later embraced the involvement of private merchants, commenting: "It's very good to commission merchants for investments. It is an extremely wonderful arrangement, if there is no coercion involved."[42]

Military Labor Force in the Jinchuan Campaigns" and "Yingyung Shengxi: Military Entrepreneurship in the High Qing Period, 1700–1800."

41 Dai, "The Qing State, Merchants, and the Military Labor Force in the Jinchuan Campaigns," 36, 70, 73, 77.

42 Quoted in Dai, "Yingyung Shengxi," 21, 25.

Although this system proved quite successful, the Qianlong Emperor, who had inherited it from his father, decided to terminate it. Corruption, in fact, had so tainted the *yingyun shengxi* system that it no longer fulfilled its original purpose. Among other malpractice, it was noted that officials ended up loaning the money to soldiers and expecting the payment of interest. Local-level officials and clerks used names of merchants to claim funds, even when there was no commercial activity in which they could be invested.[43]

Changes in the Qing management of the grain storage system throws further light on the tension between corruption and reliance on market forces. From the early years of the dynasty, Qing rulers had embraced the granary system with unprecedented vigor and diligence, eager to strengthen their image as a Confucian benevolent state committed to *minsheng* objectives, in an attempt to counteract the memory of their conquest origins. They abandoned the inefficient preparedness granary (*yubeicang*) model of the Ming – conceived as mere storage to compensate for scarcity of grain in case of famine[44] – and restored and expanded the Song's ever-normal model, establishing an empire-wide network of such granaries and charging officials with supervising the buying and storing of grain, which was then sold on the market strategically to stabilize supplies and prices.[45] This system required a constant administrative effort, reflecting, in the words of Leonard, the

[43] Dai, "Yingyung Shengxi," 14, 25, 35, 45–53.

[44] In 368, Emperor Hongwu (1368–98) ordered that four "preparedness" granaries be established in each province. This plan did not work out as intended. In general, the Ming state did not show much interest in managing food supplies, and the few granaries that had actually been established suffered from both a chronic lack of financing and the limited administrative capability of the Ming state. In this context, charity and community granaries thrived, and anti-famine preparation rested mostly on the shoulders of the local people. Wong, "Chinese Tradition of Grain Storage," 10–14.

[45] Since the fifth century BCE, storing grain had been a common strategy for both preventing famines and attempting to regularize the circulation of basic staples among the population. At that time, authors such as Fan Li (536–448 BCE) – the political adviser to the state of Yue and a successful business tycoon – and the writer of *Guanzi* presented the idea that the state should intervene to stabilize prices on the market through buying and selling grain. Wong, "Chinese Traditions of Grain Storage," 3. For a detailed discussion of the workings of the granary system under the Qing see the essays in Will and Wong, *Nourish the People.*

Qing rulers' "very activist and creative approach to the economy."[46] By the late eighteenth and early nineteenth centuries, however, the Qing granary system experienced a decline. Historian Roy Bin Wong argues that this decline was due to several reasons, including both administrative and economic considerations. In this period, the Qing came to find that their efforts to eradicate corruption among officials should also extend to the administration of the granaries. Corruption, in fact, was one of the motivations that led the Qing state to shift its focus away from the ever-normal granaries to community and charity granaries managed by local elites. The retrenchment of state intervention in the grain market was also motivated by "a great degree of skepticism toward state activism generally," not just for fear of bad governance, but also for strictly economic considerations. Some officials observed that the state's massive purchases of grain to restock the granaries caused the price of grain to rise. Others found it more expedient to stock silver instead of grain, mostly because of the difficulties in preventing spoilage and transporting the stored goods. Stored silver was to be used to purchase grain in case of emergency. This strategy, however, also proved problematic, as the state's attempt to correct grain prices would ultimately rely on the market itself since the state would buy grain at the prices set by merchants.[47] As the Qing state became increasingly involved in military operations linked to the White Lotus (*bailianjiao*, 1796–1804) and other rebellions, it increasingly employed the ever-normal granaries to supply the military or other state enterprises, leaving famine prevention measures in the hands of local elites and increasingly relying on market forces to solve regional scarcity problems.[48]

Historian Helen Dunstan confirms this diminished state intervention in grain storage during the Qianlong administration. While the granaries' purchases for storage increased until 1748, they dramatically declined after this period. At this time, grain-related policy shifted gear. State purchases of grain diminished dramatically while the state retreated from direct intervention and began instead to encourage merchants to maintain the proper flow of goods on the market and discourage them from creating bottlenecks, especially hoarding for

[46] Leonard, "The State's Resources and the People's Livelihood (*Guoji Minsheng*)," 47; Wong, "Chinese Tradition of Grain Storage," 14–15.
[47] Will and Wong, *Nourish the People*, 93–98.
[48] Will and Wong, *Nourish the People*, 93–98.

speculation. Penalties for hoarding were moderated and replaced with exhortations for the wealthy to share their stored grain on the market, a strategy that proved to be of limited success. More likely to succeed was the new policy of offering merchants opportunities to sell their hoarded grain at prices that would still allow profits. Dunstan also shows that these changes in policy were not just the whims of a few officials but a result of reports from several administrators around the empire that described the negative impact of state purchases on the market price of grain. The documentation used by Dunstan also shows that, in Beijing, Qianlong was advised by a pragmatic and competent group of officials, who worked closely to convince the emperor of the benefits of the new pro-market policies.[49] Among these officials was the powerful Fang Bao (1668–1749), who firmly believed in the crucial role played by the merchants' pursuit of profits in regulating the interregional flow of grain. According to Fang, "pursuing high prices and forsaking low ones" was a strategy that merchants "grasp[ed] without needing to be taught it." Allowing merchants to pursue profits would maximize the flow of grain into areas afflicted by scarcity and ultimately help to readjust local prices to a more regular level.[50]

The cases discussed in this section illustrate the complexity of the Qing state's relationship with the market. The commercial economy of the empire appeared to offer new solutions for maximizing the efficiency of selected administrative functions. Yongzheng's enthusiastic support for the "extremely wonderful arrangement" of entrusting private merchants with investing military funds denotes a strong belief not only in the savviness of the merchants in navigating the empire's highly commercialized economy, but also in the ability of market forces to achieve levels of efficiency in regulating the market out of reach of the government administration.[51] The Qianlong Emperor also shared this belief, declaring that "Commercial circulation has the general effect of lowering prices when they are too high."[52]

In general, therefore, Qing rulers relied on the price-regulating ability of the market but did not use this ability to create a unified economic system. Instead, they attempted to coopt the market to carry

[49] Dunstan, *State or Merchants*, 50–55, 78, and especially Chapters 3, 5, and 7.
[50] As quoted in Dunstan, "A Different Trajectory," 20. On Fang Bao's ideas of interests see also "A Different Trajectory," 31.
[51] Quoted in Dai, "Yingyung Shengxi," 21, 25.
[52] Quoted in Rowe, *Saving the World*, 198.

out selected tasks, including not only regulating prices or streamlining bureaucratic functions but also fighting corruption within the imperial administration. At the same time, they relied heavily on a brokerage system that, while intended to facilitate long-distance trade, often had the unintended consequence of interfering with the self-regulating ability of free-market competition.

Consumption

While confidence in the self-regulating power of the market built on changes originated during the Song, the pro-luxury notions of consumption that emerged in the late Ming and early Qing periods constituted a more sudden rupture with previous ideas and policies. Economic thought related to consumption, in fact, had remained more or less unchanged until the beginning of China's Industrious Revolution in the mid-1500s.

The question of whether China did experience an Industrious Revolution has been a focus of debate among historians. Recent works have counteracted de Vries' tendency to minimize similarities between the European and the Chinese Industrious Revolutions. De Vries argues that the two did not share the same characteristics and did not have the same impact on the economy. In East Asia, he explains, the "organization of the household as an economic entity," a crucial aspect of the European Industrious Revolution, did not emerge in response to market opportunities but "primarily because of demographic pressure and institutional coercion," thus minimizing the impact of changes in consumer behavior.[53] De Vries' idea of the limited market interaction

[53] Jan de Vries, *The Industrious Revolution*, 78–82. As de Vries points out, the "industrious" terminology for "labor-intensive, household-based production" was first adopted in the study of late-Tokugawa intense-labor practices, a mode of production that also came to characterize China (de Vries, *The Industrious Revolution*, 78–82). The term "Industrious Revolution," in fact, was first coined by the demographic and economic historian Akira Hayami, who uses it to describe "the rise of labor-intensive agricultural which was compatible with the rise of the market" in early-modern Japan, rather than focusing on consumer behavior; Akira Hayami, *Japan's Industrious Revolution: Economic and Social Transformations in the Early Modern Period* (Tokyo: Springer, 2016), V, 96–99; Akira Hayami, "Joron: keizaishakai no seiritsu to sonotokushutu," in *Searching for a New Historical View of the Edo Era (Atarashii Edo-Jidaishizō wo Motomete)*, ed. by Socio-Economic History and Society (Tokyo: Toyo Keizai Shimposha, 1977), 3–18.

within the Chinese Industrious Revolution has been largely disproved. Strengthening the case for the comparability of the European and Chinese industrious economies, recent studies have stressed the market orientation of the Chinese industrious household. Pomeranz, for example, argues that China experienced a similar "relevance of labor markets, markets for both time-saving and other goods, and demographic pressure."[54] While China historians generally recognize that England's agriculture was more capital-intensive than that of Jiangnan, they perceive labor in this area as more responsive to market opportunities than estimated by de Vries.[55] As early as the sixteenth century, peasants in Jiangnan planned their crops in response to the market rather than merely attempting to increase productivity per unit of land. Chinese peasants, for example, preferred to grow high-quality varieties of rice, priced for their taste, which could be sold at high prices on the market, rather than concentrating on early-ripening varieties that ensured two crops a year but sold at lower prices. In addition, they grew cheaper and faster-growing varieties, with lower market value, for the specific purpose of paying their rents, which were to be paid in grain. These choices reveal the "farmer's approach to his labor as an investment" and highlight farmers' reliance on the market and the monetized economy for maximizing income.[56] The same dynamics can be observed in Wuxi, a Jiangnan town that came to specialize in silk production in this period. Families in this area had not previously pursued sericulture but had focused on growing rice. In this period, however, they turned to sericulture in response to market opportunities that made it a much more lucrative enterprise than producing grain.[57]

Another factor contributing to increased market-based productivity was the end of the early-Ming anti-trade policies which had brought a large portion of manufacturing under the control of the state by establishing a system of "service obligations," as exemplified by the case discussed earlier of manufacturing linked to Zheng He's maritime

[54] Pomeranz, *The Great Divergence*, 98; see Chapter Two, "Market Economies in Europe and Asia," for a comprehensive discussion of this issue.

[55] Kenneth Pomeranz, "Beyond the East–West Binary: Resituating Development Paths in the Eighteenth-Century World," *The Journal of Asian Studies* 61(2) (2002), 539.

[56] John Thomas Meskill, *Gentlemanly Interests and Wealth on the Yangtze Delta* (Ann Arbor, MI: Association for Asian Studies, 1994), 19–20.

[57] Von Glahn, *The Economic History of China*, 353.

expeditions. Released from this form of servitude labor, these artisans were now able to work for themselves, selling their product on the market to make a living, while expanding both the volume and variety of goods available to the consumers.[58]

The industrious economy of this period generated a new consumer economy and a "materialist" mode of consumption, inspiring officials and intellectuals to formulate new theories that questioned the frugality paradigm. As historian Wu Jen-shu argues, in the late Ming period, China had already developed into a consumer society (*xiaofei shehui*). It was at this time that, especially in the Jiangnan region, urban elites enjoyed banquets of unprecedented sophistication in terms of the number of dishes and the quality of exotic and expensive food. The same trend can be detected in housing, clothing, and transportation. This period also saw an increased reliance on the market for purchasing not only luxury goods but also daily-need goods that had previously been produced at home. Above all, goods that were previously considered luxury items were now purchased as daily-need items by the common people. By the late Ming, luxury consumption had spread beyond the scholarly, official, and mercantile elites, also engaging people at lower levels of society.[59] The "middle people" (*zhongren*), including "small merchants from all walks of life – shop owners, restaurant owners, inn owners, and bankers – and their families ... were the ones who followed the fashions of the time and fueled luxury consumption."[60]

By the time of the Qianlong Emperor, this phenomenon was not limited to Jiangnan and other coastal areas; hinterland towns located on major trade routes also enjoyed a certain amount of luxury consumption. For example, in 1760, Wang Erjian (1703–66) – a magistrate of Ba County (Baxian) in Sichuan Province, now a district of the city of Chongqing – observed in compiling the county gazetteer that the local people were no longer frugal. They all despised common

58 Clunas, *Superfluous* Things, 144.

59 Wu Jen-shu, *Pinwei shehua: wanMing de xiaofei shehui yu shidaifu* (Beijing: Zhonghua, 2008), 23–31, 50, 128–135.

60 Wu Jen-shu and Wang Dagang, "A Preliminary Study of Local Consumption in the Qianlong Reign (1736–1796): The Case of Ba County in Sichuan Province," in *Living the Good Life: Consumption in the Qing and Ottoman Empires of the Eighteenth Century*, ed. by Elif Akçetin and Suraiya Faroqhi (Leiden: Brill, 2018), 191, 212.

clothes and crude food and preferred to eat delicacies and wear silk.[61] New shopping alleys developed, with one shop attached to the other, door to door in an unbroken chain, advertising their goods and competing with each other to attract the patronage of the shoppers who thronged the alley.[62]

It was also in the 1550s that the habit of traveling for leisure became prominent, with the consequent development of travel-related commercial services. This was caused not only by the decay of the state's traveling posts, which forced officials to rely on private establishments, but also by the gentry's new enthusiasm for leisure travel. By this time, leisure travel had become a real passion for the elites, and it was embraced as part of cultural refinement. Prices for travel, such as those for renting boats, declined so sharply that even the lower strata of the gentry, including unsuccessful examination candidates, could afford the pursuits of pleasure boating.[63] Sightseeing (*youguan*) came to be a favorite leisure activity for a larger section of the Jiangnan population, which enjoyed visiting famous temples, attending fairs and operas, riding on pleasure boats, viewing famous scenic spots, and drinking tea and wine. These new consumption habits brought about an altered landscape; teahouses and taverns proliferated, as did other establishments that catered to the throngs of sightseers.[64]

It was this new consumption economy that inspired writers to formulate new views of consumption that went beyond notions of "compensating deficiencies" with "excesses" – a formula that confined consumption to the realm of smooth circulation and equalization of resources.

Changing Views of Consumption: Lu Ji and Late-Ming Pro-Luxury Arguments

It should not come as a surprise that the earliest positive views of luxury consumption began to emerge among the literati elite of the Jiangnan region, the center of the empire's New Luxury economy and

61 Wu and Wang, "A Preliminary Study of Local Consumption in the Qianlong Reign (1736–1796)," 191, 212.
62 Wu Jen-shu, *Youyou fangxiang: Mingqing jiangnan chengshi de xiuxian xiaofei yu kongjian bianqian* (Beijing: Zhonghua shuju, 2017), 77–136.
63 Brook, *The Confusions of Pleasure*, 173–185.
64 Wu, *Youyou fangxiang*, 192–231.

kaozheng scholarly networks. Lu Ji (1515–52), the most renowned of the late-Ming pro-luxury writers, hailed from this region. Lu was born into a powerful family of officials in Songjiang – today part of Greater Shanghai. Expected to continue the family tradition and pursue a career in the imperial administration, he failed to pass the palace examination (*jinshi*), at that time essential for receiving an official appointment. As the Songjiang scholar Lin Shusheng (1509–1605) wrote in the epitaph for Lu Ji, at that time, Lu abandoned the lifestyle of his noble and powerful family to pursue a simple life of private study. This is all we know about his life. We know, however, that he was a prolific scholar who built a reputation for his brilliant essays and the eclectic nature of his intellectual interests.[65] Historian Lin Liyue places Lu Ji's works within the early developments of Statecraft scholarship (*jingshi sixiang*) in the late Ming period, an approach, she argues, that is reflected in his tendency to challenge basic notions of the Confucian tradition.[66] For example, she argues, Lu Ji disagreed with the common view that the Han Chinese and the non-Han "barbarians" (*yi*) differed in terms of levels of civilization, the former being civilized (*hua*) and the latter lowly (*bei*). Instead, Lu claimed that the main difference between these two groups rested in the fact that the Chinese lived in the "central plains" (*zhong yuan*) while the "barbarians" lived in the peripheral areas. Differences between the two were a matter of territorial division similar to that between town and countryside. In this comparison, the town represented China and naturally took the leadership over the rural periphery, the "barbarians."[67] Lu Ji's attempt at a geographical – rather than moral – differentiation between Chinese and barbarians illustrates his preference for a *kaozheng*-inspired "practical" approach, which, however, did not alter substantially the notion of Han superiority. Although Lu claimed that Heaven perceived all people, including the "barbarians," as deserving

65 Harvard University, Academia Sinica, and Peking University, *China Biographical Database* (December 19, 2018), https://projects.iq.harvard.edu/cbdb.

66 As part of the wider *kaozheng* trend, Statecraft scholarship focused on practical aspects of governance, including economic, social, and political issues. Huang Congxi and Gu Yanwu are considered early precursors of Statecraft thought. Elman, *From Philosophy to Philology*, 89–90.

67 Quoted in Lin Liyue, "Lu Ji (1515–1552) Chongshe sixiang zai tang—jianglun jinnian mingqing jingji sixiangshi yanjiu de jige wenti," *Xinshixue* 5(1) (1995), 131–153, at 134–135.

of nurture, the peripheral "barbarians" were predestined to follow the lead of the center of the "civilized" world, the Chinese empire.[68]

A *kaozheng* preference for "useful" studies appears to have been common among Songjiang's scholars. According to historian John Meskill's study of the Songjiang's literati elites, at the time of Lu Ji most Songjiang scholars had obtained only lower-level degrees and had either failed or not attempted the examination, thus forfeiting a career in the imperial administration. In general, they preferred to devote their lives to private intellectual pursuits of "useful" issues and were critical of the official *jinshi* elites, whom they identified with the declining political and social environment of the late Ming.[69]

Lu Ji's short treatise *A Critique of the Ban on Extravagance* (*Jinshebian*) challenged the idea that luxury led to poverty.[70] To discredit that point, Lu quoted the famous statement of Mencius about the circulation and exchange of products and services, which was already mentioned above – "allowing what one person has in excess to compensate for the deficiency of another" – and asked why "rulers wanted to impede" a policy that had been declared to be correct (*zheng*) by a pillar of Confucianism. Lu Ji then concluded that "luxury trade brings prosperity" (*she yi wei sheng*) by generating jobs (*jiushi*) and opportunities for profit among the people. "The so-called luxury," he explained, "does not merely allow rich merchants and prominent wealthy families to indulge in extravagance in the style of their housing, carriages, food, and clothes. If they eat grain and meat, peasants and cooks will also benefit. If they wear extravagant silk clothes, traders and weavers will also benefit."[71]

Leisure sightseeing on the West Lake (Xihu), Lu continued, captured the lively tourist and traveling business that characterized this famous sightseeing destination, generating income for boaters, dancers, cooks, and sedan carriers.[72] The West Lake was part of the city of Hangzhou,

[68] Meskill, *Gentlemanly Interests and Wealth on the Yangtze Delta*, 10, 37–38.
[69] Meskill, *Gentlemanly Interests and Wealth on the Yangtze Delta*, 10, 37–38, and the chapter "The Triumph of Abundance," 141–155.
[70] Lu Ji, "Jinshebian."
[71] Lu, "Jinshebian"; Lin, "'Jianjiatang gao' yu Lu Ji 'Fan jinshe' sixiang zhi chuanyan," 126–127. The term *bian* used in the title of Lu Ji's essay refers to a literary genre popular among *kaozheng* scholars and more precisely translated as "critical essay ... based on detachment and impartiality"; Elman, *From Philosophy to Philology*, 81.
[72] Lu, "Jinshebian."

an important trade center, but also a popular destination for leisure sightseeing and for pilgrimages to its many famous Buddhist monasteries. Guides to the "floating world" of Hangzhou were readily available, as were essays extolling the beauty of the scenery and the city's bustling fairs and festivals – including the four-day lantern festival. According to a late-Ming account, so many tourists crowded this place that those who wanted to climb up to the top of the Dragon Hill – a popular destination – had to fight the throngs of people or just give up and let the crowd transport them to the top.[73]

In this vibrant commercial context, Lu concluded, extravagance was not like hoarding. The latter, Lu declared, was like "dumping wealth into a ditch," wasting resources and causing poverty,[74] whereas luxury consumption contributed to the prosperity of the community. While these statements echoed earlier pro-spending arguments, they departed from them significantly, since they described a form of consumption that went beyond the Old Luxury. It in fact, involved what de Vries describes as a life of more comfort and leisure for a wider section of the population. In order to make a living, for example, boat renters would have to rely on sustained demand from a substantial number of sightseers. Lu also clearly defined the commercial and service sectors (boat renters, dancers, sedan carriers, and cooks) as wealth-generating and expanded the idea of wealth (*caï*) to the monetized economy.

Despite his support for luxury consumption, Lu Ji did not advocate a spendthrift attitude among consumers, but carefully distinguished between the role consumption played in the economy and in the management of the household. Frugality, he argued, was a beneficial practice for families since it helped safeguard their wealth. Frugality, however, could not lead the empire to prosperity. Rulers, who planned for the prosperity of the empire and not for that of a single household, should not ban extravagance in places like Suzhou and Hangzhou where economic circumstances were favorable.[75]

Lu Ji was also aware of the uneven economic situation of the empire, characterized by the gap between the commercialized/coastal and rural/hinterland areas. He, in fact, articulated a flexible theory of consumption that moved beyond the one-size-fits-all solution. He argued that "if prosperous, luxury can follow; if poor, retain frugality"

[73] Brook, *The Confusions of Pleasure*, 233–237.
[74] Liu, "Jinshebian."
[75] Liu, "Jinshebian."

(*xian fu er hou she, xian pin er hou jian*), calling for diversified modes of consumption according to regional circumstances. He argued that Hangzhou and Suzhou – the commercial centers of the Jiangnan economy – should be allowed to enjoy extravagant habits. In this area, "trade was a means for livelihood." Other places that did not enjoy such favorable economic circumstances should instead rely on frugality, since luxury habits would only squander their scarce resources. People in mostly agricultural places such as Ning, Shao, Jin, or Qu,[76] he argued, were very frugal, and frugality was a good choice for those who lived there. When the local economy met with difficulties, however, "half of the population needs to go seek food in other areas because if people are frugal they cannot help each other." In other words, in these localities, if agriculture suffered, there was no viable trade or service sector to fall back on. Despite this shortcoming, however, poor agricultural communities should ban luxury.[77] In Lu Ji's eyes, therefore, an economy based to a significant extent on wider activities than the "fundamental" (*ben*) agriculture was more resilient in case of crisis and could generate more wealth. Most of the wealth of the empire, he argued, came from Jiangsu and Zhejiang, although, in those areas, "who knows how many there are who do not tend the fields but still eat sorghum or who do not operate a loom but still wear embroidered silk. How is this possible? It is because habits are extravagant and those who pursue the non-fundamental economic activities are many."[78]

Lu Ji's views on the role of luxury consumption can appear contradictory at times, if not placed in context. Lu wanted to present luxury as the cause of prosperity and not as its consequence, thus he stressed the important role of luxury consumption (as demand) for the generation of wealth. What made Suzhou and Hangzhou so prosperous, he argued, was not the fact that they lay along major trade routes. It was because they had extravagant habits. Finding high demand for their goods, merchants flocked to these towns. Lu argued, "Some see that [merchants] rely on the profit of the market but do not know that it is

[76] The town of Ning is close to today's city of Qingyang in Gansu Province. Shao probably refers to a prefecture now part of the city of Tianjin in Hebei Province. Jin was a town in southern Shaanxi Province and Qu refers to a prefectural seat in today's Quzhou, in Southwestern Zhejiang Province. Liu Junren, *Zhongguo diming dacidian* (Taipei: Wenhai chubanshe, 1990), 263, 925, 951, 856.

[77] Liu, "Jinshebian." [78] Liu, "Jinshebian."

luxury that generates the market." To prove this point, Lu Ji brought up the example of his native village. Although it was "a rustic place on the seashore" that was not on the main routes of "boats and carriages," the village was known as the "Little Suzhou" because people there "particularly valued extravagance and ... relied on trade for livelihood."[79] For this reason, merchants traveled to the village and the locals could rely on trade for their living.

Lu Ji used this example to stress the stimulating effects on the economy of demand for luxury goods and not to advocate that luxury should be practiced in all "rustic" areas. Where resources were scarce, he insisted, it was important to rely on frugality in order not to squander them. "Officials should rule according to customs" (*zhangminzhe yinsu weizhi*), Lu explained, promoting frugality or extravagance according to local circumstances. If a community enjoyed a wide network of luxury consumption, constituting a vital part of its economy – even if it was just a "rustic place" – then extravagance should not be banned. If it did not, frugality should be encouraged. The latter kind of community, however, would not be as prosperous or resilient as the first. It is in this context that we should read the two seemingly contradictory, but actually complementary, statements that "if prosperous, luxury can follow; if poor, retain frugality" and that "Officials should rule according to customs."

It is also important to note that Lu Ji's "rustic" native village was Songjiang, located within the prosperous Jiangnan region and today part of Greater Shanghai. Songjiang's situation, therefore, was very different from that of more isolated and remote villages in the rural hinterland. Songjiang was a central hub for coastal shipping, being located at the junction of inland commercial channels and the sea. Transportation to and from Songjiang was also remarkably convenient. It is reported that in the prefecture, in addition to a wide network of roads, there were as many as 690 bridges and thirty-one ferries, Songjiang being a canal town similar to Suzhou. In the late sixteenth century, Songjiang experienced significant commercialization and increased prosperity among its elites.[80] Songjiang Prefecture was famous for some highly valued specialties, including the Nine Peaks

79 Liu, "Jinshebian."

80 Meskill, *Gentlemanly Interests and Wealth on the Yangtze Delta*, 25–27. See also Li Bozhong. *Jiangnan de zaoqi gongyehua* (Beijing: Zhongguo renmin taxue chubanshe, 2010), 22–27.

and Liu wines and the Huating crab. By the sixteenth century, Songjiang was also recognized as the center of the cotton industry and was famous for its cotton textiles. These products found wide circulation in the region through the commercial networks developed by Songjiang traveling merchants.[81] By Lu Ji's time, the elites in Songjiang "had long embraced a life of taste in preference to the Confucian life of will." As many observers complained, the old standards of elegance and taste – simplicity and modest deference in social intercourse and unostentatious elegance – had been replaced by a conspicuous display of wealth and consumption. Not only the great families of Songjiang Prefecture but also wider and lower social strata enthusiastically followed the latest fashions. It appears that Songjiang did not compare unfavorably to Suzhou, since Songjiang "men pursued satisfactions with special exuberance."[82]

We know that Lu Ji's *Jinshebian* essay circulated among scholars in the Jiangnan region, mostly thanks to the efforts of Zhejiang scholar and bibliophile Shen Jiefu (1553–1601), who collected Lu Ji's writings in a volume titled *Draft from the Hall of Reeds* (*Jianjiatang gao*) which he included in his private library (*cangshu jia*), thus ensuring their circulation among the Jiangnan scholarly elites.[83] The *Jinshebian* essay attracted particular attention and was included in at least two collectanea.[84] Reproduction of passages from *Jinshebian*, however, did not imply full agreement with its main arguments. The Mongol bannerman and renowned scholar, Fashishan (1752–1813), for example, appeared to disagree with Lu, although he had included passages from

81 Meskill, *Gentlemanly Interests and Wealth on the Yangtze Delta*, 20–22.

82 Meskill, *Gentlemanly Interests and Wealth on the Yangtze Delta*, 152.

83 Harvard University, Academia Sinica, and Peking University, *China Biographical Database*. For the role of private library in the development of the *kaozheng* school in Jiangnan see Elman, *From Philosophy to Philology*, 181–190.

84 Collectanea (*cong shu*) was a genre, together with encyclopedias, especially popular by the late Ming. Their main goal was to reprint and ensure the survival of manuscripts while also, as mini libraries, improving the circulation of important texts among scholars; Elman, *From Philosophy to Philology*, 190. Selected passages of Lu Ji's "Jinshebian" were included in Li Yuxiang's *Tuipeng wuyu* (printed 1571) and later in *Taolu zalu*, compiled by Fashishan. According to historian Lin Liyue, it was through Fashishan's collection that Wei Yuan (1794–1857) came to be familiar with Lu Ji's ideas. Lin Liyue, "Lu Ji (1515–1552) "Chongshe sixiang zaitang," 135.

his essay in a collectanea.[85] In his *Miscellaneous Records from the Potter's Hut* (*Taolu zalu*), closely echoing Lu Ji's own writings, Fashishan wrote that "The customs of the lower Yangzi River revere luxury ... Many ordinary people (*ximin*) in Shuzhou and Hangzhou make a living through trade. The customs of South China (*yue*) honor frugality, and the little people (*xiaomin*) of the prefectures of Ning, Zhao, Jin, and Qu cannot sustain themselves. Usually, half of their population go seeking food in the four corners."[86] Fashishan concludes this brief summary of Lu's formula of ruling according to customs with an ambiguous remark. Lu Ji's observations, he states, did indeed reflect a long-standing situation but did not validate the formula of ruling by customs. Frugality had been followed for a long time, and it was an important rule, especially for households.[87]

Lu Ji's idea of consumption, therefore, appears to have generated interest among the Jiangnan intellectual community. It is difficult, however, to assess whether other late-Ming scholars and officials who supported luxury consumption were directly inspired by Lu's *Jinshebian*, or, just like Liu, were responding independently to changes in the social and economic environment of the region. Several Jiangnan scholars also argued in favor of luxury. Among them was Ye Quan (1522–78), a native of Xiuning, Changzhou Prefecture, in Jiangsu Province.[88] Ye traveled extensively through China, and his collected

[85] A *kaozheng* bibliophile, Fashishan had compiled several collectanea and later in his career participated in the compilation of the *Siku quanshu*. Arthur W. Hummel, *Eminent Chinese of the Ch'ing Period (1644–1912)* (Taipei: SMC, 1991), 227–228. For a concise biography of Fashishan see Liu Qingshan, "Hong Liangji yu Fashishan jiayou kaoshu," *Wenhua yu chuanbo* 1 (2012), 8–12. The *Siku quanshu* (*Complete Library of the Four Treasures*) is an encyclopedic collection of more than 10,000 titles and compendiums compiled by a board of Hanlin scholars and ordered by Emperor Qianlong. It remains the largest collection of books in Chinese history.

[86] Fashishan, "Taolu zalu," in *Xuxiu siku quanshu* (Shanghai: Shanghai guji chubanshe, 1997), juan 5, 681. A note in a later (1817) reprint of "Taolu zalu" attributes this piece to Li Yuxiang's collectanea *Tuipeng wuyu*, printed in 1571. This collection included a piece identical to "Jinshebian." Li was also a resident of Songjiang and probably had occasion to read the original version of "Jinshebian." Lin, "Lu Ji (1515–1552) chongshe zai tang—jianglun jinnian mingqing jingji sixiangshi yanjiu de jige wenti," 142–143.

[87] Fashishan, "Taolu zalu," 682 and Lin, "Lu Ji (1515–1552) chongshe zai tang—jianglun jinnian mingqing jingji sixiangshi yanjiu de jige wenti," 142–143.

[88] Harvard University, Academia Sinica, and Peking University, *China Biographical Database*.

works, *A Compilation of Worthies and Erudites* (*Xianbobian*), include essays on the places he visited and their local customs as well as treatises on economic and social issues. Ye shared Lu Ji's views. In discussing the luxury prevalent in Hangzhou, Ye explained that extravagant habits were so ingrained that they had penetrated the marrow of the local population and could not be changed. On the other hand, Ye argued, these habits – among which he cited leisure trips to the West Lake as representative – generated income for a large portion of the population and for this reason should not be banned.[89] The same ideas were echoed by Wang Shixing (1547–98), a government official and writer of geographical books.[90] Wang opposed the ban on luxury and pointed out the financial gains it generated for the entire community, using again as a corroborating example the extravagant leisure trips to the West Lake, which he described as a place buzzing with people seeking all kinds of pleasures, from boat rides to dining and attending performances.[91]

As these writings illustrate, by the late Ming the Jiangnan economy was experiencing a dramatic change in the mode of consumption. Its economy came to be characterized, in the words of art historian Craig Clunas, by a "visible tension between the state's attempt to regulate consumption legally ... and the increasing lack of effect such regulations had in an 'exploding commodity context.'"[92] These changes inspired a new understanding among the Jiangnan elite of the role played by consumption in the economy.

Views of Luxury Consumption in the High Qing Period

The economic crisis that characterized the years of the Ming–Qing transition – due to the Manchu conquest and the Kangxi depression – did not displace the new views of consumption that had emerged in the late Ming. The consumption economy and pro-luxury arguments, in fact, survived the crisis and gained further momentum in the High Qing period, becoming a permanent feature of Chinese economic thought.

89 Wu Jen-shu, *Pinwei shehua: wanMing de xiaofei shehui yu shidaifu*, 39.
90 Harvard University, Academia Sinica, and Peking University, *China Biographical Database*.
91 Lin, "'Jianjiatang gao' yu Lu Ji 'Fan jinshe' sixiang zhi chuanyan," 127–128.
92 Clunas, *Superfluous Things*, 147.

One of the most vocal and well-known advocates of luxury consumption in the early Qing was Tang Zhen (1630–1704). Born in Da County (Daxian, in Sichuan Province), into a family of officials and landowners, during his youth Tang traveled extensively following his father on his official duties in Wujiang (a Jiangsu county-level town), Beijing, and Nanjing. In 1644, when Nanjing fell to the Manchus, Tang's family sought refuge in Shaoxing, Zhejiang Province, where they were to remain. In 1657, Tang Zhen passed the provincial examination, gaining the title of *juren*,[93] and was appointed magistrate of Changzhi County (Shanxi Province). His administrative career, however, came to a sudden end when he fell into disgrace, probably because he was made a scapegoat in a case of bureaucratic malfeasance. Now an impoverished and unemployed *juren*, Tang sold his family property to start a business, which, however, soon failed. Reduced to poverty, he eked out a living by engaging in small trade and renting out rooms. An accomplished scholar and would-be entrepreneur, Tang lived at the borders between the scholarly and the commercial elites.[94]

Also a Ming loyalist and *kaozheng* scholar – highly critical of Song Learning (*Songxue*) and its disregard for practical issues[95] – Tang wrote almost twenty years later than Huang, Gu, and Wang, at the tail end of the Kangxi depression, which he described in vivid terms:

> More than fifty years have passed since the founding of the Qing dynasty, and the empire grows poorer each day. Farmers are destitute, artisans are destitute, merchants are destitute, and officials too are destitute. Grain is cheap, yet it is hard to eat one's fill. Cloth is cheap, yet it is hard to cover one's skin. Boatloads of goods travel from one marketplace to another, but the cargoes must be sold at a loss. Officials upon leaving their posts discover they have no wherewithal to support their household. Indeed the four occupations are all impoverished! Now, silver and coin are the vehicles by which goods are circulated and surpluses and deficits balanced. But a family of average means may go ten days without seeing a *tael* of silver or a string of cash. With no money to facilitate the circulation of goods, farmers suffer cold

93 The title of *juren* was bestowed upon scholars who successfully passed the provincial level of the examination system.

94 Von Glahn, *Fountain of Fortune*, 222.

95 Yu Li, "Social Change During the Ming–Qing Transition and the Decline of Sichuan Classical Learning in the Early Qing," *Late Imperial China* 19(1) (1998), 31.

> and hunger, the hundred trades find no customers, and a year of bountiful harvest is no better than a year of dearth.[96]

Tang's bleak assessment of the contemporary economic situation led him to criticize Qing economic policies. Like his three predecessors, Tang condemned autocracy and corruption, supported "storing wealth among the people," and envisioned a natural economy based on free trade.[97] Tang was also an anti-silverist and argued for a return to copper cash. His opposition to the use of silver was in part motivated by his concerns with despotism, corruption, and hoarding of wealth. As he explained in one of his essays:

> Accumulation harms wealth, and silver is a material easy to accumulate. [Silver] is molded into a lovely round shape, with a glittering white surface, so everyone covets it. It is so compact that one treasury of silver is equal [in value] to a hundred treasuries of copper cash. One can keep all the silver in the world out of people's sight. High officials collect silver and carry it away month after month, so silver is disappearing [from circulation] very quickly ... The propensity of silver to be accumulated by people is as natural as the tendency of water to flow to lower ground.[98]

Tang also worried about the scarcity of silver that characterized the early Qing period and how this scarcity affected the economy:

> The flow [of silver] is like a narrow stream; how can it be of use for the world? On the contrary, copper cash, like a fountain, will never be exhausted. Currency cannot benefit the world unless it flows as abundantly as big rivers.[99]

Tang, however, differed from the previous generation of Ming loyalists on the issue of luxury consumption, reflecting not only the permanence of the new views on consumption that had emerged in the late Ming but also his own very different life experience. Huang Zongxi, for example, had denounced all kinds of consumption not linked directly with livelihood and not prescribed in the classics on rites, such

96 Quoted in von Glahn, *Fountain of Fortune*, 223; Tang Zhen, "Cunyan," in *Qian Shu* (Taipei: Heluo tushu chubanshe 1974), 114.
97 Kishimoto-Nakayama, "The Kangxi Depression and Early Qing Local Markets," 237–238.
98 Quoted in Kishimoto-Nakayama, "The Kangxi Depression and Early Qing Local Markets," 237.
99 Quoted in Kishimoto-Nakayama, "The Kangxi Depression and Early Qing Local Markets."

as extravagant expenditures for marriage – especially dowry and banquets – and Buddhist or magic rituals. Providing for all the paraphernalia required for the maintenance of Buddhism (including candles, incense, and animals for sacrifices), Huang argued, "cuts deep into the productivity of the people" and "consume[s] much of what the people produce."[100] He made the same argument for "entertainers, wine shops, and fine silk factories." "The cost of entertainers," he explained, "consumes in one night the resources of the man of moderate means. The expense of wine shops is such that one party consumes a whole year's worth of food. One suit of clothes bought at a fine silk factory costs enough to clothe ten men."[101] Observations of the lively commercial economy that had inspired Lu Ji's appreciation of luxury consumption elicited Huang's criticisms:

> In the market and stores of our cities today, nine places out of ten deal in Buddhist goods, or in goods used for magic rites, or in theatrical entertainment, or in clever contrivances and fancy accessories. Since none of them really satisfies a need of the people, to eliminate them all should be one way of remedying things.[102]

According to Huang, these kinds of consumption not only did not reflect the needs of the people but were also not conducive to wealth creation and prevented people from becoming prosperous.[103] They acted like heavy taxation, imposing an unnecessary burden on people's wealth. In order to unleash the economic potential of the people and foster their prosperity, both obstacles – heavy taxation and peripheral (*mo*) consumption – needed to be removed.[104]

Tang Zhen's pro-luxury views complicated the Ming loyalists' arguments on both consumption and despotism. Tang distinguished positive and negative forms of consumption not in terms of their utility, or

[100] Huang referred here to *Zhou Li*, *Yi Li*, and *Li Zhi*, as well as to some later modification such as Zhu Xi's *Family Rituals*. Huang and de Bary, *Waiting for the Dawn*, 160–161 and 254 (note 13).

[101] Huang and de Bary, *Waiting for the Dawn*, 160.

[102] Huang and de Bary, *Waiting for the Dawn*, 160.

[103] Huang and Shen, *Huang Zongxi quanji*, Volume 1, 40 and Huang and de Bary, *Waiting for the Dawn*, 159. In this context, De Bary translates the term *mo* as "evil outgrowths" (cit. 160), but I prefer to keep the established translation of "peripheral."

[104] Huang and Shen, *Huang Zongxi quanji*, Volume 1, 40–41, and Huang and de Bary, *Waiting for the Dawn*, 159–160.

lack thereof, toward *minsheng*, but in terms of modes of acquisition of goods. All forms of consumption, including that of luxury goods, were positive if market-based but negative if obtained through corrupted imposition by the officials. Market-based luxury consumption generated wealth, Tang explained. The "wealth of one household ... can nurture a hundred others," and "rich and poor naturally [without planning] support each other."[105] A rich family bought food and goods for celebrating weddings, births, funerals, and other life-cycle events and for making offerings to spirits and ghosts. They bought what they needed on the local market for cash. Thus silk, fish, and wine were all traded on the market, and consumption fueled a lively local trade.[106]

The acquisitions of the same goods, however, would have a negative impact on the economy if obtained through corruption or "despotic acquisition" (*nüequ*), which runs against the natural market-based system. The luxury of officials belonged to this category when goods were acquired by means of corrupt and autocratic practices and not through fair exchange on the market. Rulers and officials who indulged in luxury so obtained were, for Tang, worse than bandits and thieves, since they took away the very means of subsistence from the people, and, in so doing, they caused great damage to the economy.[107] In offering an example of such a mode of "despotic acquisition," Tang wrote:

> Outside of the east gate of Yanzhou, there is a canteen that sells goat. It employs two generations [of the family] and feeds more than ten people between wife, children, servants, etc. If [the owner] is falsely accused of having stolen a goat and is fined three piculs of grain, then those above have taken one, and those below have lost ten. This is because he has to sell his pot, and moreover he becomes unemployed. He then ends up begging on the street. This is to take one and destroy a hundred.[108]

While market-based luxury benefited the economy and contributed to the ever-important goal of supporting the people's livelihood, the luxury of officials was generally an unproductive form of despotism and corruption.

105 Tang Zhen, "Fumin," in *Qian shu* (Taipei: Heluo tushu chubanshe 1974), 106.
106 Tang, "Fumin," 106. 107 Tang, "Cunyan," 114.
108 Tang, "Fumin," 105–106. A picul was equivalent to approximately 60 kilograms.

Tang Zhen was thus able to distinguish between market-based luxury and that of corrupt officials, complicating the earlier Ming loyalists' anti-despotism arguments that denounced luxury as a unified behavior, essentially and irredeemably corrupt. With Tang Zhen we see a clear distinction emerging between negative luxury as a sign of corruption in the political sphere and positive market luxury in the private (*minjian*) economy. Rulers and officials, Tang argued, need to adopt a frugal style of life. To support his argument, he took as an example the first Ming emperor, Hong Wu (r. 1368–98), who, he argued, dressed simply in native cloth. "Clothes can be made of cotton; where is the need for brocade and embroidery? Vessels can be made of earthenware; where is the need for gold and jade? A person can be sated with rice and meat; where is the need for bear paws and Yutian rice?"[109] Rulers and officials should adopt a frugal lifestyle and avoid "despotic acquisitions," thus freeing the natural economy from the undue burden imposed by corrupt officials. In this context, luxury continued to be considered a sign of corruption among officials and frugality a mark of good government. Frugality, however, did not belong to the societal economy, where market-based luxury consumption was an expression of the people's "natural" economy and stimulated productivity and growth.[110]

Luxury consumption became the means through which, naturally (*ziran*) – free of government intervention and without planning – wealth circulated widely in society, productivity increased, and resources were balanced between rich and poor. Further describing this natural economic system, Tang wrote:

> As for the wealth of the land, there is no field that does not produce, and no person who does not make a living. As seasons pass by, there is enough for self-sufficiency without planning ... Poor and rich depend on each other without planning. This [natural economy] is the reason that the sages did not develop a technique for generating wealth. Because of this, profits emerge naturally and there is no need for [state] interference. Wealth cannot be all used up.[111]

This statement expanded the Ming loyalists' idea of an essentially "natural" Chinese economy beyond its local rural dimension to include production, trade, and services. Tang, in fact, introduced a

[109] Tang, "Fumin," 107. [110] Tang, "Fumin," 107.
[111] Tang, "Fumin," 106.

vision of the economy as a complex "natural" market system which responded to its own laws of supply and demand, both regulating production and equalizing wealth. State attempts to manage would inevitably have disastrous effects. Tang's views of the economy of the empire, in fact, come closer to the Smithian liberal market system than any other late-imperial formulation.

Support for luxury consumption continued to spread widely, especially among pursuers of Practical Studies (*shixue*).[112] The scholar Wei Jirui, mentioned earlier, also commented that the luxury consumption of the rich would create work for the poor and that, for this reason, it was important for the circulation of resources (in this sense not limited to *ben*).[113] Another pro-luxury writer among the literati was Wei Shixiao (1655–?), the nephew of the prominent scholar Wei Xi (1624–81). Following a path similar to most pro-luxury scholars, Wei had rejected the use of the stifling eight-legged style (*ba gu*) – a cumbersome literary style of prose generally linked to Neo-Confucianism and the examination system – and, rather than embarking on a career in the imperial administration, retreated to private life in the countryside to engage in practical learning.[114] In his essay, *Debate on Extravagance and Stinginess* (*Shelin shuo*), Wei argued that the luxury of rich families helped silver circulate and thus helped the people's livelihood. Luxury consumption allowed resources to be "passed down to the people" (*liu yu min*) through the market.[115] Wei's discussion summed up the popular argument that a distinction should be made between the rich, who put their wealth back into circulation among the people through their extravagant habits, and the stingy (*lin*), who instead hoarded their riches and hindered the circulation of resources. Although resonating with tropes linked to classical notions of circulation of resources, Wei's arguments reflected a deeply changed understanding of the economy which implied the elasticity of supplies as well as the utility of luxury for the economic growth of the empire. "The extravagant person wastes wealth and hurts himself," he wrote. "The stingy person accumulates

112 Practical Studies (*shixue*) was a popular late-Ming and Qing period school of thought that, like Evidential Studies (*kaozheng*), criticized Neo-Confucianism and emphasized practical and utilitarian functionality.

113 Kishimoto-Nakayama, "The Kangxi Depression and Early Qing Local Markets," 231–32.

114 Hummel, *Eminent Chinese of the Ch'ing Period (1644–1912)*, 848, 850.

115 Lin, "'Jianjiatang gao' yu Lu Ji 'Fan jinshe' sixiang zhi chuanyan," 129.

wealth and hurts the wealth [of All Under Heaven]. Hurting one's own wealth does not diminish the resources of All Under Heaven. But hurting the wealth [of All Under Heaven] exhausts all resources and impoverishes the people."[116]

Gu Gongxie (1759–1844) – a native of Wu County (Wuxian in Suzhou Prefecture, Jiangsu Province) – was also among the pro-luxury scholars who preferred to forgo a career in the imperial administration. After passing the first level of the examination, he retreated to private life. In his collection of essays, *Collected Chats from the Garden of Footsteps* (*Lüyuan conghua*), Qian Yong (1759–1844), the prominent Jiangnan calligrapher and writer of aesthetics, argued that, while in earlier times the local authorities had used public works to bring relief to the poor, today it was more convenient to use the local custom of luxury consumption to create jobs. Not following this strategy would hurt the community deeply. According to Qian, luxury was not only helpful during times of crisis but also supported the daily workings of the economy and the production of wealth. In Suzhou County, he explained, no less than ten thousand people relied on different kinds of theatrical performance each day. If leisure activities such as visits to temples, theaters, traveling boats, brothels, and cricket and quail fights were banned, there would be many poor and unemployed people who would inevitably become vagabonds, beggars, and robbers.[117] In the same collection of writings, however, Qian condemned "luxury" (*she*) as amoral in relation to politics. As was the case with Tang Zhen and most pro-luxury writers, when discussing corruption among officials, Qian maintained the traditional negative moral implications of luxury.[118]

The paradigm of positive market-based luxury and negative corrupt consumption came to influence the economic decision-making of the Qianlong Emperor. When, in 1768, bannerman and court official You Bashi (dates unknown) was on an inspection tour of the Anhui salt administration, he sent a memorial to the throne suggesting measures to end the merchants' luxury habits and to encourage frugality.

[116] Quoted in Lin, "'Jianjiatang gao' yu Lu Ji 'Fan jinshe' sixiang zhi chuanyan," 129.

[117] Qian Yong, "Conghua 1: Jiuwen," *Lüyuan conghua* (Taipei: Dali chubanshe, 1982), Section "Andun qiongre," 26–27; Wu Renshu, *Pinwei shehua*, 314.

[118] Qian Yong, "Conghua 7: Yilun," *Lüyuan conghua*, Sections "Jiaoshe" (192) and "Jian" (201–202).

Expecting the throne to support his advice, in line with the imperial state's long anti-luxury tradition, You was certainly surprised by Qianlong's response disagreeing with him. In this letter, Qianlong made his position very clear. These merchants, he argued, amassed great fortunes and spent much, but they were certainly no trouble. They actually helped to keep the masses pacified by creating job opportunities. Following the "empty notion of frugality" (*jian zhi xuming*), the emperor stated, would only lead the people to find their own ways to meet their needs – referring here to banditry and rebellion, the common survival strategies in times of scarcity feared by the state. It was better to leave the situation as it was and use the principle of "using what is plenty to supply what is scarce." The emperor commanded You to refrain from adopting anti-luxury measures.[119]

The emperor sent his reply to You in the form of a letter (*xin*), rather than an "open explanation" (*ming*). He probably did so because he was not ready to make his position official. Four main reasons arguably worked against a formal position. His support of luxury would undermine the established Confucian orthodoxy and damage the Confucian legitimacy of the dynasty. He also probably realized that the situation described by You was localized and that supporting luxury consumption was not a policy sustainable through the entire empire, as Lu Ji had suggested.[120] We can also infer that he found it difficult to openly support luxury while fighting corruption among officials. Finally, Qianlong might have considered the fact that frugality had been, historically, an important strategy for social stability, and not only because it contributed to the mandate of *minsheng* by preserving resources and regulating their distribution, mostly through sumptuary laws. It also promoted respect for social hierarchies and, because of its close association with the virtues of honesty and integrity, discouraged behavior that went against the public interest (*gong*), hence its crucial role in anti-corruption measures. Removing frugality from the official imperial policies, therefore, had the potential for seriously destabilizing consequences. Qianlong's letter to You, however, highlights the pragmatism of the imperial state; in this case, fears that unemployed people

[119] Chen Guodong, "Youguan Lu Ji de 'Jinshebian' zhi yanjiu suosheji de xueli wenti," *Xin shixue* 5(2) (1994), 162; Lin, "'Jianjiatang gao' yu Lu Ji 'Fan jinshe' sixiang zhi chuanyan," 130.

[120] Chen, "Youguan Lu Ji de 'Jinshebian' zhi yanjiu suosheji de xueli wen ti"; Lin, "'Jianjiatang gao' yu Lu Ji 'Fan jinshe' sixiang zhi chuanyan."

could turn to banditry prevailed over concerns about flouting sumptuary laws and social hierarchies.

Emperor Jiaqing (r. 1796–1820) also adhered to Qianlong's flexible approach in the early years of his reign. While never officially reversing the pro-frugality ideology of the state, he refrained from banning luxury consumption when it constituted an activity carried out on the market and contributed to improving the livelihood of the people. For example, in June 1797 – a few months after his father's death and his assumption of full control of the imperial decision-making process, but before he launched the anti-luxury Xianyu Reforms (*xianyu weixin*, 1799–1805) discussed in the next chapter – Jiaqing received a memorial accusing some high officials of leading an extravagant lifestyle. At this time, he took a flexible position on the matter of opera performances. The emperor stated that performing operas often constituted a means for making a living for common people and, therefore, it should be accepted. If the opera teams were not hired on the market and instead were kept as retainers within the *yamen* official residence, operas were a cause of grave concern and were to be banned. In the latter instances, in fact, the performances would not contribute to the people's livelihood, probably meaning that they would be paid with levied taxes as part of the official administrative expenses. In this case, Jiaqing continued, it would only be an additional instance of exploitation of the fruits of people's labor for the entertainment of big officials, a kind of consumption that Tang Zhen and the pro-luxury writers viewed as despotic and corrupt.[121]

Despite these pro-luxury statements, the Qing official policy on consumption, "revere frugality and eliminate luxury," remained unchanged and was often reiterated in official documents, its objective being focused on the traditional idea of not wasting limited resources. In the words of the Yongzheng Emperor (r. 1723–35), "consumption has regulation. To prevent exhausting [resources], we prohibit vain extravagance."[122] Support for market-based luxury consumption remained confined to specific cases as recognition of the unique economic environment of Jiangnan.

[121] "Renzong shilu" (June 15, 1799), *Qingshilu* (Beijing: Zhonghua shuju, 1985), Vol. 28, juan 45, 547. The *yamen* was both the offices of the local administration and the officials' personal residence.

[122] "Shizong shilu" (August 23, 1723), *Qingshilu* (Beijing: Zhonghua shuju, 1985), Vol. 7, juan 6, 137.

Chinese Pro-Market and Pro-Luxury Theories in Global Perspective

Pro-market and pro-luxury theories also emerged in Western Europe during the Industrious Revolution of the late seventeenth and early eighteenth centuries. By this time, Western Europe was experiencing a growth in both agricultural and manufacturing production as a result of the intensification of labor and changes in its application at the household level, as families chose to deploy their resources in market-oriented activities. This growth in productivity was sustained by the New Luxury mode of consumption, characterized by the pursuit of a more comfortable lifestyle. Among the examples provided by de Vries is the impact on consumption of the development of private and public illumination. Illumination was fueled by whale and vegetable oils, causing an expansion in whaling and in agricultural production of seeds from rape and flax, as well as in the development of seed-pressing mills. An additional factor contributed to the expansion of demand. Aspirations for a more comfortable lifestyle were accompanied by a new trend in "competitive fashion-driven" dressing, which, breaking away from the constraints of sumptuary laws, was now pursued by the "middling sort" and not just by a small elite. In other words, the New Luxury mode of consumption was characterized not only by an expansion in the availability of consumer goods but also by a changed composition and a considerable expansion of the consumer base.[123]

In the changed economic circumstances of late seventeenth-century England, "some writers, responding to the obvious, if uneven, economic growth, began to speculate upon the dynamic effect of increasing demand. In their pamphlets, the use of the word 'market' subtly changed from a reference to the point of sales to the more elusive concept of expandable spending."[124] New questions also arose on the issue of dispersion of wealth and the morality of luxury, as most famously exemplified by Bernard de Mandeville's (1670–1733) poem *The Fable of the Bees: or, Private Vices, Public Benefits* (1714). In this

123 De Vries, *The Industrious Revolution*, 128, 133, 150, 154. For a detailed discussion of the Industrious Revolution in Western Europe see De Vries, *The Industrious Revolution*, Chapter 3, 73–121, and Chapter 4, 122–185.

124 Joyce Appleby, "Ideology and Theory: The Tension between Political and Economic Liberalism in Seventeenth-Century England," *The American Historical Review* 81(3) (1976), 502.

poem, Mandeville focused specifically on luxury and argued that imposing frugality on a community would lead inevitably to a shrinking economy and widespread unemployment. The *Fable* tells the story of "A Spacious Hive well stock'd with Bees, That lived in Luxury and Ease" until, under pressure from religious censorship of depravity and corrupt lifestyle, "Honesty fills all their Hearts." As luxury habits were banned, the beehive fell into poverty and decline. The poem concluded with the famous statement that: "Bare Virtue can't make Nations live, In Splendor; they, that would revive; A Golden Age, must be as free; For Acorns, as for Honesty."[125] Although written as a satirical poem and intended as a critique of "empty" – to adopt the term Qianlong used to criticize You Bashi's idea of "frugality" – Christian virtues, rather than Confucian morality, Mandeville's writings signaled a change in perception of the role played by luxury consumption in the economy very similar to the shift marked by Lu Ji's "Jinshebian" essay in China. In both regions, the expansion of production and amount of goods available on the market as well as the development of a new mode of consumption brought intellectuals to observe a newly acquired elasticity of production and demand and, in this context, to re-evaluate older notions of frugality and morality.

In Europe, this erosion of moral arguments on luxury was accompanied by the idea that the pursuit of personal interests could be beneficial to the commonwealth; an idea originally developed as a critique of despotism by Niccolò Machiavelli (1469–1527). Machiavelli criticized the Prince who ruled under the influence of blinding and irrational passions, condemning the general population to live in gloomy uneasiness under the expectation of unpredictable dictates of the state that would ultimately damage their interests. The idea that rule by enlightened rationality and personal interests, divested of moral pretenses, would generate freedom from the whimsical passions of the aristocratic ruling elite was eventually to become the foundation of Liberalism.[126] Inspired by these intellectual developments as well as by

125 Bernard de Mandeville, *The Fable of the Bees or Private Vices, Publick Benefits. Newly Edited, with an Introduction, by Irwin Primer*, Vol. 1 (New York, NY: Capricorn Books, 1962), 25, 33, 38.

126 Albert O. Hirschman, *The Passions and the Interests: Political Arguments for Capitalism before Its Triumph* (Princeton, NJ: Princeton University Press, 1977), 18; Istvan Hont, "The Early Enlightenment Debate on Commerce and Luxury," in *The Cambridge History of Eighteenth-Century Political*

their anti-despotic beliefs, François Fénelon (1651–1715) and Jean François de Saint-Lambert (1716–1803) advocated free commerce and the end of state intervention. They presented free trade as a state of freedom in which people would no longer be subjected to the irrational whims of a despotic state and could rely on a more rational and predictable economic environment to pursue their personal interests, benefiting business and stabilizing the economy in general.

As had happened in China with the Ming loyalists, however, these European writers experienced difficulties in separating the idea of luxury from those of political corruption and despotism. François Fénelon, for example, although embracing the notion of a societal economy based on personal interests and on the free market, continued to consider all forms of luxury as a sign of an amoral and corrupt social and political system. His difficulty in distinguishing between market-based and "autocratic" luxury resembled that of earlier Ming loyalists, such as Wang, Gu, and Hong. Writing a mere generation later, Saint-Lambert and Mandeville had no difficulty applying this distinction as they introduced the idea that luxury was morally acceptable if expressed through consumption in a free market – a distinction introduced in China by Tang Zhen in the late seventeenth century. In this form, luxury consumption could actually benefit the whole community by fostering economic prosperity.

It is impossible to ignore the similarities between the developments of economic thought in Europe and China and how local intellectuals reacted in comparable ways to comparable changes in their respective economies. The similarities, however, were accompanied by significant differences. The most evident difference lies in the chronologies of the development of pro-market and pro-luxury theories in the two regions. In China, the idea that private interests could regulate the market more efficiently than the state was already well established by the late Ming, as exemplified by Qiu Jun's (1420–95) writings discussed earlier. In Europe, positive understandings of material interests were introduced in the context of the political discourse by Machiavelli in the early sixteenth century but became relevant for economic thought more than a century later. At this time, the notion of despotism came to be associated with

Thought, ed. by Mark Goldie and Robert Wokler (Cambridge: Cambridge University Press, 2006), Part IV: Commerce, Luxury, and Political Economy, 377–418; Mandeville, *The Fable of the Bees Or Private Vices, Publick Benefits.*

mercantilism, considered as promoting a despotic state intervention in the economy which hindered the development of the national economy and repressed domestic economic forces. We can ascribe this difference not just to the fact that China experienced a commercial revolution earlier than Europe did, but also to China's long tradition of able administrators, who paid particular attention to the political economy of the empire and its provisionist *minsheng* mandate. In this context, scholar officials studied closely issues of circulation (*liu*) of goods (market) – especially grain – and the various factors that affected it.

In addition, in China, the idea of the free market did not at first emerge entwined with a critique of the political system but as a strategy to achieve the empire's mandate of *minsheng* in a more efficient way. Although, historically, the issue of the efficient and equitable (*ping*) circulation of goods had carried significant political implications – as illustrated by *The Debate on Salt and Iron* and the debates over the New Policies of Wang Anshi – it had generally addressed issues of perceived malgovernance and had not challenged long-standing imperial institutions. Even the critiques of Qing despotism put forward by the Ming loyalists in the early Qing period advocated a return to "moral" Han rule rather than regime change. After Tang Zhen, pro-market ideas lost their anti-despotism edge, arguably because their proponents found a responsive interlocutor in the imperial state, especially during the Qianlong reign. In late-imperial China, therefore, the idea of a self-regulating market was based mostly on considerations of economic utility. Changes in the understanding of the economic role of consumption were also based on economic concerns. The departure from established Confucian theories of the moral value of profits (*li*) and luxury (*she*) described in this chapter was possible because the reinterpretation of both tropes remained within a higher-level framework of morality represented by the mandate of *minsheng*. In other words, the paramount importance of achieving this mandate justified and legitimized ideological innovations.

Any comparison of economic ideas of market and consumption in China and Western Europe cannot eschew the thorny debate on "the great divergence" and the recent contribution offered by historian Joel Mokyr.[127] Whereas Pomeranz approached this issue by focusing on

[127] Joel Mokyr, *A Culture of Growth: The Origins of the Modern Economy* (Princeton, NJ: Princeton University Press, 2017).

the economic conditions in the two regions, the constraints they faced, and their ability to overcome them, Mokyr brings the focus back to a supposed exceptionality of Enlightenment thought and its crucial role in the European Industrial Revolution.[128] Mokyr argues that among the most important elements of Enlightenment thought that contributed to the success of economic modernization in Europe was its ability to generate innovative ideas that broke with the status quo and bore directly on modes of production. Although he goes beyond simplistic paradigms and relies on an impressive array of relevant literature, Mokyr still assesses China as trapped in intellectual immobility. China, he concludes, did not experience the same intellectual developments as Europe and, for this reason, did not undergo a process of economic modernization similar to the European one.

In discussing the first issue, the ability to break with intellectual orthodoxy, Mokyr argues that in China the lack of opposition to the political status quo hindered China's philosophical and economic innovation. Failure to challenge the status quo ultimately prevented "challenges to entrenched knowledge."[129] Under these circumstances, he argues, "it was hard for the market for ideas to generate the kind of tradition-shattering innovations that the European cultural environment generated after 1500."[130] China's intellectual discourse remained "inherently conservative, because it was based on a learned tradition, on exegesis and philology. It was backward-looking and restorationist."[131] In an environment in which competing ideas remained confined to areas that did not pose a threat to the political status quo, "the civil service remained loyal to the Neo-Confucian orthodoxy, and there was never any danger of an intellectual undermining of the political status quo in the same way that the European Enlightenment undermined autocratic rule in Western Europe."[132]

The first two chapters of this book problematize Mokyr's description of China's political and philosophical orthodoxy and lack of innovation. The flexibility of Confucianism and the scholar officials'

128 Mokyr, *A Culture of Growth*; Pomeranz, *The Great Divergence*.
129 Mokyr, *A Culture of Growth*, 308, 340.
130 Mokyr, *A Culture of Growth*, 306–307.
131 Mokyr, *A Culture of Growth*, 308.
132 Geoffrey Lloyd and Nathan Sivin, *The Way and the Word: Science and Medicine in Early China and Greece* (New Haven, CT and London: Yale University Press, 2002), quoted in Mokyr, *A Culture of Growth*, 302–303.

constant reinterpretations of the classics to achieve diverse, competing, and innovative objectives disprove the validity of the statement endorsed by Mokyr – who here quotes Ray Huang – that "the ancient texts became 'an instrument of repressive conformity.'"[133] The imperial mandate of *minsheng*, rather than being a rigid ideology, actually provided a flexible framework for Lu Ji and Tang Zhen, among other Chinese intellectuals, to use to formulate pro-market and pro-luxury theories that responded to changes in the economic circumstances of the time, in a way very similar to that of intellectuals in Western Europe. In addition, *kaozheng* scholars were able to influence the Qing government, as clearly illustrated by their impact on grain storage and currency policies, as described, respectively, by Dunstan and Houng.[134] This development appears to require a reassesment of Mokyr's assumption that "the market of ideas" and the political status quo are fundamentally oppositional in the process of economic modernization. In addition, the fact that during the early Qing period the ideas of the Ming loyalists could still circulate through the empire, albeit covertly, seems to indicate a livelier and more daring "market for ideas" than that described by Mokyr.

Mokyr's second point of comparison focuses on the Enlightenment's "implications for scientific and technological progress," especially how changes in the intellectual realm "would feed back into the economy."[135] This aspect of Enlightenment thought, he explains, originated with Francis Bacon (1561–1626), the "philosopher of industrial sciences," who advocated the use of science for developing production as a means for improving the lives of the people. In a famous passage, he wrote, "The true and legitimate goal of the sciences is to endow human life with new discoveries and resources."[136] According to Mokyr, "the Baconian emphasis on creating communications not just within the scholarly community and between scholars and people in power, but eventually also between the realm of the scholar and those of the manufacturer, the farmer, and the navigator, redefined the

133 Mokyr, *A Culture of Growth*, 303. Here Mokyr quotes from Ray Huang, *1587: A Year of No Significance: The Ming Dynasty in Decline* (London: Yale University Press, 1982), 210.

134 For the role played by *kaozheng* scholars in policy making see Dunstan, *State or Merchants* and Hong, *China Upside Down*.

135 Mokyr, *A Culture of Growth*, 339–340.

136 Mokyr, *A Culture of Growth*, 71.

agenda of research in Europe."[137] Mokyr believes that this kind of understanding of "utility of knowledge" does not find a counterpart in China. While acknowledging that the Evidential Studies (*kao-zheng*), Statecraft (*jingshi*), and Practical Studies (*shixue*) schools of thought did indeed lead to considerable intellectual innovation, he concludes that "we should not read any modern concepts into it." Although these innovations included attention to "'practical matters' such as water control, military science, and administration, as well as knowledge that is in some sense verifiable," in his view, they were far from scientifically modern.[138] The issue of the development of the notion of "scientific utility" in China and its impact on economic innovation deserves more in-depth exploration, since the disparity of the pace of technological innovation between Western Europe and China remains a question central to the debate on the "great divergence." New studies, however, indicate a greater level of innovation in production techniques and machinery as well as in the utilization of labor than generally assumed.[139] It is important, however, to question Mokyr's assumption that intellectual developments within the Enlightenment were the crucial elements of the European success, without emphasizing the wider context of the Industrial Revolution in the terms, for example, presented by Appleby – that is, as the result of the coming together of several remarkable circumstances which included intellectual, political, religious, and economic developments.[140] It is important to keep in mind that the economic success of Western Europe was due to the conjunction of several factors, including, domestically, liberal economic policies and, internationally, the creation of a Western-centered hegemonic system based on free-trade imperialism.

137 Mokyr, *A Culture of Growth*, 322 and Chapter 17.

138 Mokyr, *A Culture of Growth*, 321.

139 See Peng Nansheng, *Zhongjian jingji: Zhuantong yu xiandai zhijian de Zhongguo jindai shougongye* (Beijing: Gaodeng jiaoyu chubanshe, 2002) and *Bangongyehua: jindai zhongguo xiangcun shougongye de fazhan yu shehui bianqian* (Beijing: Zhonghua shuju, 2007); William T. Rowe, *Speaking of Profit: Bao Shichen and Reform in Nineteenth-Century China* (Cambridge, MA: Harvard University Asia Center, 2018), Chapter 3; and Andrew B. Liu, *Tea War: A History of Capitalism in India and China* (New Haven, CT: Yale University Press, 2020), Chapter 2.

140 Appleby, *The Relentless Revolution*.

Alternative Voices: Pro-Frugality Arguments, the Rural Village, and the Problem of Corruption

Although in the High Qing period support for pro-luxury consumption became increasingly widespread, it continued to face challenges from different quarters. Some members of the Jiangnan elites tended to oppose luxury on the basis of philosophical considerations of Confucian morality or of nostalgia for earlier norms of gentlemanly taste and behavior based on modesty and self-effacement. In the late sixteenth century, for example, some commentators in Songjiang – Lu Ji's hometown – were dismayed by what they described as dramatic changes away from old values of virtue and simplicity toward a new attention to profit and material abundance.[141]

Challenges also came from scholars who based their arguments firmly on economic considerations. Most of these scholars focused on saving a declining rural economy and believed that the rural village should be protected from what they perceived to be the negative influence of the interregional market economy, especially because of its reliance on silver and the spread of luxury habits. In this context, their position was not in direct opposition with that of most pro-luxury writers, who argued that extravagant consumption could only play a positive role in prosperous and highly commercialized areas and was detrimental for poor rural areas.

Among prominent intellectuals who supported frugality were the members of the Yan–Li (*Yan–Li xuepai*) school of thought. Scholars from this group mostly came from, or gravitated to, northwestern Zhili Province – today's Hebei Province – and were practitioners of Practical Studies (*shixue*), which they distanced from its original association with *kaozheng*, criticizing it for being too involved in meaningless and pedantic philological exercises. These pro-frugality writers strongly opposed state intervention and envisioned the realization of a rural "natural economy" which went beyond that of the Ming loyalists, since they favored greatly limited trade and, in some cases, even advocated a return to basic barter.

The Yan–Li group is best represented by its founder Yan Yuan (1635–1704) and his main disciples, Li Gong (1659–1733) and Wang

141 Meskill, *Gentlemanly Interests and Wealth on the Yangtze Delta*, 44, 50, 53, 152, and the chapter titled "The Triumph of Abundance."

Yuan (1648–1710).[142] Born in Boye County, in Zhili Province, Yan Yuan had abandoned classical studies, and the possibility of a career in the imperial administration, when he was in his twenties. Originally an enthusiastic follower of Neo-Confucianism, he underwent an intellectual awakening on the occasion of the death of his step-grandparents. During this period of mourning, Yan had followed meticulously the Song text *Family Rituals* (*Jia li*), generally attributed to Zhu Xi. Later, however, he compared it with the original classic texts on rites and discovered discrepancies. He thus came to believe that Neo-Confucian scholars had greatly misinterpreted and corrupted the meaning of the ancient classics because of their unwise preoccupations with Buddhism and Daoism. Above all, they had obscured the classics' emphasis on practical issues. It was at that time that Yan began working as a physician. His medical practice, however, did not hinder him from continuing to pursue his philosophical interests. Yan was especially close to peasant life, and it is said that he himself carried out farm work. In 1679, Li Gong came to study under him, becoming his closest disciple, and was arguably more successful then Yan in propagating his philosophy, so much so that the names of both came to be associated with it, the Yan–Li school of thought.[143] Li Gong was also a native of Zhili; he came from Li County, adjoining Yan Yuan's native place of Boye. Li spent most of his life in this area, interrupted by brief periods of residence in Beijing, where he tutored the children of a few important families. During his times in Beijing, Li Gong met with renowned scholars and powerful officials, including the prominent official Fang Bao (1668–1749). It was through these connections that he, and the Yan–Li group, acquired a reputation that reverberated through the empire.[144] After he started studying under Yan Yuan, Li converted to Practical Studies, complementing his studies in philosophy and history with additional instruction in mathematics, economics, archery, playing the lute, military tactics, and ceremony. Unlike Yan Yuan, Li successfully passed the provincial examination in 1690, but he continued to support his family by teaching rather than seeking an administrative position, serving only a few short-term appointments in the educational administration of Zhili.

142 Liu Zhonghua, "Qingchu xuezhe wang yuan de jingshi sixiang ji qi xhueshu minyun," *Tangdu xuekan* 27 (2011), 75–76.

143 Hummel, *Eminent Chinese of the Ch'ing Period*, 912–915.

144 Hummel, *Eminent Chinese of the Ch'ing Period*, 475–479.

Both Yan and Li advocated a return to a natural (*ziran*) rural economic life,[145] opposing long-distance and foreign trade, which they believed "led to waste and extravagance" (*daomin zhangshe*) and ruined the people.[146] The rural economy they envisioned was based on a system of household self-sufficiency. Food and clothes were to be produced at home, and only a few essential goods would circulate through barter.[147] In their attempt to stop the use of silver in rural areas and to limit the monetization of the local economy, they also called for the payment of taxes in kind.[148] Yun Hesheng (1663–1741), another member of the Yan–Li School, argued that the use of silver should be completely eliminated and replaced with grain and cloth, the products of the peasants' daily work.[149] The recruitment of Yun as a disciple of the Yan–Li School offers an example of the importance of Li's contacts in Beijing for boosting its prestige. It was in fact during one of his stints in the capital that Li met Yun, who soon became an enthusiastic supporter of Yan and Li's brand of practical studies. A native of the Changzhou Prefecture (Jiangsu Province), he became responsible for spreading the school's ideas in the Jiangnan region.[150]

One other prominent member of the Yan–Li school was Wang Yuan. A native of Beijing, Wang moved temporarily to Jiangsu at the fall of the Ming but eventually returned to Beijing, where he participated in the writing of the Qing-sponsored *Ming History* (*Mingshi*). Originally a Ming loyalist, Wang Yuan shared with most Ming–Qing transition scholars a deep concern with re-establishing stable governance. In Beijing, he became close to the prominent official Fang Bao. It was at Fang's home that Wang Yuan met Li Gong, who later introduced him to Yan Yuan. A qualified admirer of Tang Zhen, Wang eventually converted to Practical Studies after his encounter with Li and Yan. While in Beijing in 1693, he passed the provincial examination. Being a Ming loyalist, however, he never served in the imperial administration, nor did he attempt the palace examination. Wang

145 Li Gong, "Ping shu ding," in *Congshu jicheng chubian* (Shanghai: Shangwu yinshuguan, 1937), Vol. 761, juan 11, 81–85.
146 Li, "Ping shu ding"; see also Zhao Jing, *Zhongguo gudai jingji sixiangshi jianghua* (Beijing: renmin chubanshe 1986), 569.
147 Zhao, *Zhongguo gudai jingji sixiangshi jianghua*, 569.
148 Zhao, *Zhongguo gudai jingji sixiangshi jianghua*, 568–570.
149 Zhao, *Zhongguo gudai jingji sixiangshi jianghua*, 569.
150 Hummel, *Eminent Chinese of the Ch'ing Period*, 478.

spent most of his life in Beijing and Tianjin, although he occasionally traveled to Boye to visit Yan Yuan.[151]

Wang's eclectic background influenced his views on the economy, especially his understanding of the importance of trade, on which he departed from the Yan–Li group's main line. While he adhered to most of the solutions for reviving the rural economy proposed by Yan and Li, including a return to the "well-field system" (*jingtian*), Wang declared, "We must certainly respect the fundamentals but must also not disregard what is peripheral. if in the world there were clothes but no merchants, would it still be possible to govern the empire?" This statement directly opposed Li Gong's idea that "trade cannot be valued."[152]

Also focused primarily on the agricultural economy were the members of the Household Management school of thought (*zhisheng xuepai*), most prominently Zhang Lüxiang (1611–80) and Zhang Ying (1637–1708). Like Yan, Li, and Wang, the two Zhangs also wrote in the early Qing and harbored loyalist feelings toward the Ming. They initially eschewed public life, devoting their studies to the problem of maintaining the economic prosperity of elite lineages. Both Zhangs came from the Jiangnan area, as did most pro-luxury writers. Their support for frugality can arguably be ascribed to their adherence to Neo-Confucianism and the aesthetic values and sense of morality that it implied, reflecting intellectual trends among local Neo-Confucian scholarly networks and the interests of powerful local lineages in the maintenance of the estates of elite families.

Zhang Lüxiang was a native of the village of Yangyuan in northeastern Anhui Province. He spent most of his life in the Jiangnan area, where he pursued his studies under the prominent Neo-Confucian and Ming loyalist scholar Liu Zongzhou (1578–1645). Zhang himself was one of the last followers of Zhu Xi. Rather than engaging in what he perceived to be political factionalism, Zhang retreated from public life and devoted his energies to improving his family estate. Zhang greatly

151 Hummel, *Eminent Chinese of the Ch'ing Period*, 842–844.

152 Liu, "Qingchu xuezhe wang yuan de jingshi sixiang ji qi xhueshu minyun," 77–78; Wu Baosan and Li Puguo, *Zhongguo jingji sixiangshi ziliao xuanji* (Peking: Zhongguo shehui kexue chubanshe: Xinhua shudian jingxiao 1990), 384–398; Zhao, *Zhongguo gudai jingji sixiangshi jianghua*, 580; Ye, *Gudai zhongguo jingji sixiang*, 413–414. The well-field system was a system of community-shared landholding originally mentioned by Mencius.

admired a well-known manual on farming, *Nongshu*, and decided to write a supplement, the *Bu nongshu*, an extensive manual for increasing agricultural production and promoting the prosperity of the family.[153] Zhang's focus on managing the estates of rural lineages was shared by all writers of the Household Management school, who also opposed luxury and advocated frugality. Zhang Ying, for example, in his main work *A Few Observations on Permanent Property* (*Hengchan suoyan*), especially stressed the danger of selling property, which he considered to be essential for a family's financial security. For this reason, he proposed three main rules: basing expenditures on income (*liang ru wei chu*) and ensuring that expenditures did not exceed income; avoiding living in the city in order to save money; and being frugal and focusing on increasing the productivity of the land.

Zhang Ying was a native of the same district as Zhang Lüxiang, Tongcheng. Unlike other ruralists, Zhang Ying enjoyed a successful public career. In 1667 he passed the palace examination, and he joined the Hanlin Academy in 1672. After that initial success, he was appointed to increasingly prominent positions, including chancellor of the Hanlin Academy, president of the Board of Ceremonies, and grand secretary. He retired to private life in 1701, spending the last years of his life writing poetry, editing his own works, and looking after the family's estate.[154] Zhang came from a lineage that had a long tradition of responsible landowning and of reliance on its profits to support the education and official careers of family members, a strategy shared by other prominent rural lineages.[155]

Not all supporters of frugality had direct links to the land or led a life of retirement eschewing appointments in the imperial administration. The prominent Qing official Chen Hongmou – considered the longest-serving official under the Qing as governor of various provinces – also supported frugality. A prominent representative of the Statecraft (*jingshi*) school of thought, Chen Hongmou was a native of Guilin Prefecture, in the southwestern frontier province of Guangxi. As historian William Rowe writes in his extensive study of Chen's life, thought, and

[153] Hummel, *Eminent Chinese of the Ch'ing Period*, 45–46.
[154] Hummel, *Eminent Chinese of the Ch'ing Period*, 64–65.
[155] Hilary J. Beattie, *Land and Lineage in China: A Study of T'ung-ch'eng County, Anhwei, in the Ming and Ch'ing Dynasties* (Cambridge: Cambridge University Press 1979), 37, 95; Zhao, *Zhongguo gudai jingji sixiangshi jianghua*, 594.

work, "Chen Hongmou carried the stamp of this frontier upbringing, sometimes intentionally and sometimes not, throughout his life." He appeared like a "country bumpkin" to other more sophisticated officials of his time, "shockingly ignorant of the latest aesthetic trends and scholarly debates." His background and personality, however, did not prevent him from gaining widespread admiration, since many recognized his "practical savvy in worldly affairs," which was in line with contemporary Statecraft trends. Away from Jiangnan and its regional network of libraries and scholars, Guilin was generally considered peripheral, both geographically and in terms of the intellectual debates of the time. By the time of Chen Hongmou, in fact, Guilin was a lively intellectual center especially renowned for its own version of Practical Studies. According to Rowe, Chen was representative of this "semi-peripheral" intellectual milieu, characterized by a "rigid and relatively unsophisticated moral fundamentalism ... in which an ideology of *shixue* [Practical Studies]... could readily take hold." Chen Hongmou was also influenced by the northern school of Neo-Confucianism, especially praising the works of Zhu Xi, although his support for this philosopher appears to have wavered at times. For example, in his discussion of the Chinese family, Chen chose not to cite Zhu Xi, preferring to rely on other sources, such as the works of Sima Guang.[156]

Chen's views on trade and consumption were not closely focused on the local rural economy, as were those of other pro-frugality writers. His perspective as a provincial governor brought him to formulate a more complex view of frugality and its relationships with consumption and economic growth. Departing from most of the pro-frugality writers, Chen believed in trade not just for its circulation (*liu*) function, but also as a generator of wealth. He believed that the "natural" flow of trade – free of state control – contributed to *minsheng* because it not only ensured the sustained availability of supplies but also created jobs and contributed to the accumulation of wealth.[157] This belief illustrates Chen's agreement with pro-luxury writers in regard to the importance of the commercial sector and could be seen as contradicting his 1746 "Proclamation Encouraging Frugality." This proclamation, however, was directed to rural households in Shaanxi, a target that Lu Ji himself arguably would have perceived as in need of frugal

[156] Rowe, *Saving the World*, 15, 20–24, 128.
[157] Rowe, *Saving the World*, 198–199.

practices. In it, Chen urged farmers not to spend extravagantly and distinguished between two different kinds of consumption: productive and unproductive. In the category of unproductive consumption, he included luxury spending in general, from religious to recreational purposes. Only useful (*youyong*) and profitable (*youyi*) spending was acceptable, he explained; everything else had no use (*wuyong*) and was unprofitable (*wuyi*). For Chen, however, frugality was not just a strategy for preserving wealth and preparing for periods of scarcity. Families should also save any surplus they might enjoy for reinvesting in the fields to promote further growth in production. In this sense, Chen's notion of frugality went beyond earlier distinctions between productive and unproductive consumption – such as those formulated by Huang Zongxi – as well as practices for prudent household management. It actually introduced a strategy for capital accumulation and economic growth in a predominantly agrarian setting. The utilitarian economic objectives of his *Proclamation* cannot be obscured by his ritualist deployment of moral pro-frugality tropes.[158]

Chen's call for capital investment in agriculture appears similar to those of the *physiocrates* (who also called themselves *économistes*) – including François Quesnay (1694–1774) and Anne Robert-Jacques Turgot (1727–81) – who were his contemporaries. These French philosophers developed a model that placed agriculture at the base of the French economy and advocated reinvestment of surplus in this sector. They also considered consumption, as effective demand, to be crucial for economic prosperity, because it supported productivity. Nicolas Dutot (1684–1741) – a pre-*physiocrates* French economic thinker – summed up this idea in his statement that consumption "is the essence of commerce." While supporting this theory of circulation, the *physiocrates* also believed in careful spending and the importance of saving for generating capital for meaningful reinvestment.[159]

Ironically, the inspiration for the *physiocrates* can be traced to the new interest in the Chinese economy and politics that developed at the time of Louis XV (1715–74). Quesnay, for example, was deeply interested in Confucianism and its agrarian policies. He also admired the

158 Rowe, *Saving the World*, 195–196.

159 Jerah Johnson, "The Role of Spending in Physiocratic Theory," *The Quarterly Journal of Economics* 80 (1966), 621–622, 628; Alessandro Roncaglia, *A Brief History of Economic Thought* (Cambridge: Cambridge University Press, 2017), 47–53.

highly centralized nature of the Chinese government. This admiration generated a deep contradiction between support for a free-market economy and support for an all-powerful autocratic government. The *physiocrates*, in fact, shared with Bernard de Mandeville and other European pro-market writers the idea that "self-interest" could be a basic tool for organizing the economy, thus echoing a crucial aspect of liberal *laissez faire* trends. They also believed that private property was an essential element of the economy and needed to be protected by the law. The *physiocrates*, however, took these basic ideas in a different direction from the one that eventually led to theories of liberal capitalism. They believed in the need for a strong authoritarian state, resolving the contradiction between *laissez faire* respect for individual interests and despotism by arguing that the authoritarian state should share ownership of economic assets with the common people. This co-ownership would link society and state through identical interests, thus ensuring that the government would not act against the interests of the population.[160]

Similarities between the basic tenets of the French *physiocrates* and Chen Hongmou's ideas of "productive consumption" and surplus reinvestment in agriculture testify to the rise, in both Europe and China, of the notion that agriculture could produce a "surplus" that could be reinvested to bolster production. Chen's ideas in this area also illustrate the richness of Chinese economic thought on the agricultural economy. This was not limited to conservative visions of a self-sufficient village isolated from the commercial growth of the time and focused on subsistence agriculture. Chen advocated frugality among peasant families of his region within the wider framework of generating capital for reinvestment and increasing agricultural productivity.

Although at first glance the Chinese anti- and pro-luxury writers appear to be in direct opposition, they actually agreed on one important point. Both groups distrusted government intervention in the economy, which they compared negatively to their particular vision – commercial or agricultural – of a "natural" economy. The oppositional views of these thinkers were mostly based on the focus of their observations and area of interest. They both discouraged luxury for poor rural areas and believed that economic frugality was a wise course for managing a

[160] Hirschman, *The Passions and the Interests*, 97–98; Roncaglia, *A Brief History of Economic Thought*, 47–53.

family estate. Pro-luxury writers, however, looked beyond the rural economy and reflected changes in the highly commercialized regions of the empire. Once again, the increasing gap between hinterland and coastal China greatly influenced the economic debate.

From the perspective of the Qing state, frugality remained an important policy, although it could be disregarded in the context of the Jiangnan economy, as had been the case with Qianlong's and Jiaqing's responses to the memorials advocating frugality regulations in this area. In these circumstances, frugality had become an "empty" principle; it was not empty, however, when deployed to achieve important political goals, such as counteracting scarcity of resources in rural areas and, no less a problem, containing corruption among the administration.

In the High Qing period, in fact, it appears that the state was increasingly preoccupied with limiting luxury consumption in order to control corruption in the imperial administration. As Yongzheng stated on the first day of his rule (January 5, 1723), officials should consider their position to be a duty rather than a source of pride for their rank, and each should behave like a loving parent to the people. More specifically, Yongzheng considered two qualities essential for good governance: frugality and honesty. "If [there is frugality], then one can consume and there will be no scarcity. If [there is] honesty, then the high officials cannot be concerned with their private interest, such as exploiting the life of the little people in order to satisfy the voracious desires of the high officials."[161] Yongzheng's vision of a dutiful and incorruptible administration was not to be realized, as exemplified by the corruption that plagued the *yingyung shengxi* and *shanghao* strategies discussed earlier in this chapter. Corruption, in fact, tended to be the norm, especially with the rise of Heshen (1750–99) in the imperial administration. A former Manchu guardsman, Heshen became a favorite of the Qianlong Emperor and was appointed by him to various high positions, including membership in the increasingly powerful Grand Council, which he ended up dominating. His influence grew to such an extent that the last years of the

[161] "Shizong shilu" (January 5, 1723), *Qingshilu* (Beijing: Zhonghua shuju, 1985) vol 7, juan 3, 78–79. Yongzheng's efforts to curb corruption in the imperial administration through tax reforms is discussed in depth in Madeleine Zelin, *The Magistrate's Tael: Rationalizing Fiscal Reform in Eighteenth-Century Ching China* (Berkeley, CA: University of California Press, 1992).

Qianlong reign came to be referred to as the "Heshen Regency" (1796–9). Taking advantage of his power, Heshen nominated people close to him to government posts, establishing strong political alliances throughout the imperial administration. In exchange for continuous support, Heshen demanded expensive gifts from his protégés, in this manner acquiring an immense fortune.[162] During this "regency," therefore, Heshen encouraged a culture of extravagance and personal enrichment in officialdom, creating, as discussed in Chapter 3, a strong political reaction against luxury in general.

Conclusion

The late-Ming revival of the commercial revolution consolidated ideas of the market that had been brewing since the Song period, especially the notion that personal material interests had the power to optimize the smooth circulation of goods and stabilize prices. It was, in fact, in this period that the idea of China's "natural" (*ziran*) economy, departing from its earlier formulation as a foundational (*ben*) agricultural economy, developed into a view of a market-based societal economy free from state intervention. Whether perceived as basically agricultural (as by Ming loyalists and other scholars who focused on rural revival) or commercial (as by Lu Ji, Tang Zhen, and other pro-luxury writers), all interpretations of China's natural economic community relegated the state to the sidelines. Even the small number of extreme ruralists – such as those of the Yan–Li group, who advocated a return to barter – did not contemplate any level of state regulation.

The Qing rulers embraced these views of the market as being able to efficiently regulate prices and ensure the optimal circulation of essential goods, a stance most clearly exemplified by the state's diminishing intervention in the grain storage system. They also entrusted the management of some functions of the imperial bureaucracy to private merchants. These outsourcing experiments proved successful from the economic point of view but created new opportunities for corruption and collusion between officials and merchants, often discouraging their continuation. Corruption became a critical issue which encouraged the

162 Daniel McMahon, "Dynastic Decline, Heshen, and the Ideology of the Xianyu Reforms," *Tsing Hua Journal of Chinese Studies, New Series* 38(2) (June 2008), 231–254, at 235 ff.

retreat of state intervention in such areas as grain storage but discouraged privatization in others, including military supplies and funding.

The idea of the capacity of the economy to grow, which had been developing slowly since the Song, was widely accepted by the late Qing period. It was in the context of the recognition of the elasticity of production and demand in the new industrious economy of China that scholars and officials reconsidered the economic role of luxury consumption. Despite the Ming government's determination to suppress extravagant lifestyles, the high level of commodification reached by the economy at that time fueled new habits of consumption. Artisans and service providers catering to an expanding consumer base could now depend on their trades to make a living. In the highly commercialized region of Jiangnan, the commercial sector was growing at a fast pace, presenting to observers a kind of diversified economy that could be more resilient and prosperous than one based exclusively on agriculture, as Tang Zhen poignantly remarked. This unstoppable and exuberant expansion of the commercial and monetized sectors of the economy came to be widely perceived as an important source of wealth generation for the empire.

The debates analyzed in this chapter also highlight the ability of Chinese intellectuals to respond to changes in the economy with the same pragmatism, flexibility, and insights as their European counterparts, thus further eroding the notion that Chinese thinkers were trapped in a conservative intellectual environment not conducive to innovative ideas that could pave the way to economic modernization.

3 *Scarcity Revisited: Population Growth, Frugality, and Self-Strengthening (1800–1911)*

During the first half of the nineteenth century, China witnessed a sharp economic decline, marking the end of the "prosperous age" (*shengshi*) of the High Qing period. Observing the altered economic conditions, Chinese economic thinkers pondered the causes of this decline.[*] One of the main factors they considered responsible for the current crisis was an unprecedented demographic expansion and the inability of the economy to produce enough resources to sustain the growing population of the empire, a serious threat to the *minsheng* mandate. China, they believed, was running out of resources and facing a new scarcity crisis. In this situation, all forms of luxury consumption, even if market-based, came again to be perceived as a waste of resources.

At the end of the eighteenth century the new political environment generated by Emperor Jiaqing's succession to the throne also contributed to the decline of pro-luxury arguments. Corruption among officials had long been an obstacle to the open adoption of pro-luxury policies. Luxury consumption, however, became even more politically unsustainable during the reign of Jiaqing, as calls for frugality became an important aspect of the Xianyu Reforms (*xianyu weixin*, "the reforms that embrace all," 1799–1805). The emperor presented these reforms as a restoration of moral governance to counteract the corrupting influence of Heshen. In his attempt to project an image of his reign as the polar opposite of the corrupt Heshen, Jiaqing declared that the new government was to restore enlightened rule as well as efficient and diligent administration. Overwhelming corruption, together with a lack of care for the welfare of the people, Jiaqing asserted, had made the state ineffective. For this reason, habits of frugality needed to be restored. As historian Daniel McMahon

[*] This chapter includes sections originally published in Margherita Zanasi, "Frugality and Luxury: Morality, Market, and Consumption in Late Imperial China," Frontiers of History in China 10(3) (2015), 457–485.

phrases it: "Heshen was extravagant; Jiaqing was frugal."[1] The Xianyu Reforms also signaled an attempt of the Qing government to come to terms with the Empire's new economic circumstances and the reduced financial capability of the state. Continuing the Qing's experiments in cutting administrative cost by entrusting private merchants with tasks previously performed by the imperial bureaucracy, the Jiaqing and Daoguang (r. 1820–50) administrations privatized such important functions as the maintenance of the Grand Canal and the transportation of tribute grain.

The revival of the ideas of scarcity and frugality, however, did not imply a return to traditional economic notions. At this time, frugality polices came to be framed within a notion of the economy of empire as able to grow – although not enough to keep up with the demographic expansion – and as driven by the market. In this context, scholars and officials focused their attention on new methods for increasing production that went beyond the measures traditionally taken during times of crisis, such as land reclamation efforts. Among these new strategies was the deployment of frugal consumption for the achievement of two main objectives. The first objective was to encourage the accumulation of capital, which was then to be invested in the economy to promote growth, a strategy contemplated earlier by Chen Hongmou. The second objective was redirecting demand away from luxury goods and channeling it to support the expansion of the production of basic staples in order to meet the needs of the growing population and to fight scarcity.

The idea of China's new economy of scarcity remained among the main concerns of Chinese intellectuals and officials throughout the Opium War (*Yapian zhanzheng*, 1839–42). While the arrival of Western imperialism deeply changed the political and economic landscape of the empire, it did not completely alter the main themes of the economic discourse. Domestic factors that had emerged in the late eighteenth and early nineteenth centuries, especially population growth and economic scarcity, affected Chinese officials' and intellectuals'

[1] William T. Rowe, *Speaking of Profit: Bao Shichen and Reform in Nineteenth-Century China* (Cambridge, MA: Harvard University Asia Center, 2018), 7–8; Wang Wensheng, *White Lotus Rebels and South China Pirates Crisis and Reform in the Qing Empire* (Cambridge, MA: Harvard University Press, 2014), 165–166; Daniel McMahon, "Dynastic Decline, Heshen, and the Ideology of the Xianyu Reforms," 244–248.

perceptions of both the new problems created by the imperialist intrusion and the newly imported Western economic theories. The arrival of Western imperialism, however, brought one more issue to the fore: the international trade balance. The changed framework of this trade – from China-centered protectionism to Western-centered "free-trade imperialism" – heavily penalized Chinese exports while giving an unfair advantage to Western imports. In this context, luxury consumption came to be identified with the consumption of fashionable high-quality and expensive goods imported from the West, while frugality became a strategy for encouraging the consumption of domestic products to help bridge the trade deficit. The issue of the state's financial deficit also came to assume paramount importance. The Nanjing Treaty (1842) – which marked the end of the Opium War – and other unequal treaties that followed imposed huge indemnity payments on China, ushering in the notion that the country, as a whole, was deeply in debt and that balancing national finances was an urgent goal for its survival.

Under the pressure of a large foreign trade deficit and the financial strains it generated, the overall political framework of the Chinese empire shifted from the mandate of *minsheng* to the new objective of self-strengthening (*ziqiang*), i.e. strengthening the *guo* – a term used in the late imperial period to refer to the empire and after 1911 to indicate the nation – to meet the challenges waged by foreign imperialism.[2] After the Opium War, the *guo*, as the main economic actor in the international arena, became the primary focus of debate, displacing that of the proper balance in the distribution of resources between state and societal economies as well as among members of society.

This self-strengthening focus on the *guo* and the balance of trade evokes the mercantilist theories that had emerged in Europe during the heyday of commercial capitalism (sixteenth to eighteenth centuries). Mercantilist thinkers believed that domestic trade saw the gain of one trading party reflected in the loss of the other, thus leaving national

[2] Self-Strengthening (1861–95) was a reform movement mostly led by provincial governors but supported by the imperial government in Beijing. Its goal was to strengthen China's military and economic power against the challenges coming from both foreign imperialism and devastating domestic rebellions such as the Taiping Rebellion (1850–64). For more information see von Glahn, *The Economic History of China*, 373–379.

wealth unchanged. International trade, on the other hand, contributed to bringing into the country new resources from the outside and, therefore, it was the only sector able to produce new wealth.[3] For this reason, mercantilists viewed the nation as a "joint-stock enterprise" – to use Appleby's terminology – and sought economic prosperity through domination of the international trade system.[4] The Chinese Self-Strengthening *guo*-centered approach to international trade evokes this mercantilist trend. As historian Kenneth Pomeranz comments in his study of early twentieth-century Shandong, "writings on economic development … have an almost mercantilist tone. Growth is desired because it will help preserve China's independence, not because it will promote individual welfare."[5] As Pomeranz's statement suggests, however, the Chinese imperial state acted in an international market system dominated by "free-trade" imperialism, which differed greatly from that of Europe in the seventeenth and eighteenth centuries. In other words, engaging in an international trade competition was perceived as a defensive economic strategy and not as the only way to increase national wealth. By this time, in fact, Chinese intellectuals and officials had developed a sophisticated understanding of the workings of the domestic market economy and had devised policies that took into consideration the elasticity of both production and consumption – an elasticity unrecognized by European mercantilism – as exemplified by their attempt to use frugality as a mode of consumption to stimulate production in sectors perceived as crucial for fighting both poverty (production of goods for everyday use) and imperialism (production of market substitution goods).

Western imperialism brought to China not just new economic problems, but also new concepts and terminology linked to economic liberalism. In the late Qing period, this process of knowledge transfer began gradually to change the language of the Chinese economic discourse, starting a process that was to culminate in the Republican period. These changes, however, did not dramatically alter the main

[3] Roncaglia, *A Brief History of Economic Thought*, 23; Appleby, "Ideology and Theory: The Tension between Political and Economic Liberalism in Seventeenth-Century England," 499–515.

[4] Appleby, "Ideology and Theory," 502.

[5] Pomeranz, Kenneth, *The Making of a Hinterland: State, Society, and Economy in Inland North China, 1853–1937* (Berkeley, CA: University of California Press, 1993), 47.

concerns of debates. For example, the notions of capital accumulation (*qiu cai*) and of the distinction between consumer and producer goods came to be expressed with a more specialized language but continued to be framed within the problem of China's economic scarcity, evolving from a similar understanding of productive and unproductive consumption and reinvestment of surplus by earlier scholars and officials, most notably by Chen Hongmou (1696–1771).

The End of the Prosperous Age (1800–1850s)

China historians generally see the early 1800s as a period of dramatic changes and the end of the High Qing "prosperous age." It was at this time (c. 1800), that a "great divergence" emerged between the Western European countries and China. The former were speeding up the process of industrialization, taking advantage – especially in the case of England – of a cluster of favorable as well as fortuitous circumstances, including possession of colonies (which supplied cheap resources and provided new territories for waves of migration that alleviated the pressure of population growth in the old country), fortunate geological traits (such as large deposits of coal), innovation, and a temporary weakening of political and religious authorities.[6] It was at this time that China, on the other hand, began to experience an economic decline, set in motion by a series of factors that are still topics of debate among historians.

In analyzing this period of crisis, historians have focused primarily on two issues: a new trend in the global flow of silver and China's unprecedented population growth. In the post-1800 period, China experienced an outflow of silver, reversing the earlier trend of sustained inflow that had supported the commercial economy of the late Ming and early Qing periods. Historians consider this reversal to be a result of a combination of factors, including the increase in Britain's imports of opium into China, the rise of the price of silver on international market networks, diminished global production of silver, and the

[6] Von Glahn, *The Economic History of China*, 348–354. Pomeranz, *The Great Divergence*, 326; for a detailed discussion of the economic history of this period and the scholarly debates focusing on it, see Chapter 9: "Domestic Decline and Global Challenges: Restructuring the Imperial Economy (1800 to 1900)," 348–399; Appleby, *The Relentless Revolution*.

decline of European markets for two of the most popular Chinese exports, tea and silk.[7]

The second issue, the impact of population growth on the economy of the empire, has recently generated some disagreement. Most historians argue that population's increased pressure on the land contributed crucially to the economic decline of the late Qing period.[8] According to an empire-wide count of men and women held in the sixth year of the reign of Qianlong (February 1741–January 1742), China's population was just above 100 million. Almost fifty years later (the fifty-eighth year of the Qianlong reign, February 1793–1794), it had reached 300 million, rising to roughly 430 million by the mid-nineteenth century. Most of this growth occurred in the provinces of Hunan, Hubei, and Sichuan, the Central Plains, and the southwestern frontiers, as a consequence of migrations into these regions of settlers looking for new land to cultivate. Population growth, however, was not limited to these areas. The already densely populated Jiangnan also experienced a dramatic demographic boom.[9] This demographic explosion slowed down in the late nineteenth century, mostly because of the high number of casualties in the wars against foreign imperialism and domestic rebellions – the Taiping Rebellion (1850–64) alone claimed approximately twenty million lives. The population, however, started growing again soon after and, by the end of the nineteenth century, it had already surpassed pre-Taiping levels.[10] Most recently, however, von Glahn has argued that, despite this sharp demographic upward trend, at that time "China did not yet face a Malthusian subsistence crisis" since "agricultural and industrial output kept pace with rapid population growth without any appreciable decline in per capita income."[11] Despite this

[7] Von Glahn, *The Economic History of China*, 365–367. Lin Man-Houng, *China Upside Down*, 87–114. For a detailed discussion of the post-1800 economic decline see von Glahn, *The Economic History of China*, 348–399.

[8] See, for example, Rowe, "Bao Shichen and Agrarian Reform in Early Nineteenth-Century China," 1–3; Wang, *White Lotus Rebels and South China Pirates*, 23–24; Peng Nansheng, *Zhongjian jingji: Zhuantong yu xiandai zhijian de Zhongguo jindai shougongye* (Beijing: Gaodeng jiaoyu chubanshe, 2002), 34–35; and Susan Mann Jones and Philip Kuhn, "Dynastic Decline and the Roots of Rebellion," in *The Cambridge History of China*, Vol. 10, ed. by John K. Fairbank (Cambridge: Cambridge University Press, 1978), 107–162.

[9] Von Glahn, *The Economic History of China*, 330.

[10] Li, *Fighting Famine in North China*, 3; Gao Wangling, *Qianlong shisannian* (Beijing Shi: Jingji kexue chubanshe, 2012), 23–25.

[11] Von Glahn, *The Economic History of China*, 330, 336, 330–334, 362–363.

disagreement on the role that population growth played in the economic decline of nineteenth-century China, most scholars agree that it was a greatly destabilizing phenomenon, as it pushed waves of people to the frontier lands, disrupting social order and increasing ecological decay.[12]

Adding to the two problems of silver and population was a decline in the rural economy. In addition to suffering from the higher prices of silver that further devalued the local copper-based currencies, the rural economy was disrupted by two cataclysmic events. The first was the 1815 eruption of the Indonesian volcano Tambora, which contributed to crop failures and recurring famines, depleting grain stores. The second was a change of course of the Yellow River during the years 1824–55. The river took three decades to resettle in its new course running to the north of the Shandong peninsula instead of to the south of it, and in the meantime it repeatedly flooded large portions of the Central Planes and the Huai River regions, some of the most fertile territory of the empire.[13] China also witnessed a general decline of the domestic market, as the economy focused mostly on expanding exports after the Opium War, contributing to the marginalization of inland areas not directly linked with the mostly coastal international trade networks.[14]

Population Growth, a New Economy of Scarcity, and the Imperative of Frugality

Population growth had attracted the attention of the Qing rulers since the time of Kangxi. In an edict dated December 14, 1709 – written at the end of the economic depression that characterized the first half of his reign – the emperor worried: "[Since we unified China] the number of births has increased daily and the population has grown. Arable land, on the other hand, has not grown. If we divide what a person produces . . . and what a family consumes, how can this be sufficient to support the livelihood of the people?" Kangxi believed that this was a problem for which the state "needed to begin developing a strategy."[15]

[12] Rowe, *Speaking of Profit*, 2–4; and Wang, *White Lotus and South China Pirates*, 23–33.
[13] Von Glahn, *The Economic History of China*, 361–363.
[14] Pomeranz, *The Making of a Hinterland*.
[15] Quoted in Gao, *Qianlong shisannian*, 23.

Yongzheng was also aware of the threat that population growth presented for the future prosperity of the empire. On May 30, 1723, he wrote: "The empire has enjoyed a long period of peace. The population has flourished and is abundant. The products of the land can barely provide [for it]. If, by chance, we meet with any level of scarcity, it will be difficult to feed the people. In the future, the population will grow constantly. What can we do?"[16] The problem rose to the status of imminent danger by the time of Qianlong, who addressed it soon after he succeeded his father on the throne. In November 1735, he remarked: "Population increases daily. The eight banners in Beijing and the general population in the provinces flourish and multiply. The land, however, does not increase. It is for this reason that it is difficult to meet the consumption needs of the people and to regulate what the people produce."[17] In the eyes of the High Qing emperors, therefore, population growth had the potential to create unprecedented pressure on resources, causing economic scarcity and poverty through the empire. It thus threatened to undermine the basic legitimacy of the dynasty, since it made the fulfillment of the mandate to nurture the people difficult to achieve.

Emperor Qianlong also experienced the shocking realization that the usual policies adopted by the imperial government to solve economic scarcity and fight poverty – land reclamation, tax breaks, and maintaining flood prevention and agricultural irrigation works in good order – would not be enough to face the crisis generated by the fast pace of population growth. In the edict of November 1735 mentioned above, Qianlong called for the cutting of extravagant expenditures and the adoption of frugal habits. He explained that all other possible measures to improve the situation had already been taken. The levying of taxes had been suspended. Agricultural irrigation had been repaired and improved. New land had been reclaimed and cultivated. Still, people suffered cold and hunger. In this situation, frugality was a crucial strategy for survival.[18]

[16] Quoted in Gao, *Qianlong shisannian*, 23.

[17] Quoted in Gao, *Qianlong shisannian*, 24. The banners were military and administrative divisions that serves as the basic organizational system for Manchu households.

[18] "Gaozong shilu" (November 10, 1735), *Qingshilu* (Beijing: Zhonghua shuju, 1985), Vol. 9, juan 3, 194–196.

This 1735 call for frugality appears to be in opposition to Qianlong's support for luxury consumption expressed in his 1768 letter to You Bashi. The latter, however, reflected the state's difficulties in balancing China's varied economic circumstances. Qianlong recognized the positive impact of luxury consumption in commercialized and wealthy Jiangnan and the need to optimize the use of scarce resources in the rest of the empire and especially in the rural hinterland. Qianlong's seemingly conflicting statements arguably reflected a need to adopt a flexible approach, already advocated by Lu Ji with his formula "if prosperous, luxury can follow; if poor, retain frugality." Support for luxury was deployed to achieve *minsheng* goals and avoid popular unrest in prosperous Jiangnan, where it supported the livelihood of a significant portion of the population. It was not deployed in different circumstances, where it was believed to detract from the people's livelihood.

By the time of the reign of Emperor Jiaqing, the problems created by population growth (a phenomenon that soon began to acquire its own standard terminology: *shengchi rifan*) appeared even direr and a solution more urgent. As Jiaqing stated in May 1801, "At present, the population grows daily. Even if it is possible for everyone to adopt frugality, I am still afraid there will not be enough [resources] for daily use."[19] In 1806, Jiaqing once again expressed his fears that no solution was at hand for avoiding poverty and famine. Even if crops were to be good, the people stored plenty of grain, and no natural disaster occurred, food supplies would still be insufficient because of the fast pace of population growth. According to the Ministry of Revenue, Jiaqing continued, the population of the empire had increased from the previous year by 27,720,119 people, while the total amount of grain harvested and stored had decreased by 294,248 *dan*. Only "spare consumption and reverence to frugality and simplicity" could avoid future hardships.[20] Jiaqing's statement illustrates that scarcity was no longer just an unwelcome possibility in case of crop failure but threatened to become a permanent condition. Even if crops were good, their yield would not be enough to maintain subsistence levels. This new situation called for more than the traditional strategies for fighting

19 "Renzong rui shilu" (May 19, 1801), *Qingshilu* (Beijing: Zhonghua shuju, 1985), Vol. 29, juan 82, 56–57.

20 "Renzong rui shilu" (August 15, 1806), *Qingshilu* (Beijing: Zhonghua shuju, 1985), Vol. 30, juan 172, 242–243.

scarcity. Frugality was to be pursued to a larger extent and with increased severity.

A November 1820 edict of the Daoguang Emperor urged stricter implementation of sumptuary laws. The emperor complained that even poor people indulged in unnecessary extravagance. In the case of funerals, for example, they went beyond the sanctioned rituals and "busied themselves with empty formalities, spending too much in wasteful extravagance." Certain rituals, the emperor argued, must be followed, but hosting banquets for friends, staging repeated performances, and drinking wine excessively was certainly beyond what was ritually prescribed. "The Empire regulates all marriage and funeral rites" Jiaqing continued, and everyone – officials, literati, and common people – should comply with these regulations. Military commanders and governors general should distribute regulations on weddings and funerals to their subordinates and have them circulate notices among the population at large. These regulations should reach every village and be carefully explained. Those who did not follow should be punished in an exemplary manner.[21]

This sentiment was echoed by Emperor Xianfeng (r. 1850–61), who, bemoaning the incomplete success of Daoguang's attempts to curb luxury, stresses the importance of reviving sumptuary laws and curb luxury consumption. In an 1852 memorial, the Commissioner of the Office of Transmission (*tongzhengshi*), Luo Dunyan (1814–74), complained about the luxury habits of the people, stressing its even greater danger in the context of population growth. "The empire was peaceful for a long time. All living creatures grew in great number. Officials and common people competed to value extravagance. This custom greatly affected popular feelings. It is now necessary to clearly reassert the old system in order to restore honest customs." In response, the Xianfeng Emperor decreed: "Strictly instruct every capital and provincial *yamen* [local government seats] that the people need to use the [appropriate] style of dress and that wedding and funeral ceremonies need to be regulated, according to what is recorded in the state rules. Print these regulations simply and clearly and make the common people know

[21] "Xuanzong shilu" (November 9, 1820), *Qingshilu* (Beijing: Zhonghua shuju, 1985) vol. 33, juan 26, 457–459. See also "Xuanzong shilu" (June 6, 1832), Vol. 36, juan 211 and (March 11, 1828), Vol. 35, juan 132, 15–16.

that they must carefully obey them."[22] Once again, extravagant celebrations for funerals and weddings appeared to be the main culprits, offering opportunities for extravagant consumption among the population.

Scholars and officials were also greatly concerned with population and poverty. Among them was Hong Liangji (1746–1809), generally considered the founder of modern population studies in China, a field further expanded most prominently by Yun Jing (1757–1817) and Bao Shichen (1775–1855). Hong's and Yun's works consolidated trends that had been developing for the previous half century, confirming the wide acceptance of three important ideas that were to be at the foundation of modern Chinese economic thought. The first was the perception that the Chinese economy was able to grow, although Hong believed that it could not keep pace with the demographic boom. Reflecting the *kaozheng* and Practical Studies trends that prevailed at the time, Hong and Yun addressed the problem of the low ratio of resources to population through, respectively, a mathematical approach and a sociohistorical approach. They also presented as unquestionable the idea that trade was a productive economic activity, and, in fact, they placed merchants among the "productive" groups in society. Finally, in the process of classifying different kinds of economic actors in society, they introduced the two distinct categories of "producers" and "consumers." Developing production to match population growth, they argued, was imperative for solving the scarcity problem and for the future of the empire at large since, they believed, scarcity would inevitably lead to social and political instability.

A native of Changzhou Prefecture (Jiangsu Province), as a young student Hong Liangji attended the Longcheng Academy (*Longcheng shuyuan*), one of the most prominent academies associated with *kaozheng* learning, a methodology he favored through his life. One of his earlier formative experiences was his collaboration (1771–3) with Zhu Yun (1728–81), one of the scholars and high officials most closely responsible for the compilation of the *Complete Library of the Four Treasures* (*Siku quanshu*). At the initial stage of this monumental literary compilation project, Zhu Yun hired a group of brilliant young *kaozheng* scholars to work on the editing and reprinting of ancient

22 "Wenzong shilu" (January 17, 1852), *Qingshilu* (Beijing: Zhonghua shuju, 1985), Vol. 40, juan 48, 654–655.

manuscripts. Among them was Hong Liangji.[23] This appointment set Hong on the path to a successful career in the Qing literary and educational administration, which led him to be appointed head of regional academies and, after he obtained his *jinshi* degree, a member of the Hanlin Academy and special tutor to Imperial Prince Yi Chun. His brilliant career was interrupted by one of the briefest periods of exile endured by any imperial official. In 1799, Jiaqing was offended by some critical remarks on what Hong believed to be the limited nature of his anti-corruption reform. Jiaqing immediately exiled Hong to distant Yili, in the northwestern border region of Xinjiang, but he recalled him to the capital and restored him to his positions in less than a year. An accomplished poet and calligrapher, Hong was recognized especially for his geographical works, including a volume on the geography of the empire (*Qianlong futing zhouxian zhi*).[24]

His interest in state affairs, political and economic reforms, and the geopolitics of the empire led Hong to study the problem of population growth. He concluded that the population grew exponentially, fast outpacing the linear arithmetical growth of production.[25] Predicting a dark future for China, he warned that production of resources could never catch up with population growth and that nothing could be done to rescue the country from abject poverty. Hong recognized that material life had greatly improved since ancient times because of increased productivity and improved technology, but he did not believe that these two developments could lead to a solution to China's scarcity problem. They had actually only made human life more fragile and caused a deterioration of the human spirit.[26]

Yun Jing, also a native of Jiangsu and a product of the local Jiangnan *kaozheng* and Statecraft scholarly networks, enjoyed a reputation as a competent administrator, serving as a magistrate in several counties, mostly in the Jiangnan area. Having been dismissed from his last post because of false accusations lodged by his political enemies, Yun retired from public life and devoted himself to private study.[27] Yun

[23] Elman, *From Philosophy to Philology*, 143.
[24] Hummel, *Eminent Chinese of the Ch'ing Period*, 373–375; Elman, *From Philosophy to Philology*, 158.
[25] Hu, *Zhongguo jingji sixiangshi*, Vol. 2, 619–620.
[26] Hu, *Zhongguo jingji sixiangshi*, Vol. 2, 564–566, and Zhao, *Zhongguo gudai jingji sixiangshi jianghua*, 618.
[27] Hummel, *Eminent Chinese of the Ch'ing Period*, 959–960.

Jing held a less pessimistic view of the problem of population than Hong Liangji and concentrated his attention on devising state-oriented practical solutions for increasing production. Yun did not believe that population growth was an absolute or "natural" problem (that is, one following the laws of nature). It was instead, he argued, the result of historical developments. The imbalance between producers and consumers was a problem that had only emerged in recent generations. It was fundamentally a product of social changes that had brought about the expansion of the consumer group in relation to that of the producers. In ancient times, Yun argued, those who contributed actively to supporting the community were one in ten of the population. Later, however, this ratio changed to one in thirty.[28]

Analyzing the structure of contemporary society, Yun concluded that it was roughly divided into fourteen groups of people. Among them were not only aristocrats and wealthy families, peasants, artisans, and merchants (*nong shi shang gong*) – a categorization of society into four groups of people that had been traditionally used in classical texts – but also other groups such as retainers, various kinds of servants and helpers, speculators (divided into brokers and middlemen), actors, and prostitutes. Of these groups, Yun argued, only three, peasants, artisans, and merchants, were "workers" (*weizhe*) who produced wealth. The others were mere "consumers" (*xiangzhe*). As a result, production lagged behind while consumption increased. In that situation, "Heaven cannot nurture the people, the land cannot be expanded, and goods cannot be produced with the consequence that life will no longer be possible." Yun, therefore, believed that China's problem could be solved only by transforming more societal groups into "producers" in order to increase productivity and alleviate the burden on resources created by idle consumers.[29]

The criteria used by Yun Jing to differentiate among groups in society raise a few questions. He differentiated between productive merchants (*shang*) and unproductive intermediaries and brokers (*ya* and *kuai*). Yun considered trade to be a productive economic function, but, in his view, brokers practiced only unproductive speculation that actually hurt the economy. Yun also placed actors among the unproductive

[28] Yun Jing, "Sandai yinge lun wu," in *Dayun shanfang ji* (Taipei: Taiwan Zhonghua shuju, 1965), 8b–9b.

[29] Quoted in Zhao, *Zhongguo gudai jingji sixiangshi jianghua*, 624–625; Yun, "Sandai yinge lun wu."

group, thus denying their contribution to wealth generation as part of a money- and market-based service sector, which had been recognized as productive of wealth – because it generated work for the people – in the Qianlong and early Jiaqing era. Yun Jing's inclusion of both brokers and entertainers among the unproductive forces of society reflected a growing focus on channeling all resources into the production of agricultural staples to remedy the scarcity crisis.

Yun Jing's preoccupation with the ratio between producers and consumers appears to hark back to a long-standing analysis of society and to a tenet expressed in the often-quoted passage from the *Great Learning* (*Daxue*) that detailed the basic strategy for ensuring the prosperity of the empire: "Let the producers be many and the consumers few. Let there be activity in production, and economy in [consumption]."[30] Yun Jing's concerns with the ratio between producers and consumers, however, were mostly motivated by a desire to identify the productive forces in the private economy, a trend also common among contemporary European thinkers. In his *Tableau économique* (1758), for example, the *physiocrate* François Quesnay mapped the circulation of economic resources through different groups in French society in order to identify at what stage the wealth of a nation experienced real growth. His conclusion was that only agriculture generated a surplus. All other activities, including trade, succeeded only in paying for their production costs and the livelihoods of the people involved. On the basis of this observation, Quesnay differentiated among "productive" classes (peasants) and "sterile" classes (manufacturing workers). We might expect Quesnay to have considered peasants to be the most important economic actors, since they worked in the fields to produce the all-important surplus. He bestowed this honor, in fact, on the "proprietary class," landlords and other elites, such as the clergy, who benefited from the agricultural surplus and reinvested it back in the land to generate further growth. The most important class, therefore, was not the producers but those who controlled the surplus (capital). They were not "sterile," because they reinvested capital for economic expansion, and it was this expansion that generated additional wealth. The interest of the *physiocrates* in

[30] Confucius and James Legge, *The Confucian Analects, the Great Learning, and the Doctrine of the Mean* (Dover Publications, 2013), ccliv. I have replaced the last word of Legge's translation, "expenditures," with "consumption" to render the meaning of the original term *yong* in the closing section of the quoted text.

analyzing the contribution of economic actors, therefore, was based on a recognition of the elasticity of domestic production and, in opposition to mercantilist ideas, attempted to individuate the domestic sources of growth.[31]

The identification of productive forces in society also came to be a focus of early exponents of liberalism, who were interested in understanding the location of growth. In *The Wealth of Nations* (1776), Adam Smith wrote:

> According, therefore, as this produce, or what is purchased with it, bears a greater or smaller proportion to the number of those who are to consume it, the nation will be better or worse supplied with all the necessaries and conveniences for which it has occasion.
>
> But this proportion must in every nation be regulated by two different circumstances: first, by the skill, dexterity, and judgment with which its labour is generally applied; and, secondly, by the proportion between the number of those who are employed in useful labour, and that of those who are not so employed. Whatever be the soil, climate, or extent of territory of any particular nation, the abundance or scantiness of its annual supply must, in that particular situation, depend upon those two circumstances.[32]

Adam Smith – who witnessed the very early stages of the technological revolution, though it was limited, at that time, to a better use of labor (division of labor) – considered technological innovation an important factor in a nation's "proportion" between consumption and production and could envision the advent of an age of plenty for everyone. Yun Jing, on the other hand, did not fully appreciate the possibilities of technological change – reflecting pre-Opium War China's declining innovation trends – and gave priority to the transformation of consumers into producers as the most important strategy for expanding production and solving the problem of scarcity. Among Yun's contemporaries, it was only Bao Shichen who envisioned the potential of new technologies for improving productivity.

Bao Shichen (1775–1855) – renowned calligrapher, influential scholar, and political advisor – was a harsh critic of Hong Liangji and disputed his gloomy predictions. Bao accused Hong of not

[31] Roncaglia, *A Brief History of Economic Thought*, 47–51.

[32] Adam Smith and Robert Reich, *The Wealth of Nations* (New York, NY: Modern Library, 2000), xxiii–xxiv.

having worked out satisfactorily the mathematical calculations behind the problem. Although Bao's mathematical skills might have been superior to Hong's, he based his own argument on over-optimistic projections of data. He calculated that China had four billion *mu* of arable land available, greatly exaggerating the actual figure, estimated today to have been a little over one million.[33] Bao also inflated figures related to land productivity, arguing that one *mu* could produce at least 7 *dan* of grain per year. Since one adult male could cultivate 20 *mu*, even if only one in six among China's healthy males – which he estimated to form 30 percent of the population – devoted their energies to agriculture, production would be sufficient to support the welfare of the entire empire.[34] As a consequence, Bao believed that population growth could result in more productivity since, he explained, "the empire nourishes the empire's people. It is self-evident that if population grows, so does the number of producers (*shengzhe*)."[35]

Bao's optimism was not just the result of his inflated data. He also theorized ways to improve productivity. He realized that land reclamation could not be the solution to the scarcity problem but believed that the reorganization and rationalization of production could. "It is true that there is no longer much virgin land (*kuangtu*) remaining, but the real problem is that human work capacities (*lizuo*) have not been utilized efficiently or systematically (*bu ru fa*)."[36] Bao's optimism and faith in labor organization raise the question of whether he was reacting to an increase in production resulting from new industrious agricultural and handicraft techniques and placing more hope in them than other observers did.[37] Ultimately, however, Bao's plan would meet the same kind of criticism that the English philosopher David Ricardo (1772–1823) mounted against Smith's optimist view of consistent growth. Ricardo argued that added units

[33] A *mu* is equivalent to 0.165 acres. [34] Rowe, *Speaking of Profit*, 75–81.

[35] Quoted in Rowe, *Speaking of Profit*, 82, 90–94. Zhao, *Zhongguo gudai jingji sixiangshi jianghua*, 626.

[36] Quoted in Rowe, *Speaking of Profit*, 82, 90–94; Zhao, *Zhongguo gudai jingji sixiangshi jianghua*, 626.

[37] For post-1800 technological advances in the handicraft industry see Peng, *Zhongjian jingji*, "Chapter 4: Zhongjian jishu: shougongye shengchanli de bian ge quxiang" and "Chapter 3: Jishu yu shichang: Xiangcun bangongyehua de fazhan"; Peng Nansheng, *Bangongyehua: jindai zhongguo xiangcun shougongye de fazhan yu shehui bianqian* (Beijing: Zhonghua shuju, 2007).

of labor would have a diminishing impact on productivity.[38] The rate of growth in production, therefore, would inevitably fall behind that of population growth.

Even for Bao, however, who believed in the ability of new modes of labors to significantly increase production, frugality remained a crucial policy for solving China's scarcity crisis.[39] It is difficult to find pro-luxury arguments from the late Jiaqing period. In general, no distinctions were made, even occasionally or informally, between modes of acquisition of luxury, whether they were market-based or "despotic" (*nüequ*). To contemporary observers, the Daoguang depression appeared to confirm the notion that China was running out of resources and in dire need of frugality; population growth and economic scarcity appeared to doom the empire to poverty.

Beyond Sumptuary Laws: Restructuring Production and State Intervention

The official documents and scholarly writings discussed above reveal that, while economic thinkers perceived frugality as an essential policy in the fight against scarcity, they also believed that it could not provide a satisfactory solution on its own. The new situation required new approaches that went beyond banning luxury, implementing sumptuary laws, and reclaiming new land. More effective strategies, as well as increased state intervention, were needed to rebalance the ratio between production and consumption.

This problem inspired debates as early as the late years of the Yongzheng reign. At that time, in one of his imperial lectures (*jingyan jiangyi*), Ren Qiyun (1670–1744) – a Hanlin Academy scholar and an official under both the Yongzheng and Qianlong Emperors – addressed the issues of population and scarcity. A native of Changzhou Prefecture (Jiangsu Province), Ren Qiyun was born into a poor family, but, despite these humble beginnings, he passed the *juren* (1723) and *jinshi* (1733) examinations and pursued a successful career in the imperial administration. Later, he worked closely with the royal household, holding positions such as secretary (*chunfang*), companion to the heir

[38] Robert L. Heilbroner, *The Worldly Philosophers: The Lives, Times, and Ideas of the Great Economic Thinkers* (New York, NY: Touchstone 1999), 94–100.

[39] For an in-depth discussion of the economic ideas of Bao Shichen see Rowe, *Speaking of Profit*.

apparent (*zhongyun*), and assistant in the Court of the Imperial Clan (*zongrengfu*).[40] In one of his imperial lectures, Ren discussed the scarcity of grain in the capital and its dire consequences, identifying the fast pace of population growth as one of the main culprits. In this situation, Ren suggested, the state should grant a suspension of tax collection, offer relief to the people, and pursue land reclamation. He believed, however, that these traditional measures could not bring about a definitive solution to the poverty afflicting China at that time. According to Ren, careful "long-term planning" (*jingjiu zhi ji*) was the only effective solution. Officials at the prefectural and provincial levels should calculate how much grain was needed to feed the local population and then plan accordingly. Ren himself offered a rough estimate, calculating that "a grown-up man eats three *dan* and six *dou* of rice ... [Consequently] the population of an average county will use no less than a 100,000 *dan* ... and, in a year, the population of one province will need 40 million *dan*." Once the officials had estimated their region's need for grain, they should try to match resources and population in two basic ways: increasing production and limiting consumption. Production should be focused on basic crops, eliminating wasteful ones, such as tobacco. This crop not only wasted resources that could be invested in producing grain to feed the hungry, but it also induced people to spend on unnecessary items. The money a household spent on tobacco, Ren explained, could acquire food for one or two people. Ultimately, Ren argued, only careful planning of production and adoption of a frugal lifestyle could solve China's poverty crisis.[41]

In a letter to a county magistrate named Hu, Ren offered a detailed explanation of how his plan could be implemented.[42] This letter makes it clear that Ren relied on the Qing system of power brokerage based on social groups and organizations, such as kinships and *baojia* (social units of mutual responsibility generally formed of five families), that

40 Zhao Erxun, "Liezhuan 268," in *Qingshigao* (Beijing: Zhonghua shuju, 1977), Vol. 43, juan 482, 13184–13186; Harvard University, Academia Sinica, and Peking University, *China Biographical Database*.

41 Ren Qiyun, "Jingyan jianyi wupian," in *Wangchao jingshi wenbian*, ed. by He Changling, Vol. 14, Zhiti: si, zhengbenxia (accessed through http://hanji.sinica.edu.tw/). As a measure of volume, a *dan* is equivalent to 100 liters and a *dou* to 10 liters.

42 Ren, "Guan Zhong lun" and "Yu Hu yi hou shu" in *Wangchao jingshi wenbian*, respectively Vol. 11, zhiti 5, zhi fa shang and Vol. 22, shi zheng 8, shou lin zhong.

supplemented what Mann describes as "the limits of bureaucratical control."[43] He relied on reviving and strengthening local institutions, especially the *baojia* and the *xiangyue* (district regulatory commissions). As he explained in his letter, the *baojia* and the *xiangyue* were two complementary sides of the same system, the latter providing principles to be applied by the first. The *baojia* would ensure that any illegal action would be easily detected by neighbors and reported to the authorities. The authorities would then decide on the proper punishment for both the culprits and those who failed to report them. This, Ren argued, was the way to eradicate bad customs in a local community and return it to social stability and prosperity. Ren presented these quite draconian measures as part of a larger plan for enacting Confucian virtues. Mutual surveillance should be accompanied by frequent public readings and teaching of the sixteen maxims of Kangxi's *Sacred Edict* (*Shengyu yishiliutiao*).[44] Those principles were also to inspire the regulatory committee and serve as a guideline for correct moral behavior to be followed by the members of the *baojia*.[45]

Among the bad habits that Ren's system was supposed to eradicate were not just illegal activities, such as gambling and thieving, but also luxury consumption and extravagant lifestyle. Ren's interlocutor, Hu, in fact, served as a magistrate in Yixing County (in Wuxi Prefecture in Jiangsu Province, one of the most prosperous and luxury-prone areas in Jiangnan). Ren's critique of the extravagant habits of this county evokes the same scenes of leisure consumption described by Lu Ji and Tang Zhen. People, Ren lamented, do not know frugality, and the entire region resonates with opera singing. New temples were erected everywhere, and splendidly attired women wandered around sightseeing. Throngs of people attended temple fairs. While Lu Ji and Tang

[43] Susan Mann, *Local Merchants and the Chinese Bureaucracy, 1750–1950* (Stanford, CA: Stanford University Press, 1987), 12. In this volume, Susan Mann refers to this brokerage system as "liturgical methods of governance" (12). This system of brokerage is also discussed by Prasenjit Duara, who refers to it as a "cultural nexus of power." Prasenjit Duara, *Culture, Power, and the State: Rural North China, 1900–1942* (Stanford, CA: Stanford University Press, 1991); see especially Chapter 2, "Brokering Rural Administration in Late Qing."

[44] Emperor Kangxi's *Sacred Edict* was intended to instruct the population on the basic principles of Confucian behavior.

[45] Ren, "Guan Zhong lun" and "Yu Hu yi hou shu," in *Wangchao jingshi wenbian*, respectively Vol. 11, zhiti 5, zhi fa shang, and Vol. 22, shi zheng 8, shou lin zhong.

Zhen focused on the beneficial aspects of these bustling commercial activities, Ren focused on their seediest dealings, involving gamblers and thieves as well as matchmakers, intermediaries of all kinds, and soothsayers who cheated the people.

Ren's vision of the revitalized local community, if realized, would have drastically changed its daily life. Only one opera a year would be permitted. Housing would be reasonably modest, and people would stop "revering food and wine" (*jiu shi yi wei zun*). Ren's plan to eradicate crimes and luxury relied on one important factor: the leadership of the Regulatory Committee should not be entrusted to "rich people with vulgar habits" (*bisu zhi fumin*) but to the local elderly, who, he argued, would be better positioned to know what was best for the community.[46] Those elites who had been crucial for the boom of the consumer economy in Jiangnan, therefore, would no longer play a leading role in the local society.

Bao Shichen also relied on institutions at the center of the brokerage system –"liturgical governance" or "cultural nexus," to use Mann's or Duara's expressions – which he perceived as cooperating closely with the local-level administration. In his treatise *Agricultural Administration* (*Nongzheng*), Bao detailed ways in which local officials could not just cut consumption but also increase production by deploying labor to its most efficient use, as mentioned earlier. In particular, he proposed that they employ *corvée* labor systematically to open up new land or, in areas where land was already utilized to the fullest, use *corvée* labor directly in the fields. This increased input of manpower, he believed, would generate a proportional increase in agricultural yields.[47] Here Bao seems to offer a theoretical view of the "industrious" labor-intensive mode of production that was to become a topic of discussion among today's China historians.

In addition to the expansion of production, Bao Shichen also advocated the regulation of distribution. He suggested that households be categorized according to their economic status. Wealthy households would be required to store officially regulated amounts of grain and circulate the rest on the market in order to keep supplies flowing unhindered. Heads of *baojia* would urge rich families to take care of

46 Ren, "Guan Zhong lun" and "Yu Hu yi hou shu" in *Wangchao jingshi wenbian*, respectively Vol. 11, zhiti 5, zhi fa shang, and Vol. 22, shi zheng 8, shou lin zhong.

47 Rowe, *Speaking of Profit*, 82–83.

the poorest branches of their lineages. If they failed to do so, they would be labeled "unneighborly" (*buyou*). In years of extreme scarcity, poor families in distress would be authorized by the local magistrate to ask the richest families in their area for help in the form of officially regulated loans to be repaid with minimal interest. Bao Shichen proposed to apply the same system to the county-level administration. "Wealthy counties" – thus labeled through a careful assessment of local standards of living and the resources available per household – would aid the poorest ones. This radical redistributionist plan was actually tested in the area of Nanjing, Jiangsu Province, during an especially severe and protracted drought, but it failed to bring the expected relief, mostly because of further complications, including local uprisings and massive inflows of refugees from neighboring areas. A subsequent attempt also floundered among controversies and administrative difficulties.[48]

Bao believed that the primary reason for China's agricultural decline was the imperial administrators' loss of interest in agriculture. While in earlier times officials were personally knowledgeable and involved in agricultural practices, recent administrations had left the initiative to the people, with the dire consequences of mismanagement, waste, and extravagance. The rulers, he advocated, should restore "government by fundamentals" (*benzheng*), and local officials should acquire agricultural expertise, which "can no longer be left simply to the common people."[49] This statement amounted to a critique of earlier ideas of an unregulated economy supported by both the Ming loyalist and other ruralists as well as by pro-luxury writers such as Tang Zhen. It proposed an unprecedented level of state intervention, which was, however, to be carried out in cooperation with local elites. Officials and literati landowners should work together to make sure that the land was used in the most productive way and generated the greatest impact in terms of improving people's livelihoods. Bao's view of agricultural production, although primarily targeted to fulfill *minsheng* objectives, did not exclude integration with market opportunities and encouraged sericulture and other market-oriented crops. Like Ren Qiyun, however, Bao considered the production of tobacco and wine wasteful. Tobacco, he calculated, was six times more expensive

48 Rowe, *Speaking of Profit*, 86–89.
49 Quoted in Rowe, *Speaking of Profit*, 82–83.

than grain to grow, but it only supported luxury consumption and instigated the leisure behavior of smoking, wasting time that could be employed productively. For this reason, local authorities should discourage the cultivation of tobacco and the production of wine. Bao's economic theories, in fact, exemplify the emergence of a hybrid economic system that, still relying on market forces, advocated targeted state intervention aimed at solving the problem of scarcity.[50]

Support for increased state intervention is also evident in the writings of Yun Jing. He, in fact, ascribed the growing disparity between producers and consumers and a general economic decline to a retreat of government intervention in regulating the economy and excessive reliance on the market. Problems with agriculture, he argued, began with changes in the land tenure system. In ancient times, the state owned the land and the people worked it. The agrarian economy had begun to decline when the rich came to own the land and started renting it out to the poor to work. Under this system, the renters never produced enough to feed their families, pay rent to the landlords, and meet their tax obligations. Yun Jing concluded emphatically that "this is the problem with the agricultural economy" (*ci nong zhi bing*). Yun Jing then analyzed the other two of what he perceived to be the three basic sectors of the economy: agriculture, manufacturing, and trade (*nong gong shang*). Manufacturing, he concluded, had also declined because it was no longer regulated by the state and the individual artisans did not plan their production appropriately. Lack of state regulation also plagued consumption, creating a crisis in the trade sector (*shang*). In ancient times, merchants did not ride in carriages or wear brocade, and very few people pursued excessive luxury. As a consequence, the community prospered. In his day, Yun Jing lamented, the rich competed with high officials in extravagant lifestyle, and a large portion of the population adopted luxury habits. "This, he concluded, was the problem with trade" (*ci shang zhi bing*).[51] Yun Jing's view of the economy of the empire, therefore, was the opposite of that advocated by pro-luxury writers, and its implementation would have profoundly changed the Jiangnan consumption economy.

[50] Quoted in Rowe, *Speaking of Profit*; Zhao, *Zhongguo gudai jingji sixiangshi jianghua*, 626.

[51] Quoted in Zhao, *Zhongguo gudai jingji sixiangshi jianghua*, 624–625; Yun, "Sandai yinge lun wu."

Bao's and Yun's qualified optimism regarding the ability of the state to solve the population crisis contrasted with Hong's pessimism. Hong, in fact, believed that there were no natural solutions (*tiandi tiaoji zhi fa*) or state-led solutions (*junxiang tiaoji zhi fa*) that could save China. Nature provided relief from population growth through natural disasters, such as floods and epidemic diseases, that significantly reduced the population of the empire. The effects of such cataclysmic events, however, would not last long, since "Heaven and Earth cannot prevent people from being born," even if eventually "it is not able to support them." The state, on the other hand, could launch such measures as land reclamation, relocating people to scarcely populated frontier regions, lightening the tax burden, banning superfluous and extravagant consumption, restricting accumulation of land and wealth, opening the doors of public granaries in case of scarcity, and in general striving to offer relief. These measures, he warns, would nonetheless fail to reduce the pace of population growth in the long run. Like Heaven and Earth, the state would also "be unable to limit birth." Families, he lamented, ignored warnings and regulations from the state and continued to give birth to too many children.[52]

These early Chinese discussions on the population crisis and its solutions differed significantly from those of their contemporary European counterparts, most famously represented by the publication of *Essay on Population* (1798) by the English cleric and philosopher Thomas Robert Malthus (1766–1834). Like Hong Liangji, Malthus was concerned with population growth and based his analysis on the idea of the unfavorable relationship between the geometrical growth of population and the numerical expansion of production. Malthus pessimistically concluded that nothing could be done to solve the poverty problem generated by overpopulation. Beyond this point, however, Malthus' and Hong's ideas diverged. Malthus believed that population expanded and contracted in response to the availability of resources – scarcity being the only force able to control the birth rate among workers. Increasing production and attempting to improve the living standard of the people would only provide a temporary solution. It would, in fact, make more resources available to the people,

[52] Hong Liangji, "Zhiping pian" in *Juanshige ji* (Taipei: Taiwan Zhonghua shuju, 1965) 6a–7a.

inevitably causing a new upward spike in population and a consequent return to scarcity and poverty. Attempts to solve the poverty crisis, therefore, often made the situation worse.[53] Although also pessimistic, Hong Liangji did not directly link resource availability with the size of the population, but saw the population growing geometrically in isolation from economic factors. State intervention could improve the situation, but only temporarily. In China, therefore, statist solutions emerged which contrasted with the classical liberalism of Malthus. In other words, although the Chinese and English pioneers of population studies began their analysis from a very similar quantitative calculation, the Chinese framed it within the productivist and statist trends that were emerging in China at the time, while the English tended to frame the problem in the language of "natural laws," not to be interfered with by the state, that was sweeping through Europe.

Departing from Hong's fatalism, Yun Jing and Bao Shichen believed that measures could be taken to improve the situation. Yun focused on the sociohistorical causes of the low ratio of producers to consumers and concluded that it could be adjusted with some form of social engineering promoted by the state. Bao differed from Malthus, Hong, and Yun, since, on the basis of his inflated estimates of land and productivity, he denied outright the unequal ratio of growth between people and production. He also recognized the importance of technology for improving production and solving the population crisis. From this point of view, both Yun's and Bao's theories are more comparable to Smith's optimism than Hong's, since Yun believed that it was possible to improve the ratio between producers and consumers and Bao believed that labor organization could play a crucial role in supporting a consistent upward trend in production.

A more articulated appreciation for new technologies developed steadily in the period after the Opium War, especially after Self-Strengthening efforts led scholars and officials to travel and study abroad. This was the case of the prominent scholar Yan Fu (1854–1921), who traveled widely and studied in England for three years. On his return to China, he was appointed to teaching positions at the newly established Fujian Arsenal Academy and, later, at Beiyang Naval Officers' School. These two institutions had been established during the Self-Strengthening Movement as centers not just for retraining the army in line with Western military practices but also for

[53] Roncaglia, *A Brief History of Economic Thought*, 79–83.

importing Western technologies. For this purpose, they hosted foreign advisors, taught foreign languages, and established translation bureaus. It was in this context that Yan Fu came to translate books that were influential in Western thought, including Adam Smith's *The Wealth of Nations*, Thomas Huxley's *Evolution and Ethics*, Herbert Spencer's *The Study of Sociology*, and John Stuart Mill's *On Liberty*. It was his familiarity with Western political and economic theories as well as his personal experience of life in England that brought Yan Fu to believe that technology was to play a decisive role in increasing production and solving the population problem. In his writings, he explained that the economic situation in China was still unbalanced, as production lagged behind the needs of the people. It took "the production of a hundred people to support one person" and, for this reason, scarcity was still prevalent. Only through the use of machines to improve labor efficiency, he concluded, could China's production grow and meet the needs of the population.[54]

Despite this new hope in the power of technology and the fact that, from the mid-nineteenth century on, famines, natural disasters, and warfare did indeed plague China, slowing population growth – as predicted in Hong Liangji's bleak scenario – economic scarcity and finding the optimal balance between production and consumption remained constant preoccupations for Chinese officials and intellectuals through the late Qing period. Even the arrival of Western imperialism did not overshadow these problems, which came to be integrated into the discourse on Self-Strengthening.

Reconfiguring State Finances: Empty Coffers, Corruption, and Administrative Reforms

At the beginning of the nineteenth century, it also became clear that scarcity was a problem not just for supporting the livelihood of the people and realizing the *minsheng* mandate but also for the finances of the state. This was a new problem, not faced by earlier Qing emperors, who had enjoyed more favorable economic circumstances. Kangxi often remarked on the "surplus in state finances." In 1729 Yongzheng stated: "There is abundance for the people and for the country. The

[54] Chen Yongqin, *Zhongguo jingji sixiangshi* (Zhengzhou Shi: Henan renmin chubanshe 2008), 246–249.

state coffers are full. We have already enough for the expenses of the empire."[55] By the late Qianlong and early Jiaqing period, however, the military expenses for Qianlong's campaigns in the Northwest, which brought this region under Qing control, and for subduing widespread domestic rebellions arising throughout the empire – especially the eight-year-long White Lotus Rebellion (1796–1804) – had strained the finances of the state and erased the surplus accumulated in the High Qing years.[56] In December 1821, complaining about what he perceived to be superfluous expenses by some officials, the Daoguang Emperor lamented: "As for our times, we cannot promptly handle all the repairs and regulations needed yearly. Where do we have the leisure to take care of extras?"[57] The High Qing emperors' sense of financial security had indeed given way to serious concerns that the state could no longer perform its basic duties.

According to von Glahn, one of the main problems with the financial crisis was "the rigid revenue base, tethered to the land tax rates frozen by imperial decree in 1713."[58] Even if the Qing state did tap commercial activities to a certain extent, in the late eighteenth and early nineteenth centuries approximately 70 percent of the state's revenue came from agriculture, with less than 20 percent coming from the salt monopoly and internal and maritime customs. It was only in the second half of the nineteenth century, after the Opium War, that the situation was sharply reversed. By 1893, in fact, the land tax constituted only 40 percent of revenue, followed at 19 percent by *lijin* (a tariff on domestic trade adopted in 1853, during the Taiping Rebellion of 1850–64), and by maritime customs and salt taxes at 17 percent each. The application of new taxes on commerce and consumption – especially on luxury goods such as tobacco and wine – therefore resulted in state revenue almost doubling between 1849 and 1893.[59]

In the early decades of the nineteenth century, however, the imperial state was plagued by diminished finances and sought to apply frugality

[55] "Shengzu shilu" (April 12, 1667), *Qingshilu* (Beijing: Zhonghua shuju, 1985), Vol. 4, juan 21, 297–298, and "Shizong shilu" (August 11, 1729), Vol. 8, juan 85, 134–135.

[56] Li, *China Upside Down*, 87–114.

[57] "Xuanzong shilu" (December 2, 1821), *Qingshilu* (Beijing: Zhonghua shuju, 1985), Vol. 33, juan 26, 457–459.

[58] Von Glahn, *The Economic History of China*, 362–363.

[59] Von Glahn, *The Economic History of China*, 315–316, 380.

in the imperial administration. Frugality was even to be adopted within the imperial household. When the son of Prince Yonxi started his studies, he was probably the first young member of the imperial family not to do so with much fanfare and with a new set of ornate jade paraphernalia. Turning this event into a common occurrence that did not require expensive presents and protocols was one of the measures used by Jiaqing in his attempt to return the imperial household to "honest and simple Manchu customs." Such measures were intended to restore relative simplicity to life in the forbidden city; after all, Jiaqing commented, it was impossible to avoid a few instances of extravagance. Celebrations and exchanges of presents, however, should be limited to the unavoidable ritually sanctioned occasions of the "three festivals and two birthdays" (*san jie lian shengri*, Dragon Boat, Mid-Autumn, and New Year festivals and the birthdays of Confucius and of one's teacher).[60] Although we can assume that this call to limit expenses did not really set a frugal lifestyle for the members of the imperial household, it did serve as a rhetorical example for the wider goal of implementing frugality in the imperial administration at large. Jiaqing, in fact, considered the officials in the provinces to be the most prone to extravagant lifestyles and more willing than other officials to accept bribes. These officials, the emperor lamented, complained that their salaries were not enough to cover expenses, but, in reality, they used this common refrain as an excuse to accept bribes.[61] Following in Jiaqing's steps, the Daoguang Emperor continued to pursue a stricter oversight of the administration to ensure more frugal habits. In May 1824, for example, the Imperial Censor (*yushi*) Li Yisong sent a memorial asking officials to "strictly control the ingrained habit of luxury." Li lamented that most officials in the provinces led such an extravagant and luxurious life that they exhausted resources, creating scarcity for the common people. The emperor's response was very firm, demanding thorough investigation and severe punishment of culprits, instructing Li not to be lenient and, if needed, to employ such extreme measures as dismissal from office and impeachment.[62]

[60] *Renzong shilu* (March 10, 1800), *Qingshilu* (Beijing: Zhonghua shuju, 1985), Vol. 28, juan 59, 786–787.

[61] *Renzong shilu* (March 10, 1800), *Qingshilu* (Beijing: Zhonghua shuju, 1985), Vol. 33, juan 16, 304–305.

[62] "Xuanzong shilu" (May 14, 1821), *Qingshilu* (Beijing: Zhonghua shuju, 1985), Vol. 33, juan 16, 304–305; "Xuanzong shilu" (October 17, 1820), *Qingshilu*

The promotion of administrative frugality of the Jiaqing and the Daoguang administrations was accompanied by an increased reliance on private market forces to carry out functions previously managed by the state in the hope of transferring expenses to private merchants. Jiaqing entrusted to private merchants and local elites the management of granaries and water conservation and Daoguang did so for the transportation of tribute grain and the Salt Administration. Historian Wang Wensheng describes this shift as a general "state retreat" from political and economic activism as part of a wider attempt to streamline the government administration and make it financially more sustainable by shifting responsibility for some of the paternalist, *minsheng*-oriented duties of the state to the private sector. According to Wang, these reforms were also supposed to revive the "'cultural nexus of power' protecting the state's long-term stability." The local elites, in fact, would take the initiative in grain storage and water conservation, thus "carr[ying] out tasks that contributed directly to social and economic stability."[63] Jiaqing's and Daoguang's administrative retreats were also motivated by concerns for the growing corruption in the government bureaucracy and, in this sense, built on strategies already pursued in the High Qing period.[64] Many of the reforms of the first half of the nineteenth century reveal an attempt to eliminate the wide network of sub-governmental institutions developed under the previous emperors, including local *yamen* clerks and brokers, whom the reformers perceived as the main source of corruption. According to Wang, "such 'entrepreneurial brokerages' inadvertently subverted the traditional bases of state power – the rural elite's 'protective brokerage' on the part of the state."[65] These "entrepreneurial brokerages" had developed predatory practices, as discussed in Chapter 2, ultimately "undermining the time-honored 'cultural nexus of power,'" which had characterized the symbiotic relationship

(Beijing: Zhonghua shuju, 1985), Vol. 33, juan 16, 304–305; "Xuanzong shilu" (November 9, 1820), *Qingshilu* (Beijing: Zhonghua shuju, 1985), Vol. 33, juan 6, 143.

63 Wang, *White Lotus Rebels and South China Pirates*, 256, 195, 76, respectively; Rowe, "Bao Shichen and Agrarian Reform in Early Nineteenth-Century China," 1–31, and *Speaking of Profit*, Chapters 4 and 5.

64 Wang, *White Lotus Rebels and South China Pirates*, 190, 195.

65 Wang, *White Lotus Rebels and South China Pirates*, 195. Wang refers here to the idea of Prasenjit Duara, *Culture, Power, and the State: Rural North China, 1900–1942*, 42–43.

between state and social elites.[66] In this sense, according to Wang, the Jiaqing reforms attempted to reestablish this lost connection, regain the support and involvement of the elites, and promote "a generally sustainable state–society relationship."[67] The fiscal retrenchment of the early 1800s, however, appears to have expanded the state's cooperation beyond the traditional rural elite to increasingly include those emerging commercial forces that Ren Qiyun had attempted to marginalize. The new "nexus," therefore, reflected the deep changes in the economy of the empire and recognized a shift in social elites that Ren had attempted to counteract.

Administrative streamlining, cost reduction, and circumvention of the existing corrupt bureaucratic networks motivated the 1826 reform of the Grain Tribute Administration, which switched the route that southern grain followed to Beijing (in the northern region of the empire) from the Grand Canal to a sea route, removing it from official supervision and entrusting it to private merchants. The objective of eliminating wasteful expenses by cutting both corruption and "state brokerages" remained an important motivation and inspired the privatization of the Liang-Huai Salt Administration (1834), which had long functioned as a state monopoly. The systemically entrenched corruption and loss of market due to the growing smuggling of salt made its reform imperative.[68]

Continued reliance on market forces is confirmed by the work of historian Lin Man-Houng. Lin argues that during the first half of the nineteenth century the "accommodationists" – who favored noninterventionist policies – still prevailed among the officials of the Daoguang administration, influencing how the imperial government attempted to solve the problem of the price of silver that was at the foundation of the Daoguang depression. According to Lin, the "accommodationist" officials who preferred that the state limit its role in stabilizing the circulation and value of silver – including Lin Zexu (1785–1850), Wei Yuan (1794–1856), and Bao Shichen – successfully opposed the "interventionist" policies of Wang Liu (1786–1843) that aimed to establish a paper money system which would result in strong centralization and state control. The "accommodationists," however,

[66] Rowe, *Speaking of Profit*, 108; Wang, *White Lotus Rebels and South China Pirates*, 195.
[67] Wang, *White Lotus Rebels and South China Pirates*, 195.
[68] Wong, "Chinese Tradition of Grain Storage."

lost out with the rise of the Self-Strengthening Movement that developed in the mid-nineteenth century in response to Western imperialist pressure.[69] Despite the ultimate defeat of the accommodationists, the trend toward state intervention gained more momentum in the Self-Strengthening period; however, it never came into complete contradiction with the state's efforts to cooperate with private market forces.

Facing Imperialism

The Treaty of Nanjing (1942) – and the unequal treaties with other Western European imperialist powers that followed – profoundly altered the economic landscape of China. One of the most important changes was the end of China's protectionist policies in its trade with the Western powers and the beginning of the "unequal" trade system they imposed. In China, this system relied on three Western-sanctioned institutions. The first was the imposition of huge war reparation payments (indemnities), which severely strained the already faltering imperial finances. The Treaty of Nanjing alone sanctioned an indemnity of twenty-one million silver dollars. The Boxer Protocol (1900), which closed a long string of similar war-compensation agreements, imposed 450 million silver taels (roughly equal to 330 million US dollars at the time) which was to be paid over thirty-nine years with annual interest of 4 percent.

The situation was made particularly dire by a clause included in the Treaty of Nanjing: the transfer of the Maritime Customs Service to British control. This second change had two particularly damaging consequences. China lost its ability to set its own customs duties, which, under the new British leadership, tended to cater to the interests of Britain and other Western powers. Import duties declined while export duties rose, leaving the Chinese state unable to adopt a protectionist schedule of tariffs. In addition, the indemnities were all to be paid through the Maritime Custom Service. Its total revenue was deposited into foreign banks, and only after all indemnity obligations had been met were the remaining funds transferred to the Chinese state. The imperial government, therefore, had lost control of what had, by now, became its main source of revenue, since international

[69] Lin, *China Upside Down*, Chapter 8.

trade had replaced the agricultural tax as the most significant contributor to total state revenue.[70]

A third institution established by the unequal treaties was extraterritoriality, which established territories within the empire (foreign concessions) where Chinese sovereignty was greatly curtailed. This practice of extraterritoriality became especially damaging to the economy with the Treaty of Shimonoseki (April 1895), signed to sanction the end of the First Sino-Japanese war (1894–5). Under this treaty, the victorious Japan – which was on its way to becoming the main imperialist threat to China – could establish factories on Chinese soil. These factories would act as extraterritorial entities and, therefore, would not be susceptible to Chinese laws and taxation. At the same time, however, they could avoid paying import duties, since their goods could be sold on the Chinese market without going through customs barriers.

As mentioned earlier, China's new position in the global economy led to a dramatic shift in the priorities of state policies from the overall objective of *minsheng* to that of strengthening the empire against imperialism. The nature and objectives of the Self-Strengthening reforms illustrate how, after the Opium War, new nationalist mercantilist objectives came to be incorporated within the economic discourse and merged with notions of scarcity and frugality.

Frugality and Self-Strengthening

After the arrival of Western imperialism in the mid-nineteenth century, the discourse on frugality was seamlessly incorporated into the debate on how to strengthen the empire and resist foreign intrusion. Fighting scarcity through frugality became central to many schemes for reviving China's "vital energy" (*yuan qi*), an expression popular at the time to indicate economic and social renovation. As argued by one of the main contributors to Self-Strengthening ideology and reform, Feng Guifen (1809–74) – prominent scholar, influential although unofficial political advisor, and personal assistant of Li Hongzhang (1823–1901)[71] – "if

[70] Hans J. van de Ven, *Breaking with the Past: The Maritime Customs Service and the Global Origins of Modernity in China* (New York, NY: Columbia University Press, 2014).

[71] Hummel, *Eminent Chinese of the Ch'ing Period*, Vol. 2, 241–243. Harvard University, Academia Sinica, and Peking University, *China Biographical Database.*

we want to protect the people, restore the country's vitality, and change this situation of poverty, we only need frugality."[72] Also a native of Jiangnan (more specifically of Suzhou) and an admirer of Gu Yanwu, Feng was considered one of the best Statecraft scholars of his time. It is not surprising, therefore, that he studied the social and economic problems of the times extensively, was well versed in mathematics, and developed a keen interest in Western sciences in the aftermath of the Opium War. At this time he advocated the adoption of Western technology, which he believed to be the most important lesson China should learn from the West – a view that resonated with the core principle of Self-Strengthening, "Chinese Essence and Western Technology" (*zhongti xiyong*), as succinctly expressed by the prominent official and Self-Strengthener Zhang Zhidong (1837–1909).

According to Feng, frugality was especially important at this moment of war devastation, agricultural decline, falling state finances, and a severe scarcity of resources which led to people "lying in the roads" starving. Frugality, therefore, was imperative, and it was crucial to find better solutions to restrain extravagance. Analyzing the four basic aspects of daily life traditionally linked to the problem of consumption – housing, carriages and horses, food, and clothing – Feng remarked that those who could exceed the limits in housing and carriages were actually very few, and since food could not be prohibited, the best strategy to rein in extravagance was returning the population to a simpler fashion in their dress.[73] Although this measure might appear capable of only very limited results (and it was certainly insufficient to solve China's scarcity problem), it arguably aimed a very specific criticism at Jiangnan-style New Luxury consumption and the passion of the middle people for fashion trends which openly flaunted sumptuary laws. Reformer Tang Shouqian (1856–1917) also believed that frugality had the power to solve China's many problems. A former county magistrate in Anhui, Tang later turned to political activism and business. He became a member of the Zhejiang Consultative Assembly and of the Constitutional Preparatory Committee and, in the early Republican

[72] Feng Guifen, "Chongjie jianyi." *Jiaobinlu kangyi*, in *Jindai zhongguo shiliao congkan, series 62* (Taipei: Wenhai chubanshe), Vol. 612, 133–136, also quoted in Zhao Fengtian, *WanQing wushinian jingji sixiangshi* (Beiping: Hafo Yanjing xueshe, 1939), 216.

[73] Feng, "Chongjie jianyi," 133–136.

period, established the Zhejiang Development Bank (*Zhejiang xingye yinhang*). Tang also argued that extravagance had a devastating impact on the Chinese economy, dramatically commenting that "being without simplicity is a calamity, harmful to the livelihood of the people, bad for customs, and lethal for the national economy."[74]

At the turn of the nineteenth century, even reformers and officials who had become increasingly familiar with Western economic theories – especially after Yan Fu translated *The Wealth of Nations* in 1901 – continued to support frugality against the positive interpretation of all forms of consumption promoted by the newly arrived liberal ideology. Yan Fu, for example, directly criticized the notion that market-based luxury could help sustain the livelihood of the people, since only a very small section of the population benefited from this kind of extravagant purchase:

> Some people ... say that luxury, in reality, damages the individual, but benefits the people's enterprises. This is a faulty theory. As for the benefits of luxury, they are enjoyed only by a few families that are at the receiving end of its generosity.[75]

This statement reflected the preoccupation with the limited scope of the luxury market in China. Although the New Luxury mode of consumption remained an important element of the coastal urban economies, from the Self-Strengthening perspective of the entire *guo*, it still constituted a small portion of the empire and certainly differed from the mass consumption mode (consumerism) that was emerging in Western industrialized countries at the turn of the twentieth century. Yan Fu, therefore, did not believe that, in the very different economic circumstances of China, luxury consumption had the same power to sustain economic growth as it did in the West.

Luxury consumption was also directly criticized by Liang Qichao (1873–1929), a prominent and influential reformer closely associated with Kang Youwei, who declared:

> Some of the philosophers of former times believed that, if the people's customs were extravagant and the goods they needed luxurious, production would expand. If everyone were stingy in using their wealth, then the poor would have nothing with which to support their lives. For this reason,

[74] Quoted in Zhao, *WanQing wushinian jingji sixiangshi*, 217.
[75] Zhao, *WanQing wushinian jingji sixiangshi*, 220.

they could say that luxury was not a moral evil! Little do they know that extravagant customs singlehandedly completely squander a country's wealth.[76]

Yan's and Liang's references to former philosophers who had supported extravagance confirm the popularity enjoyed by pro-luxury arguments in the late Ming and High Qing periods, challenging the common perception of the centrality of the formula "Revere frugality and eliminate luxury" in the Chinese discourse on the economy of the late imperial period.

At this time, frugality also came to assume an anti-imperialist dimension, as it was assigned an important role in remedying China's growing trade deficit. For example, Tang Shouqian (1856–1917) listed "penetration of Western goods" among the seven areas in which luxury needed to be eliminated and simplicity reinstated – the other six including the by now familiar problems of corrupt public administration, officials who overstepped their ranks, extravagant performances and entertainments, love for cigarettes and alcohol, and propensity for ostentatious luxury in the celebration of marriages and funerals. Cutting the imports of expensive luxury goods would not just erase bad customs but would also become a weapon against Western domination of the international trade system.[77]

The popularity of the idea of using frugality against imperialism is well illustrated by the writings of another official, Chen Chi (1855–1900), a member of the Reformist Faction (*weixinpai*) of Kang Youwei (1858–1927). Chen had worked with the prominent scholar, merchant, and reformer, Zheng Guanying (1842–1922) on his *Words of Warning to a Prosperous Age* (*Shengshi weiyan*), eventually writing its introduction. Chen believed that "As for the prosperity of the age, the habits of all the people, whether they are government officials or not and regardless of rank and status, must be industrious and frugal."[78] The current deterioration of customs among the Chinese people, Chen continues, was greatly aggravated by the new wave of trade with Western powers, which encouraged luxury, eroding morality and social stability in general. The Western-oriented luxury of

[76] Quoted in Lai Jiancheng, *Liang Qichao de jingji mianxiang* (Hangzhou: Zhejiang da xue chu ban she, 2010), 240.
[77] Zhao, *WanQing wushinian jingji sixiangshi*, 217.
[78] Zhao, *WanQing wushinian jingji sixiangshi*, 217–218.

the people in busy treaty ports – cities like Shanghai that the Treaty of Nanjing and other "unequal" treaties had opened to foreign residence and business – and provincial capitals had also spread to the villages, he argued, and the common people, who did not have much money, borrowed in order to buy beautiful clothes and appear elegant. Because they had difficulties repaying their debts, they started cheating and stealing. It was, therefore, important, Chen concluded, to once again enforce sumptuary laws to revive popular morals and avoid Chinese society's plunge into chaos.[79]

Other officials and scholars believed that, in the words of Self-Strengthener Zhang Zhidong, frugality was "also an important policy to perk up the management of foreign affairs."[80] Zheng Guanying was one of the most representative exponents of this idea. Having failed to pass any level of the examinations, Zheng devoted his life to trade, becoming a powerful "comprador" – a merchant who acted as an intermediary for foreign trade companies. In his *Words of Warning to a Prosperous Age* (*Shengshi weiyan*), Zheng argued that China was engaged in a "trade war" with the Western imperialist nations. It was in the trade field, and not in the military one, that the fate of China rested. As a consequence, China should not waste money strengthening the military. It should instead invest its scarce funds so as to prevail in the commercial war.[81] According to Zheng, the trade war was mostly to be fought through the manipulation of tariffs and taxes, luxury goods became important targets. Products such as wine and tobacco, which were not directly significant for the livelihood of the people, Zheng argued, should be taxed heavily, although, in general, imported goods should always be taxed more than domestic products.[82]

While the majority of the Self-Strengtheners supported frugality, others – including Wei Yuan (1794–1857) and Tan Sitong (1865–98) – put forward positive notions of luxury consumption. Wei Yuan, an official and prominent scholar especially renowned for his works in history and geography, had worked with the prominent Statecraft philosopher He Changling (1785–1848) on the compilation

79 Zhao, *WanQing wushinian jingji sixiangshi*, 218.
80 Zhao, *WanQing wushinian jingji sixiangshi*, 219.
81 Zheng Guanying, "Shangzhan 1"(586–594) and "Shangzhan 2" (595–603), "Shengshi weiyan," in *Zheng Guanying ji* (Shanghai: Shanghai renmin chubanshe, 1982).
82 Zheng, "Shengshi weiyan," Section "Nüjiao," 289.

of the first collection of Statecraft writing, *Collected Essays about Statecraft of the Qing* (*Huangchao jingshi wenbian*). During this process, he developed a strong interest in the current affairs of the empire and especially its relations with the Western powers. In this spirit, he wrote a book of geographies of foreign nations (*Haiguo tuzhi*) – first published in 1844 just two years after the Nanjing Treaty – which he intended to serve as a guide and reference book for dealing with Western countries as well as with Japan.[83]

Like most pro-luxury Self-Strengtheners, Wei Yuan encouraged frugality in general, especially among the imperial administration and within private households. He, however, believed that the market-based luxury consumption of the rich helped merchants and created opportunities for workers. In this way, it could help support the livelihood of the poor. "The *Rites of Zhou*," he wrote, "protect the rich. It protects them if they take the responsibility to give relief to their villages. It does not protect them if they are consistently stingy." Wei Yuan concluded that, if the government were to require the rich to observe frugality, "the rich would become increasingly rich and the poor increasingly poor."[84] Historian Ye Shichang argues that, in this particular statement, Wei Yuan refers directly to Lu Ji's *Jinshebian*, or at least to the passages reprinted in Li Yuxiang's *Conversations on Awakening while Pushing the Sail* (*Tuipeng wuyu*). Ye Shichang bases his argument mostly on the similarity of the rhetoric and phrasing between *Jinshebian*, *Tuipeng wuyu*, and Wei Yuan's essay on taxation and *corvée* labor.[85] Whether or not there is a direct link between Lu Ji's argument and that of Wei Yuan, it is clear that pro-luxury arguments had circulated widely since the late Ming period. Self-Strengthening thinkers were quite familiar with the "philosophers of former times [who] believed that, if the people's customs were extravagant and the goods they needed luxurious, production would expand," as Liang Qichao had phrased it in his anti-luxury statement quoted above.[86]

[83] Hummel, *Eminent Chinese of the Ch'ing Period*, 851–852.

[84] Wei Yuan, "Mo gu xia: Zhi bian 14," in *Wei Yuan ji* (Beijing: Zhonghua shuju, 1983), Vol. 2, 71–74; Chen, *Zhongguo jingji sixiangshi*, 245.

[85] Ye Shichang, "Wei Yuan yu 'Tui peng wu yu,' in *Zhongguo jingji sixiangshi lunwen*, ed. by Shanghaishi jingji xuehui zhongguo jingji sixiangshi yanyouhui, 266–269 (Shanghai: Shanghai shehui kexueyuan chubanshe, 1986). Wei Yuan, "Mo Gu Xia: Lun zhi 14."

[86] Quoted in Lai, *Liang Qichao de jingji mianxiang*, 240.

Even more vocal in his support of luxury consumption was Tan Sitong. Tan had participated in the Hundred Days reform movement (*wuxu bianfa*, July 11–September 20, 1898) and – unlike Kang Youwei and Liang Qichao, who escaped abroad – was executed when the reforms were ultimately aborted.[87] In his youth, Tan had traveled widely within China, even visiting the northwestern frontier region of Xinjiang, and had developed an interest in Statecraft as well as Western learning. While in Beijing, he met Liang Qichao and became involved in the Society for the Study of National Strengthening (*qiangxuehui*), an association led by Kang and Liang. In 1897, Tan gained some experience in implementing reforms, having the opportunity to assist the governor of his native province, Hunan, in carrying out self-strengthening measures.[88] Merging early signs of the impact of the Western idea of linear modernity – which was to assume a critical role in the debate on consumption in the Republican period (see Chapter 4) – with the long-standing objective of *minsheng*, Tan argued that luxury was a natural stage in the development of a modern society and that the circulation of wealth that it promoted helped foster social stability. Blocking this circulation would allow for an uneven accumulation of wealth and would ultimately generate chaos. Frugality, Tan continued, not only bred coarseness, but also impeded the intelligence of the people from flourishing and caused production to decline. Tan actually denounced officials' and elites' call for frugality as a stratagem used to accumulate resources for themselves rather than sharing them with the people. The elites, he complained, would rather see their grain rot in storage than share it with the poor. Although they spoke of morality, they were unmoved by the sight of gutters and streets covered with the bodies of the starving.[89]

In the Self-Strengthening period, however, support for frugality was not based just on cutting foreign imports and readdressing the balance of trade – a theme that was to remain constant through the

87 The Hundred Days reforms were a set of political, educational, and economic reforms launched by Emperor Guangxu (r. 1875–1908) in 1895 under the guidance of a group of reformist officials led by Kang Youwei. These reforms, however, met with the disapproval of more conservative groups within the administration led by the Empress Dowager Ci Xi (1835–1908) and were suppressed in a matter of months.

88 Hummel, *Eminent Chinese of the Ch'ing Period*, 702–705.

89 Chen, *Zhongguo jingji sixiangshi*, 245.

Republican era and gain renewed state attention with the Made in China Movement discussed in Chapter 4. Self-Strengthening reformers also relied on their understanding of the market and the crucial role that demand played in stimulating production. They therefore attempted to deploy frugality in support of a state-led mode of economic growth that focused on the production of *minsheng* goods, counteracting the market-based model of growth that dominated the Jiangnan region.

Deploying Frugality: Production-Driving Demand and Capital Accumulation

The arrival of Western economic ideas – at this time mostly linked to Liberalism – dramatically changed the language of Chinese debates on the economy, at times obscuring the remarkable continuities with previous debates. Whether embraced or not, familiarity with Western economic ideas generated a synthesis of selected liberal concepts and terminology with Chinese economic ideas and tropes as well as China-centered issues. In this context, frugality was deployed as a mode of consumption that could deeply influence the market and, through its power as "demand," shape the trajectory of China's economic growth. Frugal consumption could also help solve the Chinese state's by now chronic lack of funds by inducing capital accumulation in the private sector, which was expected to reinvest in Self-Strengthening enterprises. Zhang Zhidong, for example, believed that frugality could have a much deeper effect on the Chinese economy than just preserving resources and cutting imports. It could be essential for expanding production of daily-need goods. "If we don't cherish luxury," he wrote, "merchants will decrease their production costs and their profits will increase." Zhang must have been aware that the margins of profit on luxury goods were much higher than those for basic staples, regardless of production costs. He probably hoped that the higher volume of business brought by trading in the latter kind of goods would more than compensate for the higher returns of China's relatively small luxury market, which was also losing ground to imported goods. This shift of focus in consumption habits – which he clearly framed within the paradigm of supply and demand – would then, he continued, lead to increased production of useful agricultural goods: "If agriculture grows, the foundation will be prosperous. As a consequence, useful goods will easily sell … workers could enjoy regular occupation."[90]

The idea of mobilizing consumption to achieve Self-Strengthening goals was later expanded by Yan Fu and Liang Qichao. Yan Fu believed it to be crucial to China's economic development because "it is not that expenditures cannot be too large, in reality, much of it is of great value." After all, he stated, echoing Adam Smith, the goal of production was to satisfy the consumption needs of the people. If the principle of frugality were followed too closely, it would defeat the very purpose of production. Recasting often-quoted passages from the classics, Yan Fu wrote: "The classics say that, if money is not used, the main purpose of wealth is wasted." Pairing this classic quote with a contemporary notion of growth, productivism, and glut, he continued, "if there is not consumption, then the goods will pile up and the people will slowly stop having enough. In a situation in which we want to encourage profitability, is this not crippling?" Yan Fu went further to clearly theorize the crucial relationship between "capital" (*mucai*) accumulation and "expenditures" (*zhifei*). In his eyes, the problem was not whether frugality or luxury should be honored but finding the right balance between capital accumulation and consumption. Comparing the use of money to that of grain, he stated that it was wrong to consume it all and leave none to use as seeds for the new agricultural season. It was equally wrong to set aside all the grain for seeds and not to consume any. Similarly, the solution for the economy rested in finding the right balance between consumption and capital accumulation aimed at reinvestment.[91]

Yan Fu is arguably the best representative of the process of interpretation and adaptation of Western liberal ideas within the framework of strengthening the wealth and power of the *guo*.[92] In the process of translating *The Wealth of Nations*, he became well acquainted with its main concepts, which he often applied to his analysis of China's economic problems. In discussing frugal consumption, for example, he referred directly to Smith's notions of savings and capital accumulation. Criticizing those officials who dismissed frugality, he argued that even

90 Zhao, *WanQing wushinian jingji sixiangshi*, 219.
91 Chen, *Zhongguo jingji sixiangshi*, 246–247.
92 Benjamin I. Schwartz, *In Search of Wealth and Power: Yen Fu and the West* (Cambridge, MA: Belknap Press of Harvard University Press, 1964).

Adam Smith, considered frugality important – "the parents of the masses" (*qun zhi fumu*):

Although, frugality alone is not enough to solve our problems, what makes frugality valuable is that it has the ability to nurture [*yang*] and produce [*sheng*]. If there is no nurturing and no producing, then wealth is just harmful. Moreover, how can it have the effect of enriching the state and feeding the people?[93]

The value of frugality, therefore, was that it could generate capital for supporting production (*sheng*) and, in turn, production could help nurture the people (*yang*). Yan Fu based this view especially on Chapter III of Book II of *The Wealth of Nations*, titled "On the Accumulation of Capital, or of Productive and Unproductive Labour" – which he translated as: "The Work of Man that Generates Profits and that Does Not Generate Profits"[94] – in which Smith bemoaned the negative influence on the economy of the unproductive groups in society, which wasted important revenue that could have been reinvested into the economy, a theme already common among Qing philosophers.[95]

Yan Fu supported this view. He believed that it was important to accumulate capital rather than squander it in luxury consumption, and that the accumulated capital should then be liberally invested in self-strengthening enterprises, which, in turn, would ultimately benefit the people.[96] Liang Qichao also perceived frugality as a strategy for capital accumulation aimed at triggering growth. In this vein, he argued that frugality was the real key to prosperity: "It is said that the more is saved and the more goods [circulate], the more the people prosper."[97] Liang, therefore, prioritized capital accumulation and criticized luxury because it wasted "what should have been the capital for production" targeted to the elimination of scarcity and the strengthening of China's economy:[98]

In order to have production, there must be consumption. If there is no consumption then production cannot develop ... One must not consume

93 Zhao, *WanQing wushinian jingji sixiangshi*, 220.
94 Zhao, *WanQing wushinian jingji sixiangshi*, 219.
95 Smith and Robert, *The Wealth of Nations* (New York, NY: Modern Library, 2000), 360–380.
96 Zhao, *WanQing wushinian jingji sixiangshi*, 219–221.
97 Quoted in Chen, *Zhongguo jingji sixiangshi*, 247–249.
98 Quoted in Lai, *Liang Qichao de jingji mianxiang*, 240.

his capital; in this way, the principle of hardworking-frugality-saving can then be observed. In the book of Guanzi most words are about strengthening the fundamental and curbing the peripheral. It is not that there is anything bad about peripheral business, the evil is that there it develops habits of luxury that will generate problems for the people. Therefore we must pay extreme attention to the goal of revering frugality.[99]

In this passage, Liang Qichao combined citations from a classical text (now deployed as a source of nationalist legitimacy, rather than Confucian orthodoxy) with ideas of productive and unproductive consumption and of capital accumulation that had emerged earlier, most clearly with Chen Hongmou, and had come to resonate with the ideas of Adam Smith, as filtered through Yan Fu. Positive modes of consumption were expenditures such as investment and purchase of "producer goods." Negative modes, on the other hand, were those aimed at satisfying extravagant personal lifestyles.

Yan Fu's and Liang Qichao's arguments on consumption and capital accumulation followed *The Wealth of Nations* more closely than it appears at a first glance. Smith wrote his masterpiece in the mid-eighteenth century, in the early stages of capital accumulation and during a period not yet marked by consumerism but by the New Luxury mode of consumption. Smith had observed that, at the time, while the landed elites who received their surplus from rents tended to spend it on luxury consumption, the capitalist elites tended to invest almost the entirety of their surplus into production in order to survive competition from other capitalist enterprises. For Smith, therefore, saving would inevitably result in productive investment. In the industrialized West, however, this understanding of the role of frugality in the market economy was rapidly changing. As Henry Ford discovered in the mid-1910s, mass consumption was the future of capitalism, and frugality would discourage the willingness of the working people to spend. When Yan Fu translated *The Wealth of Nations* in 1901, China was in the early stage of industrialization, and Smith's original ideas of savings and capital accumulation appeared to fit more closely the needs of the economy of the empire than the mass consumption model that was emerging in the industrialized West at the time.

The Chinese discourse on consumption was complicated by a lack of specific terminology. The Chinese reformers of this period found it

99 Quoted in Lai, *Liang Qichao de jingji mianxiang*, 240.

difficult to formulate a standard translation for this economic function – the term *xiaofei* came to prevail only in the Republican period. This lack of precision in terminology was already evident in an 1892 article in the periodical *Wanguo gongbao*. In this article, the anonymous author carefully explained the difference between consumer and producer goods and their relationship to Self-Strengthening. He concluded that consumption, in general, had the effect of helping the economy grow, but consumption of luxury goods had only a marginal and temporary impact on the economy. A better way to consume was by investing capital through banks, which would then use the funds to support the construction of infrastructure as well as the production of much-needed trains and steamboats.[100] The author could easily combine under the category of consumption the two different notions of private purchases on the market with institutional (government and bank) investments in infrastructure, since he was able to use the same terms in each case: *yong* and *xiaofei*. The wide spectrum of meaning of these terms – which include using, spending, and consuming – lent the notion of consumption a wide interpretative flexibility to indicate spending in general. Private acquisitions of commercial goods and state expenses for Self-Strengthening could be equally categorized as "consumption." In this context, reinvestment of surplus and acquisition of producer goods became the positive face of luxury consumption. Tan Sitong, for example, promoted this kind of consumption. He urged the very rich to invest their money in opening factories, thus creating jobs essential to sustain the livelihood of the people. This form of investment would also lessen the problem of scarcity, generate an abundance of goods, and ensure the proper circulation of money.[101] The conflating of different kinds of expenditures under the same terminology was instrumental in placing the debate on consumption within a nationalist framework and, as such, it characterized the economic discourse in the last decades of the Qing Dynasty and the Republican years.

In this anti-imperialist context, the notion of frugality was also used to further streamline and reform the government administration, continuing a pattern started with the Jiaqing Emperor.

[100] "Fuguo yangmince: dierzhang, lunwuzhi youyi yurenzhang," *Wanguo gongbao* 4 (1892), 30–36.

[101] Chen, *Zhongguo jingji sixiangshi*, 245–246.

Self-Strengtheners Feng Guifen, Tang Shouqian, Zhang Zhidong, and Zheng Guanying, for example, used the notion of frugality to propose reducing the government administration. A favorite measure among Self-Strengtheners was the elimination of superfluous personnel. In general, the main idea was that if the local administration reduced its duties to the essentials, fewer officials would be needed and great savings could be achieved. Zhang Zhidong (1837–1909), for example, called for the state to "vigorously implement frugality" and cut "useless expenses," starting with cutting government officials' superfluous expenses, spending more carefully on public works, and simplifying rites and sacrificial offerings.[102] Two "wasteful" expenditures were generally targeted: the expenditures of the imperial household and the state's support of the eight banners. While discussions on the first issue tended to focus almost exclusively on reducing living expenses and simplifying imperial rites and ceremonies, the second issue was more difficult to tackle. Population growth among the eight banners, in fact, raised much alarm because sustaining this group required an increased amount of resources to be set aside that was therefore no longer available to the wider population. Feng Guifen's proposal was drastic. The males in the eight banners should be tested. If they proved fit for the military, they should join the army. Otherwise, they should become peasants.[103] Manchu bannermen thus became one of the most powerful symbols of the "idle consumer."

Scarcity and State Planning

Although Adam Smith's ideas resonated with Chinese notions of consumption and capital accumulation, they did not resonate in other areas, especially on the issue of the role of the state in the economy. The focus on scarcity and Self-Strengthening led to an important departure from the *laissez faire* policies of classical liberalism and its turn-of-the-twentieth-century formulations. China's situation – characterized by scarcity and not by abundance – appeared to require state intervention, as already foreshadowed in the writings of Ren Qiyun, Bao Shichen, and Yun Jing. Yan Fu, for example, argued that it was the

102 Quoted in Zhao, *WanQing wushinian jingji sixiangshi*, 218.
103 Feng, "Chongjie jianyi"; Zhao, *WanQing wushinian jingji sixiangshi*, 218, 224.

duty of the state to generate wealth and make sure it would keep up with the constant increase in population. It had been its inability to do so, he argued, that had created much hardship for the Chinese population. Even with the slowing down of population growth due to "recent wars" (referring indirectly to domestic rebellions and wars against foreign imperialist forces), the economic situation in China was still unbalanced as production lagged behind the needs of the people.[104]

Following Yan Fu's arguments, Liang Qichao also came to believe that state planning and intervention for balancing production and consumption were important to solving China's crisis. According to Liang, each year, a country had only a fixed amount of resources. The proper management of these resources was crucial for avoiding poverty and assuring increased production of wealth in the following year. In this context, Liang organized his discussion around "generating profit" (*shengli*, production) and "sharing in the benefits of production" (*fenli*, consumption). A country's production, he argued, would increase steadily if it employed capital (*ziben*) and labor (*laoli*) properly. Because China was not employing these two resources correctly, it was becoming increasingly poor. Growth could only happen if the resources produced in one year were reinvested as much as possible in production, thus increasing the total output in the following year. This could not be achieved by prioritizing consumption, which resulted in spending most resources, without generating any increase in production. In this context, not only should capital not be wasted or sit idle but the Chinese labor force should also be fully and aptly employed.[105] Planning both investment and use of resources, including labor, was therefore crucial for economic growth.

Planning should also include balancing production and expenditure/consumption, which, Liang argued, depended on how resources were invested and what kind of activities the people pursued. Echoing the work of Yun Jing, Liang divided the consumers into two basic categories – those who consumed but did not work and those who worked and consumed – concluding: "[as for] a general estimate of China's population and ... the ratio between producers and consumers ... [I see that] among 400 million people, around 210 million are consumers,

[104] Hu, *Zhongguo jingji sixiangshi*, 78–79.
[105] Liang Qichao, *Xinmin shuo* (1902), "Section 14: Lun shengli fenli." For a detailed discussion of Liang Qichao's analysis of the various groups of producers and consumers see Lai, *Liang Qichao de jingji mianxiang*, 219–220.

the rest are producers." The issue of consumption, therefore, became central to Liang's discussion of China's survival. China was poor and consequently weak and ill-equipped to survive in the struggle for survival of the fittest among nations. In this kind of environment, the fate of a country depended completely on reversing the ratio between producers and consumers: "This is the most urgent issue. The only way to save a country is to have many producers and few consumers."[106]

As these debates illustrate, solving China's poverty crisis and strengthening China's position in the international scene gave momentum to the shift in focus from the consumption of the individual and issues of "equalization" of resources among societal groups to the material needs of the *guo* as a whole. This shift contributed to the Chinese thinkers' departure from both the earlier indigenous trend of reliance on market forces and the liberal nature of Western models of modernity. Despite humanistic aspirations for freedom and socioeconomic justice and a theoretical acceptance of liberalism, most late-Qing Chinese reformers ultimately supported the idea that China's particular situation required a more interventionist state.[107] In his discussion of *The Wealth of Nations*, for example, Yan Fu wholeheartedly supported Smith's anti-mercantilist arguments. Mercantilist policies, he stated, led to oppressive economic policies and practices and Smith's economic model would certainly lead to increased freedom for a country's citizens. Self-Strengthening concerns, however, brought Yan Fu to argue that Smith's aversion to state monopolies went too far and that his free-market system would lead to inequalities in the distribution of wealth. Because of its population problem and need for an even distribution of resources, he concluded, China would adopt a stronger and more interventionist state than that envisioned by Smith.[108] Liang's economic discussion echoes a similar tension between humanistic aspects of liberalism and nation-building goals. While attracted by Smith's anti-despotism arguments, Liang also found himself caught between supporting a free market as an expression of

[106] Liang Qichao, "Xinminshuo," "Section 14: Lun shengli fenli."

[107] Schwartz, *In Search of Wealth and Power*; Zhang Hao, *Liang Chi-Chao and Intellectual Transition in China, 1890–1907* (Cambridge, MA: Harvard University Press, 1971).

[108] Hu Jichuang, *Zhongguo jingji sixiangshi* (Shanghai: Shanghai caijing daxue chubanshe, 1998), 77–78.

people's freedom and calling for some measure of protectionism and state intervention to meet China's particular needs.

Self-Strengtheners did not perceive a tension between their support for both a free market and state planning. They believed that this contradiction was resolved by the cooperation between state and economic elites. This notion had been central to the administrative reforms of the Jiaqing and Daoguang reforms, as argued earlier. A theoretical solution for this tension had already been formulated by Bao Shichen. Bao's call for the local authorities to take the lead in agricultural reforms could appear to contradict other statements in which he expressed his belief that that the best way to generate wealth was to leave the initiative to private enterprises, which in pursuing their own interests would also end up enriching the community.[109] Bao did not see his call for state activism in this area as being in contradiction with his general reliance on the private economy. In the same vein, official and reformer Kang Youwei (1858–1927), who led the Hundred Days reforms, argued that all production should be planned by the government, which should first collect data on population and average consumption and then distribute production evenly. He also advocated the establishment of provincial merchant associations (*shanghui*) which would consult with the state and manage the unified implementation of policies under the control of officials.[110] Relying on cooperation between state and the commercial elites, therefore, came to constitute a crucial trend among Self-Strengthening reformers.

Zheng Guanying also believed that the state and the private sector should join forces to fight the "commercial war" with the imperialist aggressors. The state should foster and encourage the private sector, which should focus on the nationalist goals of producing for import substitution and strengthening China's export. The government should establish a ministry of commerce linked to local Chambers of Commerce, launch new business schools, publish business journals, and, in general, help the modernization of trade practices.[111] These institutions would create a network for cooperation between state and

[109] Rowe, "Bao Shichen and Agrarian Reform in Early Nineteenth-Century China"; Zhao, *Zhongguo gudai jingji sixiangshi jianghua*, 625–627.

[110] Xia Yande, *Zhongguo jinbainian jingji sixiang* (Shanghai: Shanghai shudian, 1989), 55–66.

[111] Hsiao Kung-ch'uan, *A Modern China and a New World* (Seattle, WA: University of Washington Press, 1975), 311–312.

private economy, mobilizing private businessmen in the pursuit of national goals in a style that echoed Jiaqing's and Daoguang's administrative reform but tended toward a model of developmental state similar to that of the Meiji Restoration (1868–1912). The Self-Strengthening Movement, in fact, attempted to create a close partnership between the state and the political and economic elites for pursuit of nation-building objectives. In this context, provincial governors established new enterprises based on new technologies, such as the Kaiping mining complex established in 1877 by Li Hongzhang (1823–1901). Li, like other provincial Self-Strengtheners, took the lead in improving transportation and infrastructure, enlisting private funds and business through the strategies of "state–private joint operation" (*guanshang heban*) or "official supervision and merchant management" (*guandu shangban*). Arguably the most famous of these enterprises was the China Merchant Steamship Navigation Company (*lunchuan zhaoshangju*), launched by Li Hongzhang in 1872. Provincial leadership on economic self-strengthening was not limited to mining, transportation, and infrastructure; it extended to manufacturing and especially to the revival of traditionally strong Chinese industries aimed at import substitution. Governors Li Hongzhang, Zhang Zhidong, and Zuo Zongtang (1812–85), for example, set up cotton mills and textile factories in their provinces. The cotton industry became, together with tea and silk, one of the main targets for import substitution from the Self-Strengthening Movement through the Republican years.[112]

Despite their nation building, Self-Strengthening policies resulted in further expansion of the gap between the rural hinterland and the commercial economy of the coastal areas. Only the areas of the rural hinterland with convenient links to the main transportation routes came to be integrated into the export-oriented economic revival prioritized by Self-Strengthening. In the words of Pomeranz, in fact, when promoting agricultural reforms, "government officials were less interested in raising rural income for its own sake than in 'national strengthening.' This meant above all, promoting crops that could be used in either import-substituting or export-promoting industries."[113] Rural hinterland areas that were not directly involved in this economic

[112] Zanasi, *Saving the Nation*, Chapter 5, "Implementing Rural Reforms."
[113] Pomeranz, *The Making of a Hinterland*, 73.

effort became increasingly disconnected from the coastal commercial and industrial economy, deepening the coastal–hinterland gap, a problem that was to remain a major concern of reformers through the Republican period, as discussed in Chapter 4.

Conclusion

This chapter has explored the economic circumstances of China in the 1800s and how they came to influence Chinese intellectuals' and officials' support for state leadership of the economy. Concerns with population growth and scarcity of resources, together with dramatic changes in the way China participated in the global economy, appeared to impose productivist priorities and require some form of state planning. These new priorities, however, did not imply a lack of appreciation for the market economy, which continued to influence economic theories and policies. In this context, the Jiaqing and Daoguang reforms favoring the privatization of state functions cannot be taken as a turn toward a Western-style free-market system. As Rowe points out, these reforms still implied tight government supervision.[114] Consistent with previous Qing policies, the Jiaqing and Daoguang administrations used selected market forces to achieve targeted goals, rather than instituting a system of market economy in the manner envisioned by classical liberalism in Western Europe. In the same vein, Chinese intellectuals' and officials' recognition of the power of demand to stimulate production did not support the development of a self-regulating economic system. The power of consumption, in fact, became an economic factor that the state attempted to manipulate to obtain the desired results, in this case, the expansion of production of basic daily-need goods as a strategy for fighting scarcity.

The problems of scarcity and population growth that in China inspired a retreat from luxury consumption, and consequently from the idea of an economic growth based on market-based demand, did not feature prominently in the Western developmental experience. By the 1800s, Western European nations had faced these problems but had been able to find effective solutions through colonial expansion. Colonies provided new territories where the surplus population could

[114] Rowe, *Speaking of Profit*, 145. For a detailed description of the debates surrounding these reforms see *Speaking of Profit*, 110–129, 137–149.

migrate. They also supplied low-cost resources, both in terms of food to support the population back home and in terms of raw materials for the growing industrial sector. The Qing state had also resorted to encouraging migration to frontier areas of the empire, such as the southwestern province of Sichuan. By the eighteenth century, it had completely opened up to Han settlers the northeastern region of Manchuria, which had previously been closed off and preserved for the almost exclusive use of the Manchu conquest elite for hunting and other ritual activities intended to promote the preservation of its ethnic identity. In addition, Qianlong had expanded the borders of the empire by annexing the northwestern province of Xinjiang. This conquest, however, had been primarily motivated by the strategic objective of pacifying this troubled border region; the land itself, being in large part composed of the Gobi Desert, had not generated much relief to population pressure in China proper.

The historical narrative in this chapter also highlights an ironic chronological inversion in China of the European path to industrialization. In Europe, liberalism had emerged as a direct attack on state-controlled mercantilist policies. In China, Self-Strengthening mercantilism and notions of a developmental state emerged in response to Western free-market imperialism, which denied China the ability to compete equally on the international market. In other words, Western imperialism, while introducing the idea, if not the practice, of a free-market economy to colonies and semi-/hyper-colonies (using Sun Yat-sen's term to indicate a country, like China, that was not directly colonized but still suffered the impact of imperialism), obtained the opposite effect, ultimately generating support for more statist solutions.

4 Nation Building, Strategic Markets, and Frugal Modernity in the Early Decades of the Republic of China (1912–1930s)

The idea that China's economy was characterized by scarcity and thus differed fundamentally from the consumerist economy of plenty of the Western industrialized nations continued to influence Chinese economic thought through the sweeping political changes that accompanied the fall of the imperial system (1911) and the establishment of the Republic of China (1912).[*] At this time, however, population growth was no longer a primary concern, since wars and natural disasters in the first half of the twentieth century had slowed down the demographic expansion, as gloomily predicted by Hong Liangji. The idea that China was experiencing a scarcity crisis, however, continued to be sustained by China's persistently low productive capacity in relation to the sheer size of its population – estimated by Sun Yat-sen in his *Principle of Nationalism* (*Minzu zhuyi*) to be 400 million, a number that continued to be used as a rhetorical trope to indicate the vast Chinese masses throughout the Republican years.[1] In addition, the persistence of the imperialist threat – at this time mainly embodied by the escalation of Japan's expansionist ambitions into China's mineral-rich northeastern region – reinforced the nationalist self-strengthening goals of readdressing the unfavorable balance in foreign trade and jump-starting economic development. Finally, the idea of frugality continued to dominate the discourse on consumption as both a response to economic scarcity and a strategy for mobilizing resources in support of nation building.

In this period, the Chinese debate on market and consumption was also influenced by new evolutionary theories of modernity, which had gained popularity after Yan Fu's translation of Thomas Huxley's

[*] Parts of this chapter have already appeared in Zanasi, "Frugal Modernity: Livelihood and Consumption in Republican China," The Journal of Asian Studies 74 (2015), 391–409.

[1] I maintain the already well-established transliteration of the name of Sun Yat-sen, as I do for Chiang Kai-shek.

Evolution and Ethics (*Tianyan lun*, 1896–98). The Chinese economic crisis thus came to be framed in terms of the struggle of the Chinese race and civilization for the survival of the fittest. China's circumstances began to be evaluated through the idea of predetermined stages of progress (developmental determinism). In this context, China's economy of scarcity came to signify poverty and "backward" (*luohou*) conditions *vis-à-vis* the prosperity and "progress" (*jinbu*) achieved by wealthy industrialized nations. This new evolutionist approach introduced the concepts of "modernity" (*jindai*) and "modernization" (*jindaihua*), which came to be used ubiquitously in both the popular and official discourses on the economy.[2]

Despite its rigid linear determinism, the idea of evolutionary modernity did not solve the basic question of what modernization meant and how it should be achieved in the case of China. In the early twentieth century, a humanist interpretation identified modernity with high standards of living for the population at large. This interpretation gained popularity, especially among intellectuals with liberal tendencies, such as Liang Qichao and Cai Yuanpei (1863–1940). An alternative view prioritized the power of the nation-state, favoring the state's monopolization of resources and more intrusive forms of state intervention than the humanist solution.

It would be misguiding, however, to think that through the 1920s and the 1930s the Chinese debate on market and consumption presented a stark contraposition between two models of modernization: a liberal market-based solution versus an autocratic state-led one. In reality, the "humanist" option can hardly be defined as "liberal" by the standards of Western economic liberalism. It, in fact, incorporated some measure of state intervention and central planning. The humanist-liberal nature of this option rested mostly on its *minsheng* objective. At this time, the term *minsheng* continued to be used ubiquitously, although it did not carry the original meaning of the imperial mandate and mostly implied lifting China, as a nationality (*minzu*), out of poverty and, in general, turning its people into a civilized modern citizenry, i.e. cultured citizens with high standards of living. This humanist *minsheng* interpretation of modernity and nation building, therefore, differed from the more statist

2 For an in-depth discussion of Chinese intellectuals' adoption of evolutionary ideas in evaluating the economic situation of China in the Republican period see Rebecca E. Karl, *The Magic of Concepts: History and the Economic in Twentieth-Century China* (Durham, NC: Duke University Press, 2017).

solution, not just in the extent of state intervention but, above all, in its identification of modernity and nation building as the strengthening of the country's military power and the heavy industrial sector, while focusing light industry on production of consumer goods intended for export or import substitution rather than for the general goals of elevating domestic standards of living. The latter model, therefore, would restrict heavily the roles of both domestic consumption and the market. Both humanist and statist solutions, however, stressed China's need for a developmental state. This notion was so widely accepted that even those entrepreneurs who believed in "saving China through business" – i.e. the idea that private initiatives and market-oriented managerial practices were crucial to solving the national question – expected the state to take an active role in helping both their enterprises and the development of the Chinese economy at large.[3]

During the 1920s and 1930s, reformers and intellectuals also came to perceive "rationalization" (*helihua*), or the scientific reorganization of economic functions, as a crucial strategy for China's economic prosperity. Attention to "organization" and "rationalization" had some precedents in the late-Qing discussion on production and population growth, especially in Bao Shichen's call for more efficient use of labor discussed in Chapter 3. It came to be more widely theorized under the influence of Taylorism. In the early twentieth century, in fact, a wide variety of Western economic theories entered the Chinese economic discourse. Among them was Frederick W. Taylor's (1856–1915) popular book *The Principles of Scientific Management*, originally published in 1911 and already available in Japanese translation in 1912. In this book Taylor discussed improving production, focusing especially on increasing the efficiency of labor. This could be done, Taylor explained, by adopting a variety of measures, including providing appropriate training and better work tools, as well as introducing incentives to encourage individual workers to maximize personal productivity.[4] This book contributed to popularizing the idea

[3] See Brett Sheehan, *Industrial Eden: A Chinese Capitalist Vision* (Cambridge, MA: Harvard University Press, 2015) and Yeh Wen-Hsin, *Shanghai Splendor: Economic Sentiments and the Making of Modern China, 1843–1949* (Berkeley, CA: University of California Press, 2007).

[4] Frederick Winslow Taylor, *The Principles of Scientific Management* (New York, NY: Productivity Press, 2017); Frederick Winslow Taylor and Tamisuke Yokokawa, *Kagakuteki keieihō Genre* (Tokyo: Yokokawatamisuke, 1912).

that production could be improved by analyzing the various phases of the production process in order to better understand them and intervening to improve their efficiency scientifically.

Taylorism mostly affected the debate on production, but the idea of "rationalization" also impacted other aspects of economic thought. In China, for example, it was advocated for improving the relationships between production and consumption – intended as both individual consumption and state expenditure for nation building, as the Chinese terminology of *yong* and *xiaofei* continued to generally obfuscate this difference. At the root of this "reorganization" effort was the idea that the free market failed to channel resources where they were most needed. For this reason, market networks should be reorganized to help redirect their flow. This notion inspired the 1920s and 1930s Economic Cooperation Movement (*jingji hezuo yundong*). Cooperative societies were perceived as tools for rationalizing the relationship between production and consumption, channeling resources into the desired sectors while offering a compromise between a free market and state control.

The idea that the state should take an active role in planning the economy had domestic roots in the late Qing period, but it reemerged with renewed strength in the 1920s and 1930s as global political and economic trends called for the establishment of a state empowered with a more centralized and effective administrative function, as famously illustrated by the writings of Carl Schmitt on the "administrative state."[5] Whereas late-Qing intellectuals such as Ren Qiyun and Bao Shichen had entrusted their reform plans to the *baojia* system and the provincial and county administrations, reformers of the 1920s and 1930s assigned the task of planning, at least theoretically, to the central government. The worldwide negative impact of the Great Depression – generally viewed as a failure of the Western capitalist system – contributed to the popularity of statist solutions. They were also encouraged by the apparent success of "controlled economies" (*tongzhi jingji*) – such as those of Germany, Italy, the Soviet Union, and Japan – in mobilizing resources for nation building with an efficiency impossible for their liberal free-market counterparts.

[5] See for example Carl Schmitt and Jeffrey Seitzer, *Legality and Legitimacy (1932)* (Durham, NC: Duke University Press, 2004).

The appeal of these economic models increased among Chinese reformers and intellectuals as the national crisis deepened, especially after Japan's hunger for natural resources led it to annex Manchuria in 1931.[6] This direct military threat strengthened support for statist economic models favoring a military and heavy industrial mode of nation building at the expense of improving societal living standards. This trend found its full realization under the Nationalist regime (1927–37). In 1934, Chiang Kai-shek, as the head of this political formation, launched the New Life Movement (*xinshenghuo yundong*), which fully theorized the regimentation of China's population, rechanneling resources away from societal consumption and into industrial production and military strengthening.

In the Republican era, the state's push for frugality came into even more strident contradiction with urban consumerist trends than in the late imperial period. At this time, large treaty ports developed an impressive consumerist apparatus that relied on factors such as inventive marketing techniques, notions of material modernity, consumption-based forms of identity construction, and the development of infrastructures for leisure activities (including department stores and race tracks).[7] In the cosmopolitan environment of cities like Shanghai, entrepreneurs and merchants creatively – and successfully – combined long-standing

[6] For a detailed discussion of the escalation of Japanese imperialist aggression in China see Parks M. Coble, *Facing Japan: Chinese Politics and Japanese Imperialism, 1931–1937* (Cambridge, MA: Council on East Asian Studies, Harvard University, 1991).

[7] See, among many others, Sherman Cochran, *Inventing Nanjing Road: Commercial Culture in Shanghai, 1900–1945* (Ithaca, NY: East Asia Program, Cornell University, 2004) and *Chinese Medicine Men: Consumer Culture in China and Southeast Asia* (Cambridge, MA: Harvard University Press, 2006); Frank Dikötter, *Things Modern: Material Culture and Everyday Life in China* (London: C. Hurst & Co. Ltd., 2007); Leo Ou-fan Lee, *Shanghai Modern: The Flowering of a New Urban Culture in China, 1930–1945* (Cambridge, MA: Harvard University Press, 1999); Zhang Ning, "Cong paomating dao renmin guangchang: Shanghai paomating shouhui yundong, 1946–1951," *Zhongyang yanjiuyuan jindaishi yanjiusuo jikan* 48 (2005), 97–136, and "Pure Sport or a Gambling Disgrace? Greyhound Racing and the Formation of Modern Shanghai," in *Creating Chinese Modernity: Knowledge and Everyday Life, 1900–1940*, ed. by Peter Zarrow (New York, NY: Peter Lang, 2007), 147–181; Tani Barlow, "Buying In: Advertising and the Sexy Modern Girl Icon in Shanghai in the 1920s and 1930s," in *The Modern Girl around the World: Consumption, Modernity, and Globalization*, ed. by Alys Eve Weinbaum (Durham, NC: Duke University Press, 2008), 288–316.

Chinese business practices with new elements inspired by Western models.[8] During the Republican period, therefore, the urban consumerist economy appeared to flourish and develop unchallenged, despite the renewed attempts of the government to rein in consumption.

In the Republican period the debate on the economy differed from that of the late Qing in its multiplicities of voices, not only because of the rise of the academic discipline of economics and of professional economists, but also because of the rise of a lively urban public opinion fueled by the expansion of the print media. In this period hundreds of journals and magazines circulated in urban China, catering to the emerging urban group identities, such as the "new youth" (*xinqingnian*), women, and the new middle-class consumers, who tended to identify with the message of modernity these publications popularized.[9] These journals brought to the new urban middle-class readership a wide variety of voices: economists, government officials, editorialists, and popular commentators. The messages spread by these popular journals, however, were often in contradiction, pitching images of "consumerist" and "frugal" modernity against each other and presenting two competing images of Chinese identity.

The development of social sciences in China during this period and the professionalization of the "economist" (*jingji xuejia*) as a highly specialized expert also led to an embrace of Western terminology and an emphasis on departing from Confucian terminology and tropes, now considered to be indicative of an unscientific, and therefore "backward," approach. This change of terminology and intellectual framework, however, cannot obscure the continuity with issues related to scarcity and nation building that were the focus of late-Qing economic debates.

Outside the specialized field of economics, references to and attempts to revive Confucian economic ideas and tropes did continue

[8] See for example Sherman Cochran, "Transnational Origins of Advertising in Early Twentieth-Century China," in *Inventing Nanjing Road: Commercial Culture in Shanghai, 1900–1945*, ed. by Sherman Cochran (Ithaca, NY: East Asia Program, Cornell University, 1999), 37–58; Sheehan, *Industrial Eden: A Chinese Capitalist Vision*, and Yeh, *Shanghai Splendor*.

[9] Tsai Weipin, *Reading Shenbao* (London: Palgrave Macmillan, 2010), 1–10. *New Youth* was the title of a journal that more closely represented the New Culture Movement (mid-1910s to mid-1920s) and its idea that China's youngest generation needed to play an important role in the cultural and political renewal of China.

to emerge in some of the popular journals – although this was mostly motivated by the desire to assert a Chinese identity for new economic plans against wholesale Westernization. The main exception to this trend was the notion of *minsheng*, which continued to figure prominently in some of the humanist theories of modernization, as illustrated, for example, by the political and economic platform of the founder of the Nationalist Party (Guomindang or GMD) Sun Yat-sen (1866–1925). Confucian tropes and references to Confucian philosophical ideas also returned to play a prominent role in the late 1930s with Chiang Kai-shek, who attempted to evoke a Chinese moral and cultural identity in support of his New Life Movement.

Evolutionary Modernity: Consumption and China's Stage of Development

The popularization of the debate on consumption through the new print media is well exemplified by the editorial "Discussing the Elimination of Extravagance" (*Jie shechi shuo*), which appeared in a 1916 issue of *The World of the Chinese Women* (*Zhonghua funüjie*). Here the author, Xie Peiqiong, summarizes the main issues on which this debate focused in the early decades of the Republic. Xie, a student at the Guangzhou Women's Normal School, was not a prominent economist or editorialist, and her piece did not particularly distinguish itself from many similar commentaries that appeared in the ever-expanding number of journals catering to urban elites and the emerging middle class in Republican China. In its first paragraph, however, Xie's article succeeded in presenting some of the main intellectual elements of the contemporary debate on consumption and economic modernization at large:

> Social interactions have become increasingly complex, and the way of frugality (*jiejian*) is being lost. The European wind penetrates the East, and extravagant (*shechi*) habits are all the rage. There is even a theory that extravagance encourages industrialization. In addition, it is now believed that human existence in this world is not just a matter of going through the various stages of life, but of seeking pleasure in the superfluous things of daily life. Alas, if one is frugal, he becomes a miser![10]

[10] Xie Peiqiong, "Jie shechi shuo," *Zhonghua funüjie* 5 (1916).

In this paragraph, Xie identified three main popular themes. She first lamented the end of China's long-standing frugal habits as a result of the influence of Western-style consumerism, thus placing her discussion within a framework of foreign imperialism and national identity. She then questioned the idea at the foundation of Western liberal capitalism that consumption is a crucial factor in the process of economic modernization because it fuels industrial growth. Xie challenged this notion by introducing the idea that consumption could instead lead to economic scarcity. Quoting one of *Guanzi*'s famous passages – "Evil comes from scarcity. Scarcity comes from extravagance. Extravagance comes from lack of restraint"[11] – Xie made moral failure (extravagant consumption) the main cause of the nation's poverty and reinforced the theme of moral frugality as a trait of Chinese national identity. Finally, Xie questioned the consumerist view of standards of living. By using the negative term "extravagance" (*shechi*) to refer to a modern and imported style of consumption, she raised the issues of how modern Western-style standards of living differed from wasteful luxury and whether China should adopt the interpretation of standard of living promoted by the industrialized West.

Although expressed in contemporary terms, the three points raised by Xie – the Western corrupting origins of consumerism, economic scarcity, and the meaning of modern standards of living in China – were concerns already voiced by late-Qing reformers including Yan Fu and Liang Qichao, who had questioned the universal validity of the Western liberal model of economic modernization by arguing that it did not fit China's current economic situation. Xie's article, however, directly challenged the very intellectual foundations of this model. Xie did not ask whether Western-style consumption was suitable for China's specific situation of scarcity but implied that it was an intrinsically amoral system of dubious effectiveness. This piece also illustrates the persistent problem with terminology, since Xie never used the term consumption, as either *yong* or *xiaofei*, preferring "luxury" (*shechi*) to refer to Western-style consumerism. In this way, she could easily dismiss the importance of the demand function of Western-style consumption and associate it only with negative behavior.

Most 1920s and 1930s writers, however, supported Yan's and Liang's views, tending not to reject Western consumerism *tout court*

[11] Xie, "Jie shechi shuo," 2–3.

but to believe that, while a marker of modernity in more "advanced" (*jinbu*) economies, it would be harmful in China's specific situation of backwardness, i.e. lagging behind (*luohou*) and undeveloped (*wu fa zhan*). In the early twentieth century, the view prevailed that standards of living were linked to the natural progression of human development and that increased consumption was an inevitable product of civilization. Poverty and living at subsistence levels came to signify backwardness and were regarded as a liability in the Social Darwinian struggle among nations. In Japan, for example, the notion of "cultured living" (*bunka seikatsu*) – an enlightened lifestyle marked by higher standards of living and increased happiness – was closely associated with modernization.[12] Chinese intellectuals also shared this understanding of "cultured" economic and social modernity. The relationship between the progress of civilization and standards of living was directly addressed in a 1916 editorial, "Civilization and Luxury" (*Wenming yu shechi*), by Cai Yuanpei – the prominent educator and future minister of education, at that time just returned to China from studying in Europe and on his way to becoming chancellor of Beijing University. Cai opened this piece by pointing out that modernity had brought about big changes in everyday life; objects used by people daily, while simple and coarse in antiquity, were now complex and refined. The poverty and frugality of earlier times had been replaced by the general prosperity brought about by progress.[13]

Humanist evolutionary understandings of consumption became a central tenet of early (pre-1927) Guomindang ideology as Sun Yat-sen enshrined it in his fourth lecture on the Principle of the People's Livelihood (*minsheng zhuyi*). Here, Sun argued that "in the evolution of human civilization we can distinguish three stages in the standard of living." The first stage was characterized by the attempt to satisfy basic needs. The second stage was that of achieving comfort, and the third saw humanity pursuing luxury. Sun concluded that China was still in the first stage, since the "four hundred million throughout the nation"

12 Sheldon Garon, "Fashioning a Culture of Diligence and Thrift: Savings and Frugality Campaigns in Japan, 1900–1930," in *Japan's Competing Modernities: Issues in Culture and Democracy, 1900–1930*, ed. by Sharon A. Minichiello (Honolulu, HI: University of Hawaii Press, 1988), 322.

13 Cai Zimin (Yuanpei), "Wenming yu shechi," *Lüou zazhi* 7, November (1916), 3.

lacked the bare necessities of life.[14] China's consumption and standard of living at a subsistence level trapped the country in a premodern stage of evolution.

Although Sun Yat-sen recognized an intermediary mode of consumption before the great leap into consumerism, his idea of a stage of comfort-oriented consumption does not completely match de Vries' theory of a market-based New Luxury, since he believed that, in China, the modernization of standards of living, which he expressed in terms of *minsheng*, should be promoted by the state and should rely only marginally on the consumption power of the population. According to Sun, in fact, it was the ultimate goal of the Nationalist Revolution to provide the people with their four basic needs – "food, clothes, shelter, and means of transportation" (*shi yi zhu xing*) – at the level required in a modern nation. The first three elements of this formula had historically been at the base of the imperial mandate of *minsheng*. The last, transportation, was an addition of Sun Yat-sen's modernization of the traditional formula. In Sun's lectures, the fulfillment of these four needs became the standard of a civilized form of modernity. Taking an "evolutionary view of life in the universe," Sun concluded, the state should ensure the four basics of *minsheng* – clothes, food, housing, and transportation (*yi shi zhu xing*) – in a form appropriate for a civilized society.[15]

Those intellectuals who embraced Marxist theories also asserted the evolutionary nature of standards of living and consumption. Li Jianhua (1900–?) – Japan-trained professor of Labor Law at Fudan University in Shanghai and, after 1949, a cadre in both the labor and academic administrations of the People's Republic of China – opened a 1930 editorial by proclaiming that "the standards for luxury are not set" but evolve with the progress of the times.[16] What we now consider coarse could have been luxurious in the ancient days of Xia and Yu, the legendary founders of Chinese civilization. Yu's "house of reeds and earth," while today taken as an example of his frugality, might actually have been palatial at a time when people lived "in caves and in

14 Sun Yat-sen, "Sanmin zhuy: minsheng zhuyi, disan jiang," in *Sun Wen xuanji*, ed. by Yan Huang (Guangzhou Shi: Guangdong renmin chubanshe, 1924), Vol. 1, 654–670.

15 Sun, "Sanmin zhuy: minsheng zhuyi, disan jiang," 635–654.

16 Xu Youchun, *Minguo renwu dacidian* (Shijiazhuang: Hebei renmin chubanshe, 1991), 316.

the wild." Li, therefore, like Cai, thought that over the course of millennia, humankind had experienced significant improvements in standards of living and that these changes reflected the level of progress achieved by a society.[17]

Within this framework of evolutionary standards of living, the Western notion of consumerism as a signifier of modernity was embraced in China's treaty port culture, where an impressive consumerist apparatus was fast developing. It is here that most of the traits of consumerist modernity could be detected. In these urban centers, consumer goods assumed a decisive cultural meaning signifying the duty of the citizen to bring home "modern" goods in order to "join in a universal march toward" progress.[18] Advertising in the treaty ports employed a "modernist vocabulary" that aimed to "market a scientific commodity as both superseding old practices and as an evolutionary vehicle for social progress."[19] As a life of "material respectability" became one of the main attractions of modernity, a modern and progressive lifestyle became inconceivable without the acquisition of a series of new goods that could improve health and hygiene, make household chores easier, and contribute to the family's general comfort and happiness.[20]

Chinese intellectuals and officials, however, approaching the issue of consumption from a nation-building point of view, tended to perceive the treaty ports' style of consumption as out of step with China's lagging position on the developmental ladder. As Zhu Shikang argued in 1933, "China's most dangerous problem rests on the disparity between its modes of production and consumption. Although we have a pre-eighteenth-century level of development in manufacturing, we have developed a lifestyle based on twentieth-century expectations of consumption."[21] Liang Qichao also shared this view: "of course, expensive consumption is a reflection of the people's wealth, a suitable measure of expenditure in relation to income."[22] This point was driven home by a commentator using the name of Ming Gao. Writing in 1933 in *The Merchant's Public*

[17] Li Jianhua, "Shechi shenghuo zhi shehuixue de guancha," *Shehui xuebao*, 1.
[18] Dikötter, *Things Modern*, 2. [19] Barlow, "Buying In," 304, 305.
[20] Yeh, *Shanghai Splendor*, 8.
[21] Zhu Shikang, "Xiaofei yu minsheng," *Shenghuo* 2(3) (1933), 4.
[22] Quoted in Lai Jiancheng, *Liang Qichao De Jingji Mianxiang* (Hangzhou: Zhejiang da xue chu ban she, 2010), 240.

Opinion (*Shangren gonglun*), he lamented: "Japan has a twentieth-century production but a nineteenth-century consumption. China's problem is that it has a nineteenth-century production but a twentieth-century consumption."[23]

Most commentators, therefore, did not oppose higher levels of luxury consumption per se. They actually embraced the idea of materialist progress, as long as society moved forward equitably in purchasing power and consumption habits. It was when it exceeded the pace of societal development that consumption turned into an extravagant and negative practice. Writing in the *Journal of Social Studies* (*Shehui xuebao*), for example, Marxist Li Jianhua chastised "inappropriate, unnecessary, and hedonistic consumption (*xiaofei*) [that went] beyond the average level of life in the society of its time and place."[24] Li's idea echoed Liang Qichao's argument that "if consumption is high, but the people are suitably prosperous, balance their expenses with what they earn, and don't spend their capital, then they can still respect the principle of frugality and saving."[25] Higher standards of living and consumption above subsistence, therefore, did not necessarily result in imprudent or amoral behavior, as long as they did not lead to unnecessary strain on the individual's or family's finances and kept pace with the progress of society at large.

It was because of the gap between China's level of development and its style of consumption that luxury in China was often perceived not as a sign of civilization but only as an empty imitation of it. As the renowned Christian scholar and journalist Fan Zimei (1866–1939), using the pen name of Fan Bihui, explained in the YMCA journal *Working Together* (*Tonggong*), many Chinese believed that because luxury increased as civilization progressed, the mere exhibition of luxury habits was per se a sign of progress. This was not so, he stated; although in the United States and Europe luxury was indeed rooted in evolutionary progress, in China it was only a borrowed habit aimed at hiding the real poverty of the country.[26] Another religious publication expanded on the same issue. A 1927 editorial in the Protestant

23 Ming Gao, "Shijiu shiji xiaofei," *Shangren gonglun* (1933), 8.
24 Li Jianhua, "Shechi shenghuo zhi shehuixue de guancha," *Shehui xuebao* 2 (4) (1930), 1–2.
25 Quoted in Lai Jiancheng, *Liang Qichao de jingji mianxiang. Lianjing xueshu congshu* (Taipei: Lianjing chuban shiye gufen youxian gongsi, 2006), 240.
26 Fan Bihui, "Lun jianyue yu shechi," *Tonggong*, April 1934, 16–17.

missionary paper *The Correspondent* (*Tongwenbao*) pointed out that superfluous and leisure-related consumption was a sign of prosperity in the United States, where the economy was already developed. In China, however, "society's luxury [was] equal to squandering." The Chinese loved luxury, the author argued, but consumed on debt rather than spending extra income. Because they were not as hardworking as, for example, the Germans, they were destined to sink further into debt. Germany, in fact, was poor, but its people were famously hardworking and thus able to produce more than they consumed. Because China's general consumption continued to expand while its production lagged behind, the author concluded: "I don't know how we can survive!"[27]

Although the anti-consumerist tone of these two articles could arguably be ascribed to the influence of religious ethics, they placed their arguments in both a social science framework and a markedly nationalist perspective, deploying them in support of the commonly embraced notion of China's economic scarcity and lagging industrial production. A nation should not consume more than it produced. The opposite trend – producing more than consuming – was seen as an important characteristic of strong modern nations. These articles also touched on the idea, widely popular at the time, that China's economic problems were deepened by the intrinsic backwardness of the Chinese people – i.e. a lack of enlightenment in terms of work ethic and nationalist responsibility. This notion of the Chinese people's "backwardness" had constituted an important theme of the debate on nation building since the New Culture Movement (1910s–1920s), which focused on the regeneration of the Chinese individual as the most important strategy for national survival. In this context, as a commentator using the name of Hao Ran pointed out, the creation of a modern and civically conscious economic man was a prerequisite of China's development. It was, after all, the labor of such enlightened workers that, in Hao Ran's eyes, ensured Germany's success, and that workforce powered the most stunning economic recovery in the years after World War One.

Most intellectuals and reformers, therefore, perceived China's treaty port consumption trends not as signifying widespread progress among

[27] Hao Ran, "Yulun yiban: shehui shechi," *Tongwenbao* 41 (February 1927), 15. The author of this article, Hao Ran, is not to be confused with the later journalist and writer Hao Ran (1932–2008).

the Chinese population at large but as a privilege of a few, against a background of lagging development and scarcity. These commentators reversed the urban narrative of modernization and called on the modern urban household to abandon its luxury lifestyle. "Each family does not need to install appliances, each person does not need to make social visits, and women do not need useless clothes," declared editorialist Shen Yu in *Telecommunication Weekly* (*Dianzheng zhoukan*), a periodical sponsored by the Guomindang elder and chairman of the Reconstruction Committee (*jianshe weiyuanhui*), Jiang Renjie (1877–1950).[28]

This notion was not confined to editorialists of popular publications but was also widely shared by economists across political lines. Among them was the US-trained economist Zhu Shikang (1901–82), an Indiana University Ph.D. who had returned to China via the Soviet Union and who complemented his academic career – which included teaching at Jiaotong and Fudan universities – with stints in the economic administration of the Nationalist Government. Zhu considered issues of consumption crucial for China's economic development. Combining a Veblenian critique of conspicuous consumption with an anti-imperialist perspective, Zhu criticized extravagant consumption in imitation of Western standards of living or as a status symbol, which he often observed in China's treaty ports:

> what differences are there between Shanghai's, Paris's, and New York's theaters and big dance halls? ... those who hold a diploma in their hands ... in the evening fool around in dance halls or at dog races. Their consumption power is not very different from that of Western people ... If we discuss their productive power, however, we see that they are not willing to work in factories and cannot stand the life of the peasant.[29]

Zhu's firm opposition to this elitist and urban middle-class ("those who hold a diploma in their hands") mode of consumption was rooted in his concern for the general standards of living of the Chinese peasant population. "Rural villages," he lamented, "are in economic ruin to the point that people are starving throughout the countryside. They eat tree bark and grassroots to fill their bellies."[30] For Zhu Shikang, therefore, the gap between rural and urban conditions testified to the

[28] Shen Yu, "Zhizu zai jie shechi shuo," *Dianzheng zhoukan* 31 (March 1928), 3.
[29] Zhu, "Xiaofei yu minsheng," 4–5. [30] Zhu, "Xiaofei yu minsheng," 4.

gap between the economic conditions of the two areas and identified rural poverty as the symbol of the national condition, while representing the mode of consumption in the treaty ports as an abnormality exerting a negative impact on the nation at large.

China's consumption habits, therefore, appeared to be out of balance with its productive ability. Finding the proper balance between the two – or "rationalizing" their relationship – became an important nation-building goal which could be achieved only by reforming the current system of distribution of resources, the free market.

Rationalizing the Market: The Economic Cooperation Movement

The idea of the crucial need to rationalize production and consumption was briefly but poignantly presented in an anonymous editorial in a 1907 issue of the daily paper *Shenbao*, which declared that "consumption and production support each other. It is not possible to emphasize one over the other. If they are balanced, personal savings and the government treasury can be steadier than Mount Tai. If they are not balanced, there can be danger ... peeling the skin and sucking the marrow [of the nation] ..."[31] This attention to balancing production and consumption led some economists to criticize those who focused only on issues of production. This was the attitude of most academic economists in newly established centers for economic research. Among them were the Nankai Institute of Economics (*Nankai daxue jingji yanjiusuo*) established at Nankai University, in Tianjin, in 1927 by prominent Western-trained economists – including He Lian (1895–1975, generally known in the West by the name Franklin Ho) and Fang Xianting (1903–85) – in collaboration with the Rockefeller Foundation.[32] A second new center, the Department of Economics, was established at Beijing's Yanjing University (*Yanjing daxue*) under the directorship of the British missionary and economist John Bernard Tayler (1878–1951). In general, these economists believed that any

[31] "Shengchan yu xiaofei xiangguan shuo," *Shenbao* no. 12419 (August 26, 1907), 2–3.

[32] Margherita Zanasi, "Far from the Treaty Ports: Fang Xianting and the Idea of Rural Modernity in 1930s China," *Modern China* 30 (2004), 113–146; and Chiang Yung-chen, *Social Engineering and the Social Sciences in China* (Cambridge: Cambridge University Press, 2001).

discussion of consumption was premature until production had developed adequately. For this reason, they preferred to focus their work almost exclusively on improving industrial and agricultural output. The prestigious *Nankai Social and Economic Quarterly* (published earlier under the title of *Monthly Bulletin on Economic China*), published by the Nankai Institute of Economics, for example, did not publish one single article on consumption in the years 1934–7. Most articles focused on the agrarian crisis; on the use of cooperative societies to improve and rationalize production, especially in rural areas, with only minor comments on their possibility for consumption; and on problems of industrial capitalization and organization.[33] The journal *Chinese Economy* (*Zhongguo jingji*), published in Nanjing from 1933 to 1937, also focused on a similar array of topics, although it did not show as much interest in the cooperative society movement and tended to take a more theoretical approach to economics than the Nankai publication.[34]

These economists also shared in an effort to gain a "scientific" understanding of the Chinese economy through data collection, thus negating the validity and competence of previous "unscientific" economic writings and limiting their credibility. For this reason, they focused on collecting data through field studies, building statistics, and exploring one or another industry that was particularly relevant to import substitution in order to comprehend its workings scientifically and promote their rationalization. These studies were indeed very useful and laid the foundations of contemporary Chinese economics.[35] They shared, however, a narrow focus on China's capability for production, overshadowing the importance of issues related to domestic consumption.

Disagreeing with these economists and stressing the close relationship between production and consumption, Zhu Shikang wrote:

> our country's problem of livelihood for the population of four hundred million certainly begins with production. However, production and consumption are interconnected. If there are no economically rational methods of consumption, then production will never be able to develop. Therefore,

[33] *Nankai Social and Economic Quarterly*, Nankai daxue jingji yanjiusuo (Tientsin, China: Nankai Institute of Economics, Nankai University, 1935–7).
[34] *Zhongguo jingji* (Nanjing, Zhongguo jingji yanjiuhui, 1933–7).
[35] Chiang Yung-chen, *Social Engineering and the Social Sciences in China* (Cambridge: Cambridge University Press, 2001), Chapters 4 and 5.

the problem of consumption constitutes a crucial issue for the solution to the problem of China's livelihood.[36]

Echoing the views of some late-Qing officials and intellectuals, such as Zhang Zhidong, Zhu called for a reshaping of China's mode of consumption and for closer interconnection of demand with the production needs of the nation. Most anti-consumerism writers also supported this idea and called for the development of a system that would more effectively stimulate the production of basic staples. This system would replace the fast-growing urban-based consumerist apparatus – including marketing, advertising, and department stores – which, they believed, promoted the consumption of luxury goods which did not really reflect the needs of the nation as a whole and only wasted resources. Efforts for counteracting market-based consumption trends developed in the treaty ports became popular in the Republican period. A common strategy was the adoption of cooperative societies, as the Economic Cooperative Movement (*jingji hezuo yundong*) swept through China in the 1920s and 1930s. Cooperatives societies appeared to have great revolutionary potential, as outlined by economist Wang Shiying (1902–49), a prominent leader of the movement, in a June 1930 talk reprinted in the *Jiangsu Party Affairs Weekly* (*Jiangsu dangwu zhoukan*). A graduate of Fudan University (*Fudan daxue*), Wang held professorships at several universities, including the Shanghai Commercial Institute (*Shanghai shangxueyuan*). He later became involved with the economic cooperation efforts of the GMD, serving as an economic expert for the GMD Central Political Committee and in 1947 becoming the chair of the office for the management of the cooperative society (*hezuo shiye guanliju*) of the Nationalist Government. In June 1930, Wang's ideas appear to have been far more radical than those of the 1940s GMD, as he claimed to be directly inspired by Charles Gide – a French economist and socialist activist whose book *Consumers' Co-operative Societies* (1917) was already available in Chinese in the late 1920s.[37] Echoing Gide, Wang argued against the wasteful nature of consumerism, which, he explained, left control of the production process in the producers' hands, allowing capitalists

[36] Zhu, "Xiaofei yu minsheng," 4.

[37] Charles Gide, and Jianzu Wang, *Jite jingjixue* (Shanghai: Shangwu yinshuguan, 1929); Charles Gide, Cedric Bright Long, and James Peter Warbasse, *Consumers' Co-operative Societies* (New York, NY: A. A. Knopf, 1922).

and middlemen to decide what was to be produced. This system created much waste, because production did not necessarily reflect people's needs, and a great deal of money was spent on advertising, trying to convince people to buy items they could actually do without. If, instead, consumers controlled and managed production, Wang explained, "we can then produce goods that fit the needs!" After all, "production is the means. Consumption is the objective … goods are produced for the sake of consumption. They are not produced for the sake of production."[38]

Wang's model turned upside down the role that consumption was supposed to play in the economies of the industrialized West, at this time dominated by emerging growthist views which were to mature fully in the post–World War Two period. Growthism's focus on untargeted growth in production was diametrically opposed to Gide's. In the West, criticisms of growthism were not isolated instances but were widespread, gaining particular popularity with the writing of the British economic historian and Christian-socialist activist, R. H. Tawney. In his 1920 book *The Acquisitive Society* – already available in Chinese translation in 1928[39] – Tawney advocated the establishment of a "functional society" in which "the producers shall stand in a direct relation to the community for whom production is carried on, so that their responsibility to it may be obvious and unmistakable, not lost, as at present, through their immediate subordination to shareholders whose interest is not service but gain."[40] Production, therefore, should serve society and not capitalist interests.

Echoing Tawney's model of a "functional" system of industrial production, Wang, and other supporters of cooperative societies, wanted to ensure that China's productive resources were directed

38 Wang Shiying, "Xiaofeipai yu shengchanpai," *Jiangsu dangwu zhoukan* 24 (June 29) (1930), 80–81.

39 Richard Henry Tawney, *The Acquisitive Society* (Charleston, SC: BiblioBazaar, [1920] 2008); Richard Henry Tawney and Wu Zhizhuang, *Jindai gongye shehui de binli* (Shanghai: Shangwu yinshuguan, 1928). Tawney was later invited by the Institute for Pacific Relations to visit China, and in 1932 he published a report on the economic situation, *Land and Labor in China*, that pioneered the field of Chinese economic history in the English-speaking world. Richard Henry Tawney, *Land and Labor in China* (Boston, MA: Beacon Press, [1932] 1966); Margherita Zanasi, "Western Utopias, Missionary Economics, and the Chinese Village," *Journal of World History* 24(2) (2013), 359–387.

40 Tawney, *The Acquisitive Society*, 180.

toward lifting the people's standards of living rather than catering to the "wasteful" habits of an urban elite and leaving the rural masses in abject poverty. As he explained in a 1934 article in *Cooperation Monthly* (*Hezuo yuekan*), this tighter integration between demand and production could be achieved through the formation of consumer cooperative societies that would take over the functions generally played by the merchants, get involved in production decision-making, and better serve the needs of the people.[41] Like Wang, many supporters of the Economic Cooperation Movement also perceived cooperative societies as the most efficient way to maximize resources, to balance consumption and production by giving consumers a measure of control over the production apparatus, and to eliminate the "middle man," generally represented as a predatory figure who manipulated prices for personal profit.[42]

The objective of bypassing market-based production crossed political divides. Cooperative societies were widely adopted in experimental reform programs sponsored by various private and state entities, including Communist sympathizers. Owing to a general emphasis on production, however, only a few among the many cooperative societies established in the early decades of the Republican period addressed the problem of consumption. Earlier experiments with cooperative societies were carried out in the context of the movement for rural reconstruction launched by a variety of individual reformers and organizations to solve the problems of agricultural decline and poverty in the countryside. Among these reform attempts were the Mass Education Movement and the rural reconstruction experiment launched in Zouping (Shandong Province) by philosopher and educator Liang Shuming (1893–1988). In this context, cooperative societies aimed to

41 Wang Shiying, "Xiaofeizhe de faxian," *Hezuo yuekan* 6 (6) (June 15, 1934), 4–5.

42 For a variety of reform projects relying on cooperative societies see among others Charles Wishart Hayford, *To the People: James Yen and Village China* (New York, NY: Columbia University Press, 1990); Guy S. Alitto, *The Last Confucian: Liang Shu-ming and the Chinese Dilemma of Modernity* (Berkeley, CA: University of California Press, 1986); Margherita Zanasi, "Fostering the People's Livelihood: Chinese Political Thought between Empire and Nation," *Twentieth-Century China* 30(1) (2013), 6–38, and *Saving the Nation: Economic Modernity in Republican China* (Chicago, IL: University of Chicago Press, 2006); Kate Merkel-Hess, *The Rural Modern: Reconstructing the Self and State in Republican China* (Chicago, IL: University of Chicago Press, 2016).

improve the lives of the peasant by improving agricultural production (mostly through the adoption of cooperative societies), increasing literacy, and reviving social customs.[43] The vast majority of cooperative societies established in the 1930s, however, had a more extractive nature. This was the case, for example, with the Cotton Control Commission (*mianye tongzhi weiyuanhui*) established in 1933 by the National Economic Council (*quanguo jingji weiyuanhui*), a central economic planning organization of the Nationalist Government. The main purpose of this network of societies was to increase the production of crops linked to manufacturing and channel them directly into urban industrial production. Improving the livelihood of the peasants was not a primary objective.[44]

Constructing a Modern Mode of Consumption for China: Nationalist Morality and Utilitarianism

Rationalizing the relationship between production and consumption required an assessment of what kind of consumption would fit China's needs best, i.e. in which directions resources and the power of demand should be directed. The ideal mode of consumption for China, as it emerged from the debates among economists and popular commentators, was characterized by two qualities: personal frugality and nationalist morality (adherence to nation-building goals). Echoing notions developed by Hong Liangji, Yun Jing, and Liang Qichao, most writers built their vision of China's own mode of consumption around the notion of balancing consumption and production at the level of the individual. These themes are clearly illustrated by Hao Ran's comparison, already mentioned, between unenlightened lazy Chinese consumers and industrious Germans and by Zhu Shikang's condemnation of the fondness of the middle class for dance halls and dog races and their distaste for hard work.[45] These commentators presented production as an important modern virtue and luxury consumption

[43] Alitto, *The Last Confucian: Liang Shu-Ming and the Chinese Dilemma of Modernity*, Chapters 9 and 11; Hayford, *To the People: James Yen and Village China*, Chapter Seven. For more examples of the use of cooperative societies for rural reconstruction see Merkel-Hess, *The Rural Modern: Reconstructing the Self and State in Republican China*, especially Chapter 3.

[44] Zanasi, *Saving the Nation*, Chapter 4.

[45] Hao, "Yulun yiban: shehui shechi"; Zhu, "Xiaofei yu minsheng."

as a moral weakness, pressing the case for the transformation of the economic habits of the Chinese. Writing in 1936 in the *Youth Monthly* (*Qingnian yuekan*), editorialist Shou Nan, for example, described the current urban consumption habits as a personal moral failure: "The average person, in pursuing the satisfaction of all kinds of desires, acts rashly and without control, to the point that immoral extravagance penetrates our customs, disdaining moral frugality."[46] Although the Republican debate had embraced a social science approach and moved beyond the Confucian rhetoric of frugal morality – at least temporarily, until the New Life Movement reintroduced it – frugality remained closely related to the notion of morality, at this time defined in terms of national sentiment and personal contribution to nation building.

As illustrated by Xie Peiqiong's piece quoted earlier, "the way of frugality" also came to be presented as a native Chinese moral trait, a bulwark against Western decadence.[47] Many intellectuals agreed with Zhu Shikang's argument that the urban elites' imitation of a Western lifestyle created a major problem for China's economy. Echoing an argument popular among countries that confronted Western influence in their search for a locally rooted development model, Chinese anti-consumerism intellectuals identified the cities as the site of negative Western influence. It was there that long-standing Chinese social and consumption practices met with Western consumerism, creating a dangerous hybrid – a "double style of life" (*nijū seikatsu*) according to a popular Japanese expression. An anonymous editorial in the popular magazine *The Generalist* (*Yiban*), for example, complained that Chinese luxury was rooted in the extravagant habit of having two of everything. Chinese people would own Chinese-style clothes but could not do without one or two additional Western-style sets. Even celebrations often led to double expenditure. Because of the use of both the Chinese lunar calendar and the Gregorian calendar, Chinese people celebrated the New Year twice. Some people held two styles of wedding ceremonies, Chinese and Western, or, if they smoked a pipe, would have both a traditional Chinese one and an imported Western one. The anonymous editorialist concluded: "This is the foundation of extravagance in China."[48]

[46] Shou Nan, "Xiaofei jieyue," *Qingnian yuekan* 2(2), November 15 (1936), 2.
[47] Xie, "Jie shechi shuo."
[48] "Yiban de hua: Shechi de zhongguoren," (September 1928), 150.

It was in this nationalist context that movements to support frugal habits began to appear in the early Republican period. Frugality, for example, was an important aspect of the student culture at Beijing University on the eve of the May Fourth Movement. Organizations such as the Frugal Study Society (*tongxue jianxuehui*) and the Student Savings Bank (*xuesheng chuxu yinhang*) sought to encourage thrift.[49] Frugality also was an essential part of the emerging new discipline of home economics and women's education, in which "Economic understanding, including budgeting, accounting, management, and … 'efficiency' were tied directly to the moral concept of frugality."[50]

Depictions in popular magazines of the modern woman, however, illustrate the tension between two competing cultures of consumption: one of frugal modernity and one of evolutionary materialism. In popular magazines, alongside images of the modern frugal housekeeper, women were also depicted as symbols of a modern consumerist lifestyle. Ubiquitous ads represented beautiful females using luxury merchandise such as high-quality cigarettes or imported nail care products. In the words of Tani Barlow, these images "inhabited contemporary consciousness of what it took to be modern and female." Women became the prototype of the modern luxury consumer who crowded new kinds of shopping venues, such as the Sincere Department Store, which claimed to keep shoppers "on an evolutionary track with all current commodities."[51]

Frugality came to be increasingly identified with nationalist and moral attitudes. Cai Yuanpei, the chancellor of Beijing University, for example, was an enthusiastic promoter of austerity in his crusade against corruption and the "failure of China's attempt at Western-style constitutional government." In this context, frugality was deployed as a critique of capitalist consumerism and of the general

[49] Timothy B. Weston, *The Power of Position: Beijing University, Intellectuals, and Chinese Political Culture, 1898–1929* (Berkeley, CA: University of California Press, 2004), 135; Fabio Lanza, *Behind the Gate: Inventing Students in Beijing* (New York, NY: Columbia University Press, 2010), 61–66.

[50] Helen M. Schneider, *Keeping the Nation's House: Domestic Management and the Making of Modern China* (Vancouver: UBC Press, 2011), 105.

[51] Barlow, "Buying In," 307, 311. For an in-depth discussion of gender roles and luxury consumption see Lingling Lien, *Dazao xiaofei tiantang: Baihuo gongsi yu jindai Shanghai chengshi wenhua* (Taipei: Zhongyanyuan jinshisuo, 2017), 338–382.

corruption in China's political and economic life.[52] The Nationalist Party (Guomindang or GMD) also attempted to control personal consumption through nationalist propaganda. The National Goods Movement (*guohuo yundong*), if successful, would have greatly limited conspicuous consumption by putting fashionable imported goods – the main staple of urban extravagance – beyond the reach of consumers.[53] The movement, in fact, would have facilitated the redirection of consumption along the lines advocated by Zhu Shikang.

Caught between competing narratives of consumption as a sign of modernity, on the one hand, and as an elitist expression of negative imperialist influence out of step with China's level of progress, on the other, Chinese intellectuals also attempted to find a satisfactory definition of consumption levels and living standards that could be modern while also appropriate to China's dire economic circumstances. In this context, the notion of public utility emerged as an acceptable characteristic of a modern style of consumption for China. According to many commentators, current consumerist trends not only failed to reflect China's economic circumstances but also failed to contribute to the public good. Li Jianhua supported this argument by placing it in a historical-materialist narrative. According to Li, the rise of a small wealthy elite had led to the emergence of a leisure class (*youxian jieji*), which began to engage in a life of conspicuous leisure (*xianrande xiankong*) and conspicuous consumption (*xianrande xiaofei*).[54] In ancient times, Li argued, this kind of consumption was justified by a need for increasingly complicated and splendid rituals to boost the leadership position of this class. As the trappings of power, therefore, it had political utility. Because the upper class, however, continued to live in leisure even in modern times, consuming goods produced by the lower classes, "this kind of consumption became simply an expression of the abundance of wealth of the leisure class. Therefore, it came to have no utility. It was simply a kind of luxury!" This was the pattern, Li concluded, followed by consumption in contemporary China, where

52 Cai Yuanpei (Zimin), "Wenming yu shechi," *Lüou zazhi* (November 15, 1916), 1–3; Lanza, *Behind the Gate*, 64; Weston, *The Power of Position*, 145.

53 Karl Gerth, *China Made: Consumer Culture and the Creation of the Nation* (Cambridge, MA: Harvard University Asia Center 2003); Dikötter, *Things Modern*.

54 Li, "Shechi shenghuo zhi shehuixue de guancha," 2–3.

it was a sign not of progress but of a persistent form of traditional exploitation and corruption.[55]

This theme of public utility was developed also by the prominent educator Yu Ziyi (1886–1970), who in 1925 commented that consumption had increasingly become a means for the rich and powerful to establish their status and therefore had no social utility. Yu complained, for example, about warlords' and government officials' use of cars. One would think that they were off to some important meeting, but they were actually going to visit friends and play cards. "In reality, their time is not worth a penny ... it is [just] waste. However, it seems that if they don't have a car, they would appear to be poor, and if the car does not go fast, they lose personal prestige." These people, Yu continued, were wasting the possibilities offered by important scientific and technological discoveries. They turned new inventions, intended to improve life, into tools for boosting personal prestige. "The objective of those who manufacture cars is to save time and increase efficiency" and not for people to "put on airs."[56] Modern consumption, in Yu's eyes, needed to be the expression of the new scientific efficiency that came with progress and to be aimed at benefiting society at large – not just a decadent pastime of the urban elites. In this context, Hao Ran, editorializing in the Protestant *Tongwenbao*, agreed with Yu and Li, comparing "society's luxury ... to the act of squandering" because, in China, luxury expenditure was not for "the good of public interest."[57]

These criticisms of luxury consumption as squandering resources and not being in step with either the country's economic conditions or the individual's income evokes Thorstein Veblen's (1857–1929) critique of the "conspicuous consumption" mode of capitalism, which he claimed promoted unproductive economic practices that did not contribute to the economy in general.[58] Veblen's *The Theory of the Leisure Class* (1899) became available in Japanese and Chinese translations in, respectively, 1924 and 1932, and inspired writers such as Li Jianhua and Yu Ziyi, who responded in ways similar to Veblen to the materialism of Western consumerism, which, they believed, betrayed

[55] Li, "Shechi shenghuo zhi shehuixue de guancha," 4.
[56] Yu Ziyi, "Shechi," *Shenghuo* 1 (1925), 78.
[57] Hao, "Yulun yi ban: Shehui shechi," 15.
[58] Thorstein Veblen, *The Theory of the Leisure Class* (Oxford: Oxford University Press, [1920] 2008).

the original liberal notion of social improvement.[59] The translation of Veblen's work marked a change in the terminology of the Chinese critique of the materialist aspect of consumption as the terms "leisure class" (*youxian jieji*), "conspicuous leisure" (*xianrande xiankong*), and "conspicuous consumption" (*xianrande xiaofei*) came to appear frequently in specialized and popular journals.[60] This kind of critique of the materialist nature of consumption, however, predated Veblen's notoriety in China, being rooted in late-Qing themes of the relationship between productive and unproductive consumption. In his 1916 editorial titled "Civilization and Luxury," for example, Cai Yuanpei differentiated between two kinds of luxury: one that contributed to civilization and one that just wasted resources. Cai argued that the comfort and ease of modern travel was a positive aspect of modern consumption. The same was the case with new libraries and schools, which made knowledge available to the people and enabled the improvement of the human spirit. Although such infrastructures were built at great expense, they were not to be considered luxurious, because the results they generated were far greater than the money spent on constructing them. For Cai, public utility remained an important issue even when discussing personal consumption. He differentiated between consumption balanced by adequate contribution to the public good and wasteful egotistical luxury. If an individual spent more than the average person and did not counterbalance his expenditures with an adequate amount of socially useful output, Cai wrote, he was indulging in extravagant luxury.[61] China needed, therefore, to adopt a mode of spending based on a frugal fulfillment of personal needs when it came to individual consumption and, in general, contributing to the modernization of both economy and society. Although Cai's modernization program relied on state intervention, it still reflected humanistic notions of modernity. Cai, in fact, placed "public utility" in the context of nation building and subordinating the individual's consumption habits to this greater-good goal so as to contribute to the development of a "cultured living," marked by

[59] Veblen, *The Theory of the Leisure Class*; Thorstein Bunde Veblen and Shinzo Ono, *Yukan kaikyuron* (Tokyo: Jiryusha, 1924); T. Weibulin and Hu Yimo, *Youxian jieji lun: Shehui zhidu zhi jingjixue de yanjiu* (Shanghai: Zhonghua shuju, 1932).

[60] Li, "Shechi shenghuo zhi shehuixue de guancha," 2–3.

[61] Cai, "Wenming yu shechi," 38–39.

a general improvement of society's educational opportunities and general comfort.

By the mid-1930s, however, an important shift occurred. The idea that nation building rested on state-led industrialization and military buildup became prevalent, displacing more humanist interpretations such as Cai's. This alternative interpretation of nation building and of the role frugality played in it resonated especially among Nationalist leaders and was to find full realization in the New Life Movement.

Frugal Modernity: The New Life Movement

The New Life Movement was launched officially in February 1934 in Nanchang, the provincial capital of Jiangxi, as a tool for strengthening the military efforts of Chiang Kai-shek's fifth anti-Communist campaign. The New Life Movement became an integral part of the military strategies adopted in this area.[62] In its early stages, the movement was the special brainchild of Chiang and his longtime secretary and associate Chen Lifu (1900–2001), reflecting both leaders' view of a wider Confucian-inspired revitalization of society.[63] The New Life Movement, in fact, did not just support war objectives but also appropriated notions of Confucian virtue and personal morality in an attempt to reshape social habits nationwide. In this context, it placed anti-consumerist frugality at the center of the Nationalists' plan for socio-economic modernity, nation building, and the construction of national identity. Summarizing this basic New Life Movement principle, Chiang stated: "plain and simple are two important guidelines of the New Life Movement. They are also the basis for implementing hard work and frugality. The opposite of plain and simple is extravagance and waste, which definitively hinder nation building."[64]

[62] Zhang Li, "Jiangxi nongcun fuwu shiye 1934–1945," in *Kangzhan jianguoshi yanjiu taohui lunwen ji, 1937–1945* (Nangan: Zhongyang yanjiuyuan jindaishi yanjiusuo, 1985), 1035–1057; Federica Ferlanti, "The New Life Movement in Jiangxi Province, 1934–1938," *Modern Asian Studies* 44(5) (2010), 961–1000.

[63] Chiang's wife (Song Meiling) and the YMCA later came to be involved in the implementation of the movement. Ferlanti, "The New Life Movement in Jiangxi Province, 1934–1938," 6, 8, 12–15.

[64] Chiang Kai-shek, "Xinshenghuo yundong sanzhounian jinian gao quangguo tongbao shu (February 19, 1937)," in *Zongtong Jianggong sixiang yanlun zongji* (Taipei: Zhongguo guomindang zhongyang weiyuanhui dangshiwei yuanhu, 1984), 210.

Although the intellectual framework of the New Life Movement was rooted in earlier debates on consumption and frugality, it introduced new elements that reflected anti-liberal trends developing worldwide at that time. It especially reflected the globalizing Fascist movement and its anti-Communist concern for social stability and the regimentation of economic resources. The issue of social order had long been a particular preoccupation with Nationalist leaders and intellectuals. Writing in 1928 in the Nationalists' publication *Electrical Administration Weekly* (*Dianzheng zhoukan*), commentator Shen Yu expressed deep concern with this issue. Distressed by the present-day corruption of society, which manifested itself in widespread extravagant consumption and the flouting of social hierarchies, Shen borrowed the Song Dynasty historian Sima Guang's lamentation on the excesses of his time to convey his dissatisfaction:

> Foot soldiers dress like scholars. Peasants wear silk shoes. At home, the gentry drinks wine [of a higher quality] than that prescribed by rules. If meat and fish dishes are not expensive and rare, if there is not a wide variety of dishes, and dishes [are not so plentiful that they] fill the table, people do not dare to invite guests. Indeed, if this is not the case, people vie to criticize [the meal], considering it vulgar and stingy. Alas! Customs have declined to this point![65]

For Shen, during his era, Chinese society had reached an even greater degree of extravagance and waste than that observed by Sima Guang and posed a serious threat to social order because it reflected lack of restraint and moral weakness among the Chinese population. The problem, Shen explained, lay in the fact that people were never content with their status. Influenced by the general extravagance of contemporary society, they aspired to ascend the socioeconomic ladder by any means necessary, even if those means were amoral and caused misery for many others.[66] Only the re-establishment of frugal habits could eradicate this feeling of discontent and curb the rampant corruption and social instability that afflicted Chinese society.

In addition to the growing popularity of the idea that curbing consumption would help stabilize society, a new interpretation of Sun Yat-sen's principle of "people's livelihood" (*minsheng*) – an important trope for Nationalist political legitimacy – paved the way

[65] Shen, "Zhizu zai jie shechi shuo," 1. [66] Shen, "Zhizu zai jie shechi shuo," 1.

for the authoritarian view of frugality as a means of economic mobilization that came to be embodied by the New Life Movement. This new conceptualization reversed Sun's vision of people's livelihood. Sun had identified progress with improvement in the material life of the people and considered the state primarily responsible for fulfilling this goal. In his four lectures on the Principle of the People's Livelihood (*minsheng zhuyi*), for example, Sun envisioned the state playing an active role in providing the four basic necessities of the people – clothing, food, housing, and transportation (*yi shi zhu xing*). He delineated a system in which state factories "would manufacture the clothing needed by the people," thus ensuring that this basic necessity of livelihood would be met.[67] Sun also argued for similar direct state intervention in the satisfaction of the other three basic needs, making raising standards of living the primary objective of China's modernization efforts. The New Life Movement reversed Sun's view that livelihood was a primary responsibility of the state and an area in which the state's resources needed to be invested. Chiang Kai-shek reinterpreted Sun's trope of the four material needs of the people. He argued that transportation not only represented Sun's idea of the development of the transportation (*xing*) infrastructure of the new modern Chinese nation but also signified "moral" (*yi*) and "honest" (*lian*) behavior.[68] As Chiang explained in his "Outline for the New Life Movement" (*Xinshenghuo yundong gangyao*), "*xing* is the movement of walking, but it can also be behavior," and this meaning, he argued, guided all four elements of the formula.[69]

By placing personal behavior at the center of the formula for standards of living, Chiang and Chen strengthened the link between material and spiritual modernity. Personal behavior became an important modernizing force that could revolutionize everyday life by changing people's actions as they related to their basic material needs.[70] In this context, the New Life Movement transformed Sun's trope of *yi shi zhu xing* from a description of people's daily basic economic needs and the parameters for improving livelihood into a matter of personal attitude

67 Sun, "Sanmin zhuyi: minsheng zhuyi, disi jiang (1924)," 670.
68 Chiang Kai-shek, "Xinshenghuo yundong gangyao (May 15, 1934)," in *Zongtong Jianggong sixiang yanlun zongji*, 154–170.
69 Chiang, "Xinshenghuo yundong gangyao," 161, 169.
70 Chiang, "Xinshenghuo yundong gangyao," 155.

toward material life, an important building block for a system of mass mobilization of economic resources.[71]

To bring about this transformation, Chiang and Chen evoked the four traditional Confucian virtues of *li*, *yi*, *lian*, and *chi* (rites/manners, righteousness, honesty, and sense of shame) and deployed them to define, albeit in a seemingly contradictory way, proper modern behavior. "The New Life Movement," Chiang wrote, "advocates the regulation of life [through the application of] '*li*, *yi*, *lian*, *chi*.'" The consistent practice of these virtues would gradually transform the daily habits of the people and encourage the development of moral habits in the pursuit of basic material needs. These virtues, Chiang reasoned, would become the core rules in "acting toward people, handling affairs, carrying oneself, and dealing with goods."[72] More specifically, Chiang explained, the way things are obtained should be "honest" (*lian*). The way the quality of things is chosen should be "righteous" (*yi*), befitting, Chiang explained, a person's era, status, and place. Everyone should regulate his food, housing, clothing, and behavior according to his age, environment, and rank and follow the basic principles of "not vulgar but not excessive; not grand but not stingy." In addition, Chiang continued, "consumption" of goods should follow "rites" (*li*), by which, in this case, he meant "properly managed (*li*)," by virtue of adhering to the principle of "neat and clean, plain and simple."[73] Consumption, therefore, was always to be guided by the basic principle of frugality but was also shaped by social status and determined by consideration of age and rank, thus ensuring social order. In this context, moral consumption behavior "that fits the current age" became the measure of economic modernity, shifting the focus away from generally higher levels of material standards of living.[74]

To support his point of view about the greater importance of the moral dimension of life over its material aspect, Chiang cited a famous saying by the Song Dynasty Neo-Confucian philosopher Cheng Yi

[71] Chiang Kai-shek, "Xinshenghuo yundong sanzhounian jinian gao quangguo tongbaoshu (February 19, 1937)," in *Zongtong Jianggong sixiang yanlun zongji*, 203, and "Xinshenghuo yundong dier qimude he gongzuo baogao yaozhi (February 19, 1936)," in *Zongtong Jianggong sixiang yanlun zongji*.

[72] Chiang, "Xinshenghuo yundong gangyao," (May 15, 1934), 158–159.

[73] Chiang, "Xinshenghuo yundong gangyao," (May 15, 1934), 162–163, 167.

[74] Chiang, "Xinshenghuo yundong gangyao" (May 15, 1934), 155.

(1033–1107): "losing moral integrity is a serious matter; dying of hunger is a trivial matter."[75] Chiang used Cheng Yi's statement, however, not to describe the moral standards of chaste women and government officials, as Cheng Yi had primarily intended it, but to demand sacrifices from the people in support of the state. In other words, as historian Arif Dirlik argues, whereas Confucian thought "had placed moral responsibility with the ruler ... New Life ideology placed the burden [of moral responsibility] on the population."[76]

The New Life Movement's priority for a nationalist mode of consumption reflected not only Chiang's own understanding of nation building in terms of a German-style military-oriented industrialization but also emerging trends of autarky and planned economy that, in the 1930s, led to similar changes in the perception of consumption elsewhere, especially among Fascist countries such as Italy.[77] In 1932, for example, the Italian government launched new regulations establishing the Ente Nationale della Moda (National Organization for Fashion), which was to oversee the implementation of new standards in clothing, especially for women, promoting consumption of national products and a Fascist vision of a native and simple modern style for the Italian woman.[78]

In 1937, aware that the model of frugal nation building was becoming a worldwide trend, Chiang remarked:

> Today, when any nation experiences difficulties in national reconstruction, without exception both government and society make hard work and thriftiness their basic principles and value highly the plain and simple. Then one can see that [they] have [successfully] used material resources, time, and labor to save the nation.[79]

Chiang thus used international trends to legitimize his condemnation of consumption beyond the frugal lifestyle as anti-nationalist in nature.

[75] Chiang, "Xinshenghuo yundong gangyao" (May 15, 1934), 162-3.

[76] Zhang Ning, "Cong paomating dao renmin guangchang: Shanghai paomating shouhui yundong, 1946–1951," *Zhongyang yanjiuyuan jindaishi yanjiusuo jikan* 48, June (2005), 971.

[77] Renzo de Felice and Michael Arthur Ledeen, *Fascism: An Informal Introduction to its Theory and Practice* (New Brunswick, NJ: Transaction Books, 1976), 69.

[78] Eugenia Paulicelli, *Fashion under Fascism: Beyond the Black Shirt* (New York, NY: Berg, 2004), 45.

[79] Chiang, "Xinshenghuo yundong sanzhounian jinian gao quangguo tongbao shu," 210.

The New Life Movement appeared to offer a solution to the question that had generated the earlier debate on consumption, that is, what kind of modern living standards China should pursue in order to be in step with its level of economic development and to avoid wasting precious and scarce resources, while, at the same time, achieving its nation-building goals and preserving some measure of native identity. In this sense, the New Life Movement can be seen as the last step in the process of the gradual development of anti-consumerist trends that dated back to the late Qing period. The New Life Movement, however, overturned the liberal understanding of modernity based on the development of the societal economy and rising standards of living that had been an important theme of the early twentieth-century debate. Although it prioritized nation building, the early debate, in fact, was marked by attempts to find a balance between these liberal themes and China's lagging industrialization and poverty. Attempts to depart from the liberal market and rationalize the relationship between production and consumption, for example, had focused on the ultimate goals of improving the people's standard of living by eliminating poverty and, in general, by channeling resources into the production of daily-need goods. The New Life Movement, instead, confined consumption to a marginal role and merged early anti-consumerist themes into a new view of frugality that went against basic notions of economic liberalism. The movement upheld a conservative form of social hierarchy while carrying out mass mobilization geared to channeling resources away from the social economy and into military state building and while limiting the role of the market in the drive for economic growth.

The evolution of the discourse on frugality in China and Japan followed a similar pattern. In the 1930s in Japan, as well, the idea of frugality became a tool for the mobilization of economic resources. These similarities suggest that the increasing sense of economic and political crisis that emerged in the interwar years deeply affected the East Asian region, strengthening interventionist and anti-liberal interpretations of livelihood and consumption. This sense of crisis was a product of a changed international environment, one marked by the deterioration of international trade and the spreading effects of the Great Depression. It, however, also resonated with domestic circumstances. On the one hand, Japan was embarking on its imperial expansion, which it perceived to be essential to its economic survival. China, on the other hand, increasingly feared Japanese imperialism and national annihilation. This atmosphere of life-or-death crisis and the sense that immediate national goals transcended the needs of the individual helped the New Life Movement and the 1930s frugality campaigns in Japan to further develop a system of economic mass mobilization that had first emerged in many countries in support of the war effort during World War Two.[80]

Marxism, Evolutionary Development, and Nation Building: Blurring Political Divides

Starting in the 1930s, the Chinese discourse on the economy had changed significantly in both tone and scope. By this time, Chinese intellectuals were discussing Western economics with an increasingly sophisticated understanding – if not with increased acceptance – of Western theories, following the further development of the discipline of economics within China's academic institutions as well as a new wave of translations of specialized Western texts. In 1931, economists Wang Yanan (1901–69) and Guo Dali (1905–76), for example, published a new translation of *The Wealth of Nations*, wanting to offer a more accessible and accurate version of the original work than the one produced by Yan Fu.[81] While a few Marxist works had been already translated in the late 1920s, it was only in 1930 that Chen Qixiu (1886–1960) – a professor at Beijing University, which hosted the first group for the study of Marxism – produced a translation of the massive *Das Kapital*.[82] A wider variety of Western schools of thought also came to attract the attention of Chinese intellectuals. In 1935, for

[80] Garon, "Fashioning a Culture of Diligence and Thrift."

[81] Luo Weidong, "Scholarship on Adam Smith in China," *The Adam Smith Review* 9 (2015), 237–251; Karl, *The Magic of Concepts*; Felix Boecking, "Adam Smith in Tianjin: Yang Jingnian's Translation of *The Wealth of Nations*," in *Annual Meeting of the Association for Asian Studies* (Washington, DC, 2018).

[82] Chen Wangdao (1891–1977) published a full Chinese version of *The Communist Manifesto* in April 1919, although fragments had been appearing since 1909.

example, Zhou Binglin started teaching the ideas of Alfred Marshall (1842–1924), while Wang Yanan focused his attention on the Austrian School.[83]

It is also in the 1930s that, as the launching of the New Life Movement testifies, we find a political radicalization of the discourse on the economy, not only in terms of a sharper ideological divergence between the Marxists and the liberal humanists but also in terms of radicalization within the two groups. Fascist trends became predominant among Nationalist thinkers, overwhelming more moderate voices. At the same time, leftist intellectuals came to more closely identify with the Communist Party.

Despite this radicalization, the ideas of frugality and the need to rationalize the relationship between production and consumption were widely shared across political groups. In this period the GMD's and Chinese Communist Party's (CCP) theoretical formulations of their economic positions did present important differences, especially on the issues of private property and the adoption of a market system. In practice, however, these two groups followed very similar strategies aimed at the rationalization of the market through cooperative societies, although differences in their ultimate goals remained only temporarily and thinly obscured. Leftist intellectuals such as Chen Hansheng (1897–2004), for example, saw cooperative societies as a measure against the bourgeoisie's monopolization of the means of production as well as a strategy for cutting out merchant intermediaries and guaranteeing the workers lower prices for producer and consumer goods and better returns for the sale of their products. The Nanjing Government, instead, intended to use cooperative societies to channel rural resources into urban industrial development.[84] These different goals inevitably came to a head when the Nationalist authorities became suspicious of the large number of leftist reformers active in establishing and managing cooperative societies. As a consequence, in

83 Paul B. Trescott, *Jingji Xue: The History of the Introduction of Western Economic Ideas into China, 1850–1950* (Hong Kong: Chinese University Press, 2007), 234; Karl, *The Magic of Concepts*, Chapter 3.

84 Chen Hansheng, Chin Chien-yin, and Zhongguo jingji tongji yanjiu suo, *Industrial Capital and Chinese Peasants: Chen Han-Seng. A Study of the Rural Economy of Wuhing, Chekiang (1939)* (New York, NY: Garland, 1980) and Chen Hansheng, *Gung Ho! The Story of the Chinese Cooperatives* (New York, NY: American Institute of Pacific Relations, 1947); Zanasi, *Saving the Nation*, Chapter 5.

1935, the GMD brought the Cooperation Movement under its control and transformed it into a state network for extraction of local resources.[85] The leftist initiative in the area of cooperative societies clashed with the Nationalists once again during the Second Sino-Japanese War (1937–45) when the GMD purged the leftist leaders of the Chinese Industrial Cooperative Movement (CIC or INDUSCO).[86]

Similarities between CCP and GMD economic strategies in this period were also due to the fact that notions of evolutionary development – at the very core of Marxist theories – deeply impacted leftist intellectuals, whether they were articulated in terms of historical materialism (as exemplified by Li Jiahua's narrative of the utility of luxury) or in the liberal and humanistic terms of Cai Yuanpei. In a 1916 article, for example, Li Dazhao (1888–1927) – a prominent Marxist intellectual and a founder of the CCP – gave precedence over class struggle to the idea that the entire population of China had become the "proletariat" of Western imperialist powers.[87] At this time, in fact, Leninism appeared to be of more interest to Chinese Marxists than Marx himself, since the 1917 Bolshevik Revolution and the Leninist theories that supported it – especially Lenin's *Imperialism: The Highest Stage of Capitalism* – had suddenly made Marxism (in the hyphenated mode of Marxism-Leninism) relevant for China, a predominantly agricultural and unindustrialized country which Marx's historical materialism condemned as a very unlikely locale for a Communist revolution. Before the 1930s, most of the Marxist works translated into Chinese dealt with Lenin and the national question. A translation of Lenin's *The State and Revolution* (1917) was published in 1922, and in 1928 *New Youth* published an *Outline of*

85 For a detailed discussion of the GMD vision of China's corporativist economy and their appropriation of the Economic Cooperation Movement see Zanasi, *Saving the Nation*, Chapters 4 and 5.

86 Hansheng, Chien-yin, and Zhongguo jingji tongji yanjiusuo, *Industrial Capital and Chinese Peasants*. The CCP did not perceive cooperative societies simply as a tool for rationalizing the market or as an economic model capable of mobilizing economic resources at a time of scarcity, which is demonstrated by the CCP's adoption of cooperative societies in the immediate postwar years as a tool for basic economic reconstruction; Lu Yan, "Challenges of Transition: Chinese Industrial Cooperatives from War to Peace," in Annual Meeting of the Association for Asian Studies (Washington, DC, March 2018). By the mid-1950s, the CCP was using them as a first step toward the complete elimination of the market system and the nationalization of the economy.

87 Trescott, *Jingji Xue*, 226.

Leninism. Also at Beijing University was the US-trained economist Ma Yinchu (1882–1982), who later joined the CCP and incurred the party's displeasure over his population theories in the mid-1950s. In the early Republican period, Ma was highly critical of Marxism because he believed that China's main problem was a chronic lack of capital. For this reason, he favored the idea of a National Innovation System developed by the German economist Friedrich List (1789–1846).[88] Evolutionary notions of development and anti-imperialist feelings, therefore, mitigated differences between the left and the Nationalists to the point that many intellectuals came to identify decisively with one or the other only at the end of the 1930s.

The idea of frugality was also very popular among CCP sympathizers and left-leaning reformers and intellectuals in general. As luxury came to be identified with corruption and anti-nationalism, leftist groups began to advocate "diligence and frugality" (*qinjian*) as the proper way of life for all Chinese people with nationalist aspirations. The already mentioned Frugal Study Society (*tongxue jianxue-hui*) organized at Beijing University is a good example of this trend among politically committed students. "Diligence and frugality" were also embraced by anarchist groups, as exemplified by the Diligent Work–Frugal Study Movement (*liufa qingong jianxue hui*). This work–study program sent many Chinese to work and study in France and Belgium between 1912 and 1927. Originally organized by Chinese anarchists, it was attended by many Communist Party members and sympathizers who were later to rise to positions of power within the CCP, including Zhou Enlai (1898–1976) and Deng Xiaoping (1904–97).[89]

As early as January 1934 Mao Zedong (1893–1967) announced the importance of frugality in the CCP economic program, denouncing luxury as corruption and advocating thrift among government and party officials and the population at large:

> Thrift should be the guiding principle in our government expenditure. It should be made clear to all government workers that corruption and waste are very great crimes. Our campaigns against corruption and waste have

[88] Trescott, *Jingji Xue*, 226.

[89] Marilyn Avra Levine, *The Found Generation: Chinese Communists in Europe during the Twenties* (Seattle, WA: University of Washington Press, 1993) and Tsai Weipin and Lin Pei-yin, *Print, Profit, and Perception* (Leiden: Brill, 2014).

> already achieved some results, but further efforts are required. Our system of accounting must be guided by the principle of saving every copper for the war effort, for the revolutionary cause and for our economic construction.[90]

In theory, the CCP deployed frugality as a temporary nation-building strategy aimed at achieving the objective of a Communist economy of plenty. The ever-elusive goal of mass prosperity, however, became a distant and elusive mirage – as huge cornucopias carried by happy peasants and bursting with produce appeared as a frequent trope on propaganda posters – that contrasted starkly with Mao's renewed call for personal sacrifice in support of such movements as the Great Leap Forward (1958–60). Mao recognized the tension between China's poverty and the CCP's promises of riches for all. In his February 1957 essay "On the Correct Handling of Contradictions among the People," Mao asserted:

> We must see to it that all our cadres and all our people constantly bear in mind that ours is a big socialist country but an economically backward and poor one, and that this is a very great contradiction. To make China rich and strong needs several decades of intense effort, which will include, among other things, the effort to practice strict economy and combat waste, i.e., the policy of building up our country through diligence and frugality.[91]

Despite very different political objectives, especially the complete elimination of the market – rather than its manipulation or "rationalization" –Mao's deployment of frugality ultimately came to closely resemble that of the Nationalists not only in the New Life Movement but also in post-1949 Taiwan. Its main objective, in fact, was the mobilization of resources in support of a statist vision of nation building, putting raising standards of living on the back burner.

Conclusion

In the early decades of the twentieth century, anti-consumerist trends in China developed around two main issues. The first issue was the identification of China's luxury consumption as fundamentally

[90] Mao Zedong, "Our Economic Policy" (January 23, 1934), *Selected Works*, Vol. I, 145.

[91] Mao Zedong, "On the Correct Handling of Contradictions among the People" (February 27, 1957), *Selected Works*, Vol. 5, Chapter 11, On Practicing Economy (accessed through the Marxist Internet Archives).

different from Western consumerism and out of balance with the country's economic circumstances, characterized by scarcity. Since the Opium War, this problem had been reframed in nationalist terms and was no longer articulated in terms of the mandate of nurturing the people. The problem of scarcity had become one of "backwardness" endangering not just the livelihood of the people but also that of the entire nation in the Social Darwinian battle for the survival of the fittest. New tropes of frugal morality became an integral function of the modern sentiments of nationalism.

The second issue concerned the tension between globalizing Western liberal notions of economic modernity and China's nation-building priorities. The early Republican debates on consumerism and standards of living illustrate how the struggle to balance liberal and consumerist modernity with local economic conditions created deep contradictions between a supposedly universalist élan for modernization and China's specific needs. The notion of frugal modernity that emerged in the early Republican years appeared to resolve this contradiction by offering an alternative to the outright importation of Western consumerism, since it was designed to fulfill China's nation-building goals and satisfy the specific developmental needs of its economy of scarcity. The New Life Movement drastically radicalized this vision of modern productivist consumption, transforming individual frugality into a tool for the mass mobilization of resources. This radicalizing trend found its culmination in the Communist regime after 1949, since the Nationalists never had the administrative reach or the political power to enforce its policies to their full potential.

Even before global anti-liberal trends radicalized the discourse on market and consumption in the 1930s, the adoption of a Western-style free-market economy was challenged by Chinese intellectuals' and officials' perceptions of China's circumstances. The notion that the country was experiencing a different economic environment from that of the industrialized West pointed to the beginning of China's difficult relations with a free-market economy. This view led to what Wang Yanan described as either recognition of China's supposed failure to catch up on a Western-defined developmental ladder or an assertion of China's exceptionalism, two outcomes he considered equally problematic.[92] Although the developmentalist approach adopted by most

[92] Karl, *The Magic of Concepts*, 3.

Chinese economists in the Republican period did indeed create this conundrum, it also highlighted the dilemma faced by many countries attempting to develop at that time. These countries found themselves trapped in an international environment dominated by economic and military powers pursuing economic advantages in their territories. In this context, the question arose of whether a country should attempt development based on a modern globalized economy, mostly located in urban areas and forming isolated islands within a poorer and less developed national territory. This path to development implied support for free trade and consumerist policies, but it did not have the potential to promptly solve the problems that most worried the local economists: failure in nation building and in protecting the domestic industrial sector, the decline of the rural economy, and the increase in national poverty. The alternative was to attempt to limit the influence of the consumerist urban islands on the national economy and attempt a more nationally integrated and protectionist form of development. The latter option was ultimately adopted, to various degrees, by the Republican and Communist governments, requiring the establishment of some form of developmental state to direct the mode and direction of economic growth.

The Chinese critique of consumerism did not unfold in isolation but rather contributed to a global debate over capitalism. At the end of the nineteenth century and in the early twentieth century, consumerist forms of capitalism became the target of scathing critiques. Popular works such as those of Veblen, Gide, and Tawney criticized this system as amoral, economically dysfunctional, and an elitist deviation from the original goal of industrialization, which they defined as improving the standard of living of the population at large. Consumption was the reason for and the ultimate goal of production. In the capitalist consumerist system, in contrast, consumption served to support unlimited levels of growth in production beyond the satisfaction of demand and as a tool for further accumulation of capital aimed primarily at producing financial wealth for a few. These critiques were particularly effective because they marked a departure from earlier religious and moralist accusations against luxury and constituted the first attacks against consumerism based on a social science approach, drawing specifically on the fields of sociology and economics. These critiques raised the question of the proper relationship between modern standards of living and consumerism and denounced the current consumerist trends as the commercialization of progress and of leisure time at the expense of more egalitarian and uplifting forms of consumption.[93] These issues were particularly relevant for Chinese intellectuals and reformers as they pondered the problem of how to find a model of economic modernization that would fit China's economic and nationalist objectives.

[93] Daniel Horowitz, *The Morality of Spending: Attitudes toward the Consumer Society in America, 1875–1940* (Chicago, IL: I. R. Dee, 1992).

Conclusion

The decision to adopt a *longue durée* (1500s–1930s) approach to the history of thought on market and consumption in modern China inevitably implies a close focus on the historical development of just two notions: a narrow focus which did not sufficiently reflect the complexity of the Chinese discourse on the economy at large and the variety of problems it addressed (not least those of taxation, land tenure, and currency). This approach, however, served its intended purpose of tracing long-term transformations in the complex interrelations between historical circumstances, intellectual interpretations, and political objectives. In the case of Qing China, the political objective was embodied in the mandate of *minsheng*, as not just a rhetorical commitment to the welfare of the population of the empire but also a prerequisite for economic and political stability. From its establishment, the Qing state embraced this classical Confucian mandate with particular enthusiasm and pragmatism, as illustrated by its reformulation of *minsheng* into the *guoji minsheng* (state finances and people's livelihood) formula, which firmly linked the strategic importance of the prosperity of the societal economy to the financial stability of the state.

The adoption of the mandate of *minsheng* did not imply a rigid approach to the political economy of the empire. *Minsheng*, in fact, was an objective and not a predetermined economic formula. For this reason, achieving it could accommodate innovative strategies as scholars and officials re-evaluated the role played by different economic functions in promoting the prosperity of the empire. The Confucian philosophical framework that inspired this mandate was also more flexible than it is generally credited to have been. Beginning in the Northern Song period, for example, we witness a reformulation in positive terms of the role of private interests (*li*) – a concept that had been perceived as working against the realization of the classical Confucian vision of a harmonious and humanist economy and society since the Warring States period. In response to the expansion of interregional market networks and the increased commercialization of the economy, scholars and officials such as Dong Wei formulated a positive view of the pursuit of private interest (*li*) when it could be done by competing freely on the market. In such a case, it greatly contributed to the maximization of the circulation (*liu*) and the equalization (*ping*) of resources. It was the industrious economy of the late Ming and early Qing periods, however, that produced the most dramatic changes in the Chinese interpretation of the imperial economy, the nature of its wealth (*cai*), and the economic forces that produced it. The commercial and monetized economy came to be perceived as contributing to the production of wealth, rather than just playing a pivotal role in its distribution. Although seemingly challenging Confucian orthodoxy – or the version of it that prevailed at that time – these reconceptualizations of basic Confucian principles were ultimately justified by the role they played in achieving the main objectives of the *minsheng* mandate.

By the time of the establishment of the Qing Dynasty in 1644, the idea that the economy could grow and the notion of the efficiency of the market in regulating prices and circulating goods through the empire were already widely accepted. The Qing administration relied on these capabilities of the market to an unprecedented extent, especially in its attempts to improve military logistics and the distribution of grain, as well as to streamline the overburdened bureaucracy by outsourcing some of its tasks, such as the transportation of southern tribute grain to the capital. The Qing state also experimented with using private market forces to combat corruption in the bureaucracy, a strategy that often backfired, since it created new opportunities for collusion between officials and merchants, as was the case with the *yingyung shengxi* system discussed in Chapter 2.

Qing rulers did not embrace the idea of allowing New Luxury demand to influence the direction and the areas of economic growth for the empire as a whole, although they pragmatically and unofficially supported it in highly commercialized areas such as Jiangnan. Frugality, in fact, remained an important policy for both maintaining social stability and for fighting bureaucratic corruption. An additional reason for the Qing's continued support of the policy of *chong jie chu she* (revere frugality and eliminate extravagance) was that the economic circumstances of the empire were uneven because of the gap between the economies of the coastal and rural hinterland regions.

In these circumstances, we can argue that the state perceived the consumption economy of Jiangnan as a special case that deviated greatly from the agricultural norm of the empire – a realization that did not prevent it from relying heavily on its economic resources. In addition, from the end of the Qianlong reign, the importance of the rural economy became an even more urgent priority for the Qing state as agriculture experienced a decline while population grew at a fast pace and economic scarcity contributed to the devastating rebellions which arose in the rural areas that bordered China proper, mainly the White Lotus and the Taiping rebellions.

The growing gap between the coastal commercial economy and that of the rural hinterland emerges as a consistent concern of scholars and officials beginning in the mid-1500s. This situation attracted the attention of Lu Ji, who advocated different consumption policies in different economic circumstances. It also influenced the anti-silverists of the Ming–Qing transition period. Protecting the rural village from the negative effects of the coastal commercial economy – mostly its use of silver and its habits of luxury consumption – remained a consistent concern for the Qing anti-luxury writers. The vantage point of observation (whether centered on commercialized coastal areas or the rural hinterland), the nature of the economy they observed, and the problems they intended to solve greatly influenced the economic ideas of scholars and officials, their writings testifying to the difficulty in integrating the economic modes prevailing in different regions of the empire. The coastal–hinterland gap deepened after the Opium War, mostly because of the Self-Strengthening reforms' stress on reversing the unfavorable balance of trade. The objective of bridging this gap, however, came to hold a central position in economic discourse in the Republican period. At this time Chinese intellectuals and reformers debated the nature of China's modern identity. Did the consumerist and globalized treaty port economy constitute the new soul of modern China? And, if so, should the state's nation-building efforts be based on the development of a Western-style demand-based market economy? Or did economic modernity require lifting China as whole out of poverty and "backwardness"? This perception of modernization required solving the poverty crisis in the rural hinterland while curbing luxury consumption in the treaty ports in order to redirect resources toward nation-building-related production. The Nationalist state (1927–49) opted for the latter solution, which appeared to better serve its anti-imperialist and defensive nation-building objectives.

A second issue also constituted a major concern for scholars and officials, historically: the extent of state intervention in the economy. Controversies over this problem emerged as early as the Former Han Dynasty and continued through the imperial period, as exemplified by the *Debate on Salt and Iron* and the dispute over Wang Anshi's New Policies. By the late Ming period, the idea that the state should not intervene in the economy had become widely accepted and, during the High Qing era, it also came to influence state policies. At the turn of the nineteenth century, however, the problems generated by economic decline and the demographic boom changed this trend. Scholars and officials feared a return to economic scarcity and, for this reason, envisioned an increased role of the state in planning both the production and the distribution of resources. This shift did not imply an end of state reliance on private market forces. The Jiaqing and Daoguang emperors actually expanded the practice of privatizing selected functions of the administration, such as the transportation of tribute grain. At this time scholars and officials also began to envision forms of state intervention that went beyond historical precedents and attempted to directly influence local decisions on planting crops, regulating consumption – beyond sumptuary laws and luxury bans – and using labor in innovative ways, as illustrated by the reform plans of Ren Qiyun and Bao Shichen. These early interventionist plans relied on coopting local elites and social organizations such as the *baojia* for the realization of state goals. The late-Qing ideas of state intervention, in fact, developed within the Qing system of power brokerage described in Chapter 3 and did not envision a sharp division between state and society.[1] The Qing administrative apparatus, in effect, did not have the capability for direct state intervention, especially in comparison with the system for a "controlled economy" established in the 1930s by the Nationalist Government. The increasing sense of crisis created by imperialist intrusion further discouraged the adoption of market-based solutions, as

[1] Susan Mann, *Local Merchants and the Chinese Bureaucracy, 1750–1950*, 12. In this volume, Mann refers to this brokerage system as "liturgical methods of governance" (12). Prasenjit Duara, *Culture, Power, and the State: Rural North China, 1900–1942*; see especially Chapter 2, "Brokering Rural Administration in Late Qing."

the newly imported theories of economic liberalism did not appear to offer a suitable model for a defensive nation-building.

As argued in Chapter 2, the retreat from pro-market policies initiated in the Jiaqing period cannot be seen as a failure to advance on a supposedly linear trajectory of development by bringing some form of "proto-liberal" ideas to maturity in a full-fledged system of economic liberalism. The Qing-period understanding of the power of competing private interests to regulate the market and the appreciation of growth-inducing commercial demand did not generate a comprehensive ideology or a vision of an all-encompassing economic system. These ideas instead inspired ad hoc solutions to solve specific problems. Different circumstances appeared to require different solutions and, in this vein, the always-pragmatic Qing rulers adopted all tools at their disposal, deploying them to solve specific problems according to the specific capability of each tool. In this context, despite the persistent misconception that Confucian orthodoxy acted as an obstacle to change in imperial China, ideology appears not to have played a major role in the decision-making process of the Qing state.

China's choice of statist solutions in the period after the Opium War should also be placed in a global context. Historically, state intervention played an increasingly important role in the industrialization attempts that followed the English Industrial Revolution. As early as the 1960s, economist Alexander Gerschenkron – answering that monument to developmental determinism that was W. W. Rostow's *The Stages of Economic Growth, A Non-Communist Manifesto* – explained that different historical periods required different approaches to development. More specifically, countries that attempted industrialization at a later stage than England could not rely solely on market forces but required increased intervention from the state (Germany) or financial institutions (France).[2] England's industrialization, in fact, had changed the external conditions faced by any country aspiring to economic development. In other words, as the global market changed, so did the requirements for industrialization.[3] This was much more the case with countries that faced Western imperialism. They soon discovered that adopting a Western-style

[2] Walt Whitman Rostow, *The Stages of Economic Growth, A Non-Communist Manifesto* (Cambridge: Cambridge University Press, 1960).

[3] Appleby, *The Relentless Revolution*, 163–166.

free-market and consumerist system contributed to making them economically vulnerable *vis-à-vis* industrialized powers and that political and economic independence required an interventionist state and protectionist policies. This was the path chosen by Japan, setting a particularly poignant example for China, since it proved successful in ridding Japan of Western imperialist interests and asserting Japan's national power on the global scene. This nineteenth-century trend toward an increased role of the state in planning economic development, however, did not imply an inevitable descent into the authoritarian Fascist corporativism of the Nationalist Government (1927–49) or the realization of a Communist economy attempted during the Mao period (1949–76). In this sense, we can draw a parallel with Russia. Gerschenkron argues that in this country pro-state choices developed before the Soviet revolution and had more complex roots than simply the political ideology of the Communist Party of the Soviet Union.[4] In the case of China, we also witness the growth of pro-statist policies well before the establishment of the CCP and later of the PRC. In both cases the excesses of the two Communist parties can be understood as the coming together of long-term domestic economic trends, extremist political objectives, and the increasingly radicalized global environment of the pre- and post-World World Two periods.

The choice faced by the late-imperial scholars and officials, on the other hand, was not one of starkly opposed economic models: a liberal one and an authoritarian one marked by state control. Instead, they envisioned a hybrid form of market with ad hoc government intervention aimed at solving China's problems of poverty and interference from imperialist powers. In this sense, it anticipated forms of developmental states originated in Japan during the Meiji Restoration and later developed in the postwar period – a more liberal version of state interventionism than its 1930s system of controlled economy.[5]

4 Alexander Gerschenkron, *Economic Backwardness in Historical Perspective: A Book of Essays* (Cambridge, MA: Belknap Press of Harvard University Press, 1962).

5 Chalmers A. Johnson, *MITI and the Japanese Miracle: The Growth of Industrial Policy: 1925–1975* (Stanford, CA: Stanford University Press, 2012); William C. Kirby, "Engineering China: Birth of the Developmental State, 1928–1937," in *Becoming Chinese: Passages to Modernity and Beyond*, ed. by Wen-hsin Yeh (Berkeley, CA: University of California Press, 2000), 137–160.

Finally, this book raises the question, recently asked by William Rowe, of whether the early 1800s mark "the transition era into modern Chinese history."[6] It is at this time, in fact, that a new set of political and economic preoccupations emerged. From the point of view of political economy, in fact, it was in this period that the issue of population growth and of the hinterland–coastal gap as well as a trend toward state intervention emerged as the fundamental elements of China's modern economy. They remained main concerns of Chinese economists and political leaders, affecting economic decision-making from the late Qing through the Republican and PRC periods. Such recognition would implicitly lead to a redefinition of Chinese economic modernity, a thorny issue much debated among scholars. Currently, views on this issue are divided primarily along fields of expertise. Qing historians tend to focus on the introduction of liberal economic elements, such as unregulated markets and forms of consumption above subsistence. The field of Republican China, instead, has moved away from the search for "sprouts of capitalism" and pro-market policies as signs of a bourgeoning modernity to focus, instead, on the emergence of a modern centralized and interventionist developmental state as a central characteristic of modern China.[7] This divergence reveals the danger posed by the compartmentalization of academic disciplines according to what Daniel Lord Smail and Andrew Shryock describe as the creation of "isolated time bands."[8] The *longue durée* approach taken in this book has attempted to bridge this historiographical gap by tracing continuities between the late imperial and the Republican periods. Improved communications between scholars of the Qing and Republican periods will significantly contribute to achieving a better understanding of the process of economic modernization in China.

[6] Rowe, *Speaking of Profit*, 9.

[7] Kirby, "Engineering China." For the impact on China historiography of the idea of "sprouts of capitalism" see Paul A. Cohen, *Discovering History in China: American Historical Writing on the Recent Chinese Past* (New York, NY: Columbia University Press, 2010).

[8] Daniel Lord Smail and Andrew Shryock, "History and the 'Pre,'" *The American Historical Review* 118 (2013), 709–737.

Glossary

Ai Gong	哀公
anmin	安民
ba	霸
ba gu	八股
bailianjiao	白蓮教
Ban fa	版法
Bao Shichen	包世臣
baochuan	寶船
baojia	保甲
Baxian	巴縣
bei	卑
ben	本
benzheng	本政
bi you suo sun, ze ci you suo yi	彼有所損，則此有所益
bisu zhi fumin	鄙俗之富民
Boye	博野
bu gan wei tian xia xian	不敢為天下先
Bu nongshu	補農書
bu zai guan ze zai min	不在官則在民
bunka seikatsu	文化生活
buyou	不友
cai	財
Cai Yuanpei	蔡元培
cang fu yu min	藏富於民
cangshu jia	藏書家
Chang'an	長安
changpingcang	常平倉
Changzhi xian	長子縣
Changzhou fu	常州府
Chen Chi	陳熾

Chen Hansheng	陈翰笙
Chen Hongmou	陳宏謀
Chen Lifu	陳立夫
Chen Qixiu	陳啓修
Chen Wangdao	陳望道
Cheng ma	乘馬
Cheng Yi	程頤
Chi mi	侈靡
Chong jian chu she	崇儉黜奢
chunfang	春坊
ci	慈
ci nong zhi bing	此農之病
ci shang zhi bing	此商之病
dan	石
Daodejing	道德經
Daoguang	道光
daomin zhangshe	導靡長奢
Daxian	達縣
Daxue	大學
Deng Xiaoping	鄧小平
Dianzheng zhoukan	電政週刊
Dong Wei	董煟
dou	斗
fajia	法家
Fan Bihui	范皕誨
Fan Li	范蠡
Fan Zimei	范子美
Fang Bao	方苞
Fang Chengmo	范承謨
Fashishan	法式善
Feng Guifen	馮桂芬
fenli	分利
gong	公
gongshi	貢士
gongtianfa	公田法
Gu Gongxie	顧公燮
Gu Yanwu	顧炎武
Guan Zhong	管仲
guandu shangban	官督商辦

Guangxu	光緒
guanshang heban	官商合辦
Guanzi	管子
guo	國
Guo Dali	郭大力
guohuo yundong	國貨運動
guoji misheng	國計民生
Guomindang	國民黨
Haiguo tuzhi	海國圖志
Han Fei Zi	韓非子
Hangzhou	杭州
Hanlin yuan	翰林院
Hao Ran	浩然
He Changling	賀長齡
He Lian	何廉
helihua	合理化
Hengchan suoyan	恆產瑣言
Heshen	和珅
hezuo shehui yundong	合作社會運動
hezuo shiye guanliju	合作事業管理局
Hezuo yuekan	合作月刊
Hong Liangji	洪亮吉
hua	華
Huang He	黃河
Huang-Lao	黃老
Huang Zhen	黃震
Huang Zongxi	黃宗羲
Huangchao jingshi wenbian	皇朝經世文編
Jia li	家裏
jian	儉
jianbing	兼併
jianbing zhi jia	兼並之家
jian zhi xuming	儉之虛名
Jiang Renjie	張人傑
Jiangnan	江南
jianguo	建國
Jiangsu dangwu zhoukan	江蘇黨務週刊
Jianjiatang gao	蒹葭堂稿
jianshang	奸商

jianshe weiyuanhui	建設委員會
jiaomin	教民
Jiaqing	嘉慶
jie	節
Jie shechi shuo	戒奢侈說
jiejian	節儉
jin	金
jinbu	進步
Jinchuan	金川
jindai	近代
jindaihua	近代化
jingji hezuo yundong	經濟合作運動
jingji xuejia	經濟學家
jingjiu zhi ji	經久之計
Jinshebian	禁奢辨
jingshi	經世
jingshi sixiang	經世思想
jingtian	井田
jingyan jiangyi	經筵講義
Jinshi	進士
jiu shi yi wei zun	酒食以為尊
Jiuhuang huomin shu	救荒禍民書
jiushi	就業
junshu	均輸
junxiang tiaoji zhi fa	君相調劑之法
junzi	君子
juren	舉人
Kaifeng	開封
Kang Youwei	康有為
Kangxi	康熙
kaozheng	考證
kuai	儈
laoli	勞力
li (interests)	利
li (manage)	理
li (rites)	禮
Li Dazhao	李大釗
Li Gong	李塨
Li Hongzhang	李鴻章

Li Jianhua	李劍華
li, yi, lian, chi	禮義廉恥
Li Yisong	李肄頌
Li Yuxiang	李豫享
lian	廉
Liang Qichao	梁啟超
liang ru wei chu	量入为出
Liang Shuming	梁漱溟
Liao Jin	遼金
lijin	釐金
Lin Shusheng	林樹聲
Lin Zexu	林則徐
liu	流
liu yu min	流於民
Liu Zongzhou	劉宗周
liufa qingong jianxue hui	留法勤工儉學會
liutong	流通
Longcheng shuyuan	龍城書院
Lu Ji	陸楫
Lu Tan	盧坦
lunchuan zhaoshangju	輪船招商局
Lunyu	論語
Luo Dunyan	羅惇衍
luohou	落後
Lüyuan conghua	履園叢話
Ma Yinchu	馬寅
Mao Zedong	毛澤東
Mencius	孟子
mianye tongzhi weiyuanhui	棉業統制委員會
ming	明
Ming Gao	鳴皋
Mingshi	明史
Mingyi daifang lu	明夷待訪錄
minjian	民間
minjian shiyi	民間市易
minsheng	民生
minsheng zhuyi	民生主義
minzu	民族
Minzu zhuyi	民族主義

mo	末
mucai	母財
Nankai daxue jingji yanjiusuo	南開大學經濟研究所
nijū seikatsu	二重生活
Ning	寧
nong shi shang gong	士農工商
Nongshu	農書
Nongzheng	農政
nüequ	虐取
ping	平
pingtiao	平糶
pingzhun	平準
qi	氣
Qian Shu	潛書
Qian Yong	錢泳
qiangxuehui	強學會
Qianlong	乾隆
Qianlong futing zhouxian zhi	乾隆府廳州縣志
qinjian	勤儉
qingmiao	青苗
Qingshilu	清實錄
qingzhong	輕重
qiu cai	求財
Qiu Jun	丘濬
Qu	衢
quanguo jingji weiyuanhui	全國經濟委員會
qun zhi fumu	羣之父母
Ren Qiyun	任啟運
Renzong	仁宗
san jie lian shengri	三節兩生日
sanbao	三寶
Sang Hongyang	桑弘羊
shang	商
Shanghai shangxueyuan	上海商學院
shanghao	賞號
shanghui	商會
Shangren gonglun	商人公論
Shao	紹
Shaoxing	紹興

she	奢
she yi wei sheng	奢易為盛
shecang	社倉
shechi	奢侈
Shehui xuebao	社會學報
Shelin shuo	奢吝說
Shen Jiefu	沈節甫
Shen Yu	慎予
Shenbao	申報
sheng	生
shengchi rifan	生齒日繁
shengli	生利
shengshi	盛世
Shengshi weiyan	盛世危言
Shengyu yishiliutiao	聖諭一十六條
shengyuan	生員
shengzhe	生者
Shenzong	神宗
shi yi zhu xing	食衣住行
shishi qiushi	實事求是
shixue	實學
Shou Nan	壽南
Siku quanshu	四庫全書
Sima Guang	司馬光
Songjiang	松江
Songxue	宋學
Shujing	書經
Tang Shouqian	湯壽潛
Tang Zhen	唐甄
Taolu zalu	陶廬雜錄
tiandi tiaoji zhi fa	天地調劑之法
tianming	天命
Tianyan lun	天演論
tong gong yi shi, xian bu zu	通功易事，羨補不足
Tongcheng	桐城
Tonggong	同工
Tongwenbao	通問報
tongxue jianxuehui	同學間學會
tongzhengshi	通政使

Tongzhi	同治
tongzhi jingji	統治經濟
Tuipeng wuyu	推篷寤語
Wang Anshi	王安石
Wang Erjian	王爾鑑
Wang Fuzhi	王夫之
Wang Liu	王鎏
Wang Shixing	王士性
Wang Shiying	王世穎
Wang Yanan	王亚南
Wang Yuan	王源
wangdao	王道
Wanguo gongbao	萬國公報
Wei Jirui	魏際瑞
Wei Shixiao	魏士傚
Wei Xi	魏禧
Wei Yuan	魏源
Weixinpai	维新派
weizhe	為者
Wenming yu shechi	文明與奢侈
wu wei	無為
Wujiang	吳江
wuyi	無益
wuyong	無用
Wuxi	無 錫
Wuxian	吳縣
Wuxu bianfa	戊戌變法
Xian fu er hou she, xian pin er hou jian	先富而後奢，先貧而後儉
Xianbobian	賢博編
Xianfeng	咸豐
xiangyue	鄉約
xiangzhe	享者
xianrande xiankong	顯然的閑空
xianrande xiaofei	顯然的消費
xianyu weixin	咸與維新
xiao	孝
xiaofei	消費
xiaofei shehui	消費社會

xiaomin	小民
Xie Peiqiong	謝佩瓊
Xihu	西湖
ximin	細民
xin	信
xinfa	新法
xing	性
Xinjiang	新疆
xinqingnian	新青年
xinshenghuo yundong	新生活運動
Xinshenghuo yundong gangyao	新生活運動綱要
Xiongnu	匈奴
Xiuning	休寧
xuesheng chuxu yinhang	學生儲蓄銀行
Xunzi	荀子
ya	牙
yahang	牙行
yamen	衙門
Yan Fu	嚴父
Yan Yuan	顏元
Yan–Lin xuepai	顏李學派
Yantie lun	鹽鐵論
yang	養
yangmin	養民
Yangyuan	楊園
Yangzi	揚子 (or *chang jiang* 長江)
Yanzhou	兗州
Yapian zhanzheng	鴉片爭戰
Ye Quan	葉權
yi (barbarian)	夷
yi (moral, righteous)	義
Yi Chun	奕純
yi shi zhu xing	衣食住行
yi we li	以義為利
Yiban	一般
yicang	義倉
yingyung shengxi	營運生息
yitiao bianfa	一條鞭法
Yixing	宜興

yong	用
Yongzheng	雍正
You Bashi	尤拔世
You Rou	有若
youguan	游觀
youxian jieji	有閑階級
youyi	有益
youyong	有用
Yu Ziyi	俞子夷
yuan qi	元氣
yubeicang	預備倉
Yue	越
yushi	御史
yutian	玉田
Zhang Lüxiang	張履祥
Zhang Ying	张英
Zhang Zhidong	張之洞
Zhanguo	戰國
zhangminzhe yinsu weizhi	長民者因俗為治
Zhejiang xingye yinhang	浙江興業銀行
zheng	正
Zheng Guanying	鄭觀應
Zheng He	鄭和
zhifei	支費
zhiguo	治國
zhisheng xuepai	治生學派
zhong ben yi mo	重本抑末
zhong yuan	中原
Zhongguo jingji	中國經濟
Zhonghua funüjie	中華婦女界
zhongren	中人
zhongti xiyong	中體西用
zhongyun	中允
Zhou Binglin	周炳琳
Zhou Enlai	周恩來
Zhou li	周禮
Zhu Shikang	祝世康
Zhu Yun	朱筠
ziben	資本

ziqiang	自強
ziran	自然
Zizhi tongjian	資治通鑑
zongrengfu	宗人府
Zouping	邹平
Zuo Zongtang	左宗棠

Bibliography

Alitto, Guy, *The Last Confucian: Liang Shu-ming and the Chinese Dilemma of Modernity* (Berkeley, CA: University of California Press, 1986).

Appleby, Joyce, "Ideology and Theory: The Tension between Political and Economic Liberalism in Seventeenth-Century England," *The American Historical Review* 81 (1976), 499–515.

The Relentless Revolution: A History of Capitalism (New York, NY: W. W. Norton & Co., 2011).

Arrighi, Giovanni, *Adam Smith in Beijing: Lineages of the Twenty-First Century* (London and New York, NY: Verso, 2008).

The Long Twentieth Century: Money, Power, and the Origins of Our Times (London; New York, NY: Verso, 2010).

Bailey, Paul John, and Lin, Pei-yin, *Print, Profit, and Perception: Ideas, Information and Knowledge in Chinese Societies, 1895–1949* (Leiden: Brill, 2014).

Barlow, Tani, "Buying In: Advertising and the Sexy Modern Girl Icon in Shanghai in the 1920s and 1930s," in *The Modern Girl around the World: Consumption, Modernity, and Globalization*, ed. by Alys Eve Weinbaum (Durham, NC: Duke University Press, 2008), 288–316.

Beattie, Hilary J., *Land and Lineage in China: A Study of T'ung-Ch'eng County, Anhwei, in the Ming and Ch'ing Dynasties* (Cambridge: Cambridge University Press, 2009).

Boecking, Felix, 'Adam Smith in Tianjin: Yang Jingnian's Translation of *The Wealth of Nations*', in *Annual Meeting of the Association for Asian Studies* (Washington, DC, 2018).

Bol, Peter K., "Government, Society, and State: On the Political Vision of Ssu-Ma Kuang and Wang An-Shih," in *Ordering the World: Approaches to State and Society in Sung Dynasty China*, ed. by Robert P. Hymes and Schirokauer Conrad (Berkeley, CA: University of California Press, 1993), 128–192.

Bonner, Michael, "Poverty and Economics in the Qur'an," *Journal of Interdisciplinary History* 35 (2005), 391–406.

Borokh, Olga, "Liberal Economic Thought in Republican China," in *Liberalism and Chinese Economic Development: Perspectives from Europe and Asia*, ed. by Gilles Campagnolo (New York, NY: Routledge, 2016), 63–83.

Boserup, Ester, *The Conditions of Agricultural Growth: The Economics of Agrarian Change under Population Pressure* (New Brunswick, NJ: Aldine Transaction, 2005).

Brokaw, Cynthia Joanne, *The Ledgers of Merit and Demerit: Social Change and Moral Order in Late Imperial China* (Princeton, NJ: Princeton University Press, 2014).

Brook, Timothy, *The Confusions of Pleasure: Commerce and Culture in Ming China* (Berkeley and Los Angeles, CA: University of California Press, 2011).

Cai Yuanpei (Zimin), "Wenming yu shechi," *Lüou zazhi* (November 15, 1916), 1–3.

Chaffee, John W., *The Thorny Gates of Learning in Sung China: A Social History of Examinations* (Albany, NY: State University of New York Press, 1995).

Chakrabarty, Dipesh, *Provincializing Europe: Postcolonial Thought and Historical Difference* (Princeton, NJ, and Oxford: Princeton University Press, 2008).

Chen Guodong, "Youguan Lu Ji de 'Jinshebian' zhi yanjiu suosheji de xueli wenti," *Xinshixue* 5 (1994), 159–179.

Chen Hansheng, *Gung Ho! The Story of the Chinese Cooperatives* (New York, NY: American Institute of Pacific Relations, 1947).

Chen Hansheng, Chin Chien-yin, and Zhongguo jingji tongji yanjiu suo, *Industrial Capital and Chinese Peasants: Chen Han-Seng. A Study of the Rural Economy of Wuhing, Chekiang (1939)* (New York, NY: Garland, 1980).

Cheng Yi and Cheng Hao, *Ercheng yishu* (Shanghai: Shanghai guji chubanshe, 2000).

Chen Yongqin, *Zhongguo jingji sixiangshi* (Zhengzhou: Henan renmin chubanshe 2008).

Chiang Kai-shek, "Xinshenghuo yundong gangyao (May 15, 1934)," in *Zongtong Jianggong sixiang yanlun zongji* (Taipei: Zhongguo guomindang zhongyang weiyuanhui dangshiwei yuanhui, 1984a), 154–170.

"Xinshenghuo yundong dier qimude he gongzuo baogao yaozhi (February 19, 1936)," in *Zongtong Jianggong sixiang yanlun zongji* (Taipei: Zhongguo guomindang zhongyang weiyuanhui dangshiwei yuanhui, 1984b), 63–71.

"Xinshenghuo yundong sanzhounian jinian gao quangguo tongbao shu (February 19, 1937)," in *Zongtong Jianggong sixiang yanlun zongji* (Taipei: Zhongguo guomindang zhongyang weiyuanhui dangshiwei yuanhu, 1984c), 207–212.

Chiang Yung-chen, *Social Engineering and the Social Sciences in China* (Cambridge: Cambridge University Press, 2001).

Chin, Tamara T., *Savage Exchange: Han Imperialism, Chinese Literary Style, and the Economic Imagination* (Cambridge, MA: Harvard-Yenching Institute, 2014).

Clunas, Craig, *Superfluous Things: Material Culture and Social Status in Early Modern China* (Honolulu, HI: University of Hawaii Press, 2016).

Coble, Parks M., *Facing Japan: Chinese Politics and Japanese Imperialism, 1931–1937* (Cambridge, MA: Council on East Asian Studies, Harvard University, distributed by Harvard University Press, 1991).

Cochran, Sherman, "Transnational Origins of Advertising in Early Twentieth-Century China," in *Inventing Nanjing Road: Commercial Culture in Shanghai, 1900–1945*, ed. by Sherman Cochran (Ithaca, NY: East Asia Program, Cornell University, 1999).

Inventing Nanjing Road: Commercial Culture in Shanghai, 1900–1945 (Ithaca, NY: East Asia Program, Cornell University, 2004).

Chinese Medicine Men: Consumer Culture in China and Southeast Asia (Cambridge, MA: Harvard University Press, 2006).

Cohen, Paul A., *Discovering History in China: American Historical Writing on the Recent Chinese Past* (New York, NY: Columbia University Press, 2010).

Confucius and Lau, D. C., *The Analects [of] Confucius* (Harmondsworth: Penguin Books, 1979).

Confucius and Legge, James, *The Confucian Analects, the Great Learning, & the Doctrine of the Mean* (Mineola, NY: Dover Publications, 2013).

Dai Yingcong, "The Qing State, Merchants, and the Military Labor Force in the Jinchuan Campaigns," *Late Imperial China* 22 (2001), 35–90.

"Yingyung Shengxi: Military Entrepreneurship in the High Qing Period, 1700–1800," *Late Imperial China* 26 (2005), 1–67.

De Bary, William Theodore, and Huang Zongxi, *Waiting for the Dawn: A Plan for the Prince: Huang Tsung-hsi's Ming-i-tai-fang lu* (New York, NY: Columbia University Press, 1993).

De Bary, William Theodore, Bloom, Irene, Chan Wing-tsit, and Adler, Joseph, *Sources of Chinese Tradition, Vol. 1* (New York, NY: Columbia University Press, 1999).

De Felice, Renzo, and Ledeen, Michael Arthur, *Fascism: An Informal Introduction to Its Theory and Practice* (New Brunswick, NJ: Transaction Books, 1976).

De Vries, Jan, *The Industrious Revolution: Consumer Behavior and the Household Economy, 1650 to the Present* (Cambridge and New York, NY: Cambridge University Press, 2009).

Dikötter, Frank, *Things Modern: Material Culture and Everyday Life in China* (London: C. Hurst & Co. Ltd., 2007).

Dirlik, Arif, "The Ideological Foundations of the New Life Movement: A Study in Counterrevolution," *Journal of Asian Studies* 34 (1975), 945–980.

Dreyer, Edward L., *Zheng He China and the Oceans in the Early Ming Dynasty, 1405–1433* (New York, NY: Pearson Longman, 2010).

Duara, Prasenjit, *Culture, Power, and the State: Rural North China, 1900–1942* (Stanford, CA: Stanford University Press, 1991).

Dunstan, Helen, *State or Merchant: Political Economy and Political Process in 1740s China* (Cambridge, MA: Harvard University Press, 2006).

"A Different Trajectory: Market-Consciousness in Chinese Political Economy, 800–1800," *Journal of Chinese History* (n.d.), 1–29, doi:10.1017/jch.2019.21.

Ebrey, Patricia Buckley, *Women and the Family in Chinese History* (London: Routledge, 2005).

Elman, Benjamin A., *From Philosophy to Philology: Intellectual and Social Aspects of Change in Late Imperial China* (Cambridge, MA: Harvard University Press, 1984).

On Their Own Terms: Science in China, 1550–1900 (Cambridge, MA: Harvard University Press, 2005).

Civil Examinations and Meritocracy in Late Imperial China (Cambridge, MA: Harvard University Press, 2013).

Eltis, David, and Engerman, Stanley L., "The Importance of Slavery and the Slave Trade to Industrializing Britain," *The Journal of Economic History* 60 (2000), 123–144.

Elvin, Mark, *The Pattern of the Chinese Past: A Social and Economic Interpretation* (Stanford, CA: Stanford University Press, 1973).

Ermis, Fatih, *A History of Ottoman Economic Thought: Developments before the Nineteenth Century* (Abingdon and New York, NY: Routledge, 2014).

Fan Bihui, "Lun jianyue yu shechi," *Tonggong* (April 1934), 16–20.

Fashishan, "Tao lu za lu," in *Xuxiu siku quanshu* (Shanghai: Shanghai guji chubanshe, 1997).

Feng Guifen, "Chong jie jian yi." *Jiaobinlu kangyi*, in *Jindai zhongguo shiliao congkan, series 62* (Taipei: Wenhai chubanshe), Vol. 612, 133–136.

Ferlanti, Federica, "The New Life Movement in Jiangxi Province, 1934–1938," *Modern Asian Studies* 44 (2010), 961–1000.

Frank, Andre Gunder, *ReOrient: Global Economy in the Asian Age* (Berkeley, CA: University of California Press, 2008).

"Fuguo yangmince: dierzhang, lunwuzhi youyi yurenzhang," *Wanguo gongbao* 4 (1892), 30–36.

Gale, Esson M., *Discourses on Salt and Iron: A Debate on State Control of Commerce and Industry in Ancient China* (Taipei: Ch'eng Wen, 1973).

Gallagher, John, and Robinson, Ronald, "The Imperialism of Free Trade," *The Economic History Review* 6 (1953), 1–15.

Gao Wangling, *Qianlong shisannian* (Beijing: Jingji kexue chubanshe, 2012).

Garon, Sheldon, "Fashioning a Culture of Diligence and Thrift: Savings and Frugality Campaigns in Japan, 1900–1930," in *Japan's Competing Modernities: Issues in Culture and Democracy, 1900–1930*, ed. by Sharon A. Minichiello (Honolulu, HI: University of Hawaii Press, 1988), 312–333.

Gerschenkron, Alexander, "Backwardness in Historical Perspective," in *Backwardness in Historical Perspective: A Book of Essays*, ed. by Alexander Gerschenkron (Cambridge, MA: Belknap Press, 1976), 5–30.

Gerth, Karl, *China Made: Consumer Culture and the Creation of the Nation* (Cambridge, MA: Harvard University Asia Center, 2003).

Gide, Charles, and Jianzu Wang, *Jite jingjixue* (Shanghai: Shangwu yinshuguan, 1929).

Gide, Charles, Long, Cedric Bright, and Warbasse, James Peter, *Consumers' Co-operative Societies* (New York, NY: A. A. Knopf, 1922).

Giersch, C. Patterson, "Commerce and Empire in the Borderlands: How Do Merchants and Trade Fit into Qing Frontier History?," *Frontiers of History in China* 9 (2014), 361–383.

Gordon, Andrew, "Consumption, Leisure and the Middle Class in Transwar Japan," *Social Science Japan Journal* 10 (2007), 1–21.

Gordon, Barry, "Aristotle and Hesiod: The Economic Problem in Greek Thought," *Review of Social Economy Review of Social Economy* 21 (1963), 147–156.

Guanzi, Liu Xiang, and Rickett, W. Allyn, *Guanzi: Political, Economic, and Philosophical Essays from Early China*. Vol. 2 (Princeton, NJ: Princeton University Press, 1998).

Hao Ran, "Yulun yiban: Shehui shechi," *Tongwenbao* 41 (February 1927), 15 (1273).

Harvard University, Academia Sinica, and Peking University, *China Biographical Database*, https://projects.iq.harvard.edu/cbdb.

Hayami, Akira, "Joron: keizaishakai no seiritsu to sonotokushutu," in *Searching for a New Historical View of the Edo Era (Atarashii Edo-Jidaishizō wo Motomete)*, ed. by Socio-Economic History and Society (Tokyo: Toyo Keizai Shimposha, 1977), 3–18.

Japan's Industrious Revolution: Economic and Social Transformations in the Early Modern Period (Tokyo: Springer, 2016).

Hayford, Charles Wishart, *To the People: James Yen and Village China* (New York, NY: Columbia University Press, 1990).

Heilbroner, Robert L., *The Worldly Philosophers: The Lives, Times, and Ideas of the Great Economic Thinkers* (New York, NY: Touchstone, 1999).

Hirschman, Albert O., *The Passions and the Interests: Political Arguments for Capitalism before Its Triumph* (Princeton, NJ: Princeton University Press, 1977).

Hong Liangji, *Juanshige ji* (Taipei: Taiwan Zhonghua shuju, 1965).

Hont, Istvan, "The Early Enlightenment Debate on Commerce and Luxury," in *The Cambridge History of Eighteenth-Century Political Thought*, ed. by Mark Goldie and Robert Wokler (Cambridge: Cambridge University Press, 2006), 377–418.

Horowitz, Daniel, *The Morality of Spending: Attitudes toward the Consumer Society in America, 1875–1940* (Chicago, IL: I. R. Dee, 1992).

Hsiao Kung-ch'uan, *A Modern China and a New World* (Seattle, WA: University of Washington Press, 1975).

Hu Jichuang, *Zhongguo jingji sixiangshi* (Shanghai: Shanghai caijing daxue chubanshe, 1998).

Huang, Philip C., *The Peasant Family and Rural Development in the Yangzi Delta, 1350–1988* (Stanford, CA: Stanford University Press, 1990).

Huang, Ray, *1587: A Year of No Significance: The Ming Dynasty in Decline* (London: Yale University Press, 1982).

Huang Zongxi and Shen Shanhong, "Ming yi dai fang lu," in *Huang Zongxi quanji* (Hangzhou: Zhejiang guji chubanshe, 1965), 1–47.

Hummel, Arthur W., *Eminent Chinese of the Ch'ing Period (1644–1912)* (Taipei: SMC, 1991).

Hymes, Robert P., "Moral Duty and Self-Regulating Process in Southern Sung Views of Famine Relief," in *Ordering the World: Approaches to State and Society in Sung Dynasty China*, ed. by Robert P. Hymes and Schirokauer Conrad (Berkeley, CA: University of California Press, 1993), 280–309.

Johnson, Chalmers A., *MITI and the Japanese Miracle: The Growth of Industrial Policy: 1925–1975* (Stanford, CA: Stanford University Press, 2012).

Johnson, Jerah, "The Role of Spending in Physiocratic Theory," *The Quarterly Journal of Economics* 80 (1966), 616–632.

Johnson, Wallace S., "Sumptuary Laws in Chinese Law," in *The Oxford International Encyclopedia of Legal History*, ed. by Stanley Nider Katz (Oxford: Oxford University Press, 2009).

Karl, Rebecca E., *The Magic of Concepts: History and the Economic in Twentieth-Century China* (Durham, NC: Duke University Press, 2017).

Keay, John, *China: A History* (London: Harper Press, 2008).

Kirby, William C., "Engineering China: Birth of the Developmental State, 1928–1937," in *Becoming Chinese: Passages to Modernity and Beyond*, ed. by Wen-hsin Yeh (Berkeley, CA: University of California Press, 2000), 137–160.

Kishimoto-Nakayama, Mio, "The Kangxi Depression and Early Qing Local Markets," *Modern China* 10 (1984), 227–256.

Lai Jiancheng, *Liang Qichao de jingji mianxiang* (Hangzhou: Zhejiang da xue chu ban she, 2010).

Lanza, Fabio, *Behind the Gate: Inventing Students in Beijing* (New York, NY: Columbia University Press, 2010).

Laozi and Lau, D. C., *Tao te ching* (Baltimore, MD: Penguin Books, 1963).

Lears, T. J. Jackson, *Fables of Abundance: A Cultural History of Advertising in America* (New York, NY: Basic Books, 1994).

Lee, Leo Ou-fan, *Shanghai Modern: The Flowering of a New Urban Culture in China, 1930–1945* (Cambridge, MA: Harvard University Press, 2001).

Lenin, Vladimir Ilyich, "Imperialism, the Highest Stage of Capitalism," in *Selected Works* (Mowscow: Progress Publisher, 1963), 667–766.

Leonard, Jane Kate, *Wei Yuan and China's Rediscovery of the Maritime World* (Cambridge, MA: Council on East Asian Studies, Harvard University, Distributed by Harvard University Press, 1984).

"The State's Resources and the People's Livelihood (*Guoji minsheng*): The Daoguang Emperor's Dilemmas about the Grand Canal Restoration, 1825," in *To Achieve Security and Wealth: The Qing Imperial State and the Economy, 1644–1911*, ed. by Jane Kate Leonard and John R. Watt (Ithaca, NY: East Asia Program, Cornell University, 1992), 47–73.

Leonard, Jane Kate, and Watt, John R., *To Achieve Security and Wealth: The Qing Imperial State and the Economy, 1644–1911* (Ithaca, NY: East Asia Program, Cornell University, 1993).

Levine, Ari, "Che-tsung's Reign (1085–1100) and the Age of Faction," in *The Cambridge History of China, The Sung Dynasty and Its Precursors, 907–1279, Part 1*, ed. by Denis Crispin Twitchett and Paul Jakov Smith (Cambridge: Cambridge University Press, 2009), 556–643.

Levine, Marilyn Avra, *The Found Generation: Chinese Communists in Europe during the Twenties* (Seattle, WA: University of Washington, 1993).

Li Bozhong, *Jiangnan de zaoqi gongyehua* (Beijing: Zhongguo renmin taxue chubanshe, 2010).

Li Gong, "Ping shu ding," in *Congshu jicheng chubian* (Shanghai: Shangwu yinshuguan, 1937).

Li Jianhua, "Shechi shenghuo zhi shehuixue de guancha," *Shehui xuebao* 2 (4)(1930), 1–11.

Li, Lillian M., *Fighting Famine in North China: State, Market, and Environmental Decline, 1690s–1990s* (Stanford, CA: Stanford University Press, 2007).

Lien Lingling, *Dazao xiaofei tiantang: baihuo gongsi yu jindai Shanghai chengshi wenhua* (Taipei: Zhongyanyuan jinshisuo, 2017).

Liang Qichao, *Xinminshuo* (1902).

Lin Liyue, "Lu Ji (1515–1552) Chongshe sixiang zaitang–jianglun jinnian mingqing jingji sixiangshi yanjiu de jige wenti," *Xinshixue* 5 (1995), 131–153.

"'Jianjiatang gao' yu Lu Ji 'Fan jinshe' sixiang zhi chuanyan," *Mingren wenji yu Mingdai yanjiu xuehui* (Taipei: Zhongguo Mingdai yanjiu xuehui, 2001), 121–134.

Lin Man-Houng, *China Upside Down: Currency, Society, and Ideologies, 1808–1856* (Cambridge, MA: Harvard University Asia Center, 2006).

Lin, Zoe Shan, "'Favoring Their Own': Grain Embargoes in Southern Song China," *Journal of Song-Yuan Studies* 46 (2016), 169–208.

Liu Junren, *Zhongguo diming dacidian* (Taipei: Wenhai chubanshe, 1990).

Liu Qingshan, "Hong Liangji yu Fa Shishan jiayou kaoshu," *Wenhua yu chuabo* 1(212), 8–12.

Liu, Andrew B., *Tea War: A History of Capitalism in India and China* (New Haven, CT: Yale University Press, 2020).

Liu, William Guanglin, *The Chinese Market Economy, 1000–1500* (Albany, NY: State University of New York Press, 2015).

Liu Zhonghua, "Qingchu xuezhe wang yuan de jingshi sixiang ji qi xhueshu minyun," *Tangdu xuekan* 27 (2011), 75–80.

Loewe, Michael, "The Former Han Dynasty," in *The Cambridge History of China. Vol. 1, The Chin and Han Empires 221* BC–AD *220*, ed. by Denis Crispin Twitchett and Michael Loewe (Cambridge: Cambridge University Press, 2008), 103–122.

Lowry, S. Todd, *Pre-Classical Economic Thought: From the Greeks to the Scottish Enlightenment* (Boston, MA: Kluwer, 1995).

Lu Ji, "Jinshebian," *Jianjiatang gao* in *Jilu huibian, Vol. 204* (Taipei: Taiwan shangwu yinsuguan, 1969), 2–4.

Lu Yan, "Challenges of Transition: Chinese Industrial Cooperatives from War to Peace," in *Annual Meeting of the Association for Asian Studies* (Washington, DC: 2018).

Lu Zuqian, Zhu Xi, Chan Wing-tsit, and American Council of Learned Societies, *Reflections on Things at Hand: The Neo-Confucian Anthology* (New York, NY: Columbia University Press, 1967).

Luo Dajing, *Helin yulu* (thirteenth-century edition of Wang Ruilai, Beijing: Zhonghua shuju, 1983).

Luo Weidong, "Scholarship on Adam Smith in China," *The Adam Smith Review* 9 (2015), 237–251.

MacCormack, Geoffrey. "Filial Piety and the Pre-T'ang Law," *Fundamina: A Journal of Legal History* 8 (2002), 137–164.

Mandeville, Bernard, *The Fable of the Bees or Private Vices, Publick Benefits. Newly edited, with an introduction, by Irwin Primer*. Vol. 1 (New York, NY: Capricorn Books, 1962).

Mann Jones, Susan, and Kuhn, Philip, "Dynastic Decline and the Roots of Rebellion," in *The Cambridge History of China*, ed. by John K. Fairbank (Cambridge: Cambridge University Press, 1978), 197–62.

Mann, Susan, *Local Merchants and the Chinese Bureaucracy, 1750–1950* (Stanford, CA: Stanford University Press, 1987).

Mao Zedong, "Be Concerned with the Well-Being of the Masses, Pay Attention to Methods of Work (January 27, 1934)," in *Selected Works of Mao Zedong*, Marxist Internet Archives www.marxists.org/reference/archive/mao/selected-works/volume-1/mswv1_10.htm (accessed on December 10, 2019).

"Our Economic Policy (January 23, 1934)," in *Selected Works of Mao Zedong*, Marxist Internet Archives www.marxists.org/reference/archive/mao/selected-works/volume-5/mswv5_58.htm (accessed on December 10, 2019).

"On the Correct Handling of Contradictions among the People (February 27, 1957)," in *Selected Works of Mao Zedong*, Marxist Internet Archives www.marxists.org/reference/archive/mao/selected-works/volume-5/mwv5_58.htm (accessed on December 10, 2019).

McMahon, Daniel, "Dynastic Decline, Heshen, and the Ideology of the Xianyu Reforms," *Tsing Hua Journal of Chinese Studies, New Series* 38 (June 2008), 231–255.

McMorran, Ian, *The Passionate Realist: An Introduction to the Life and Political Thought of Wang Fuzhi (1619–1692)* (Hong Kong: Sunshine Book Company, 1992).

Mencius, Bloom, Irene, and Ivanhoe, P. J., *Mencius* (New York, NY: Columbia University Press, 2011).

Merkel-Hess, Kate, *The Rural Modern: Reconstructing the Self and State in Republican China* (Chicago, IL: University of Chicago Press, 2016).

Meskill, John Thomas, *Gentlemanly Interests and Wealth on the Yangtze Delta* (Ann Arbor, MI: Association for Asian Studies, 1994).

Meyer-Fong, Tobie, *Building Culture in Early Qing Yangzhou* (Stanford, CA: Stanford University Press, 2003).

Ming Gao, "Shijiu shiji xiaofei," *Shangren gonglun* 17 (1933), 7–8.

Mitchell, Timothy, *Rule of Experts: Egypt, Techno-Politics, Modernity* (Berkeley, CA: University of California Press, 2012).
Mokyr, Joel, *A Culture of Growth: The Origins of the Modern Economy* (Princeton, NJ: Princeton University Press, 2017).
Nankai Social and Economic Quarterly (Tientsin, China: Nankai Institute of Economics, Nankai University, 1935–7).
Needham, Joseph, *The Grand Titration: Science and Society in East and West* (London: G. Allen and Unwin, 1969).
O'Bryan, Scott, *The Growth Idea: Purpose and Prosperity in Postwar Japan* (Honolulu, HI: University of Hawaii Press, 2009).
Paulicelli, Eugenia, *Fashion under Fascism: Beyond the Black Shirt* (New York, NY: Berg, 2004).
Peng Nansheng, *Zhongjian jingji: Zhuantong yu xiandai zhijian de Zhongguo jindai shougongye = An Economy of Intermediate Form; The Handicraft Industry between Tradition and Modernity in Modern China, 1840–1936* (Beijing: Gaodeng jiaoyu chubanshe, 2002).
Bangongyehua: jindai zhongguo xiangcun shougongye de fazhan yu shehui bianqian (Beijing: Zhonghua shuju, 2007).
Pomeranz, Kenneth, *The Making of a Hinterland: State, Society, and Economy in Inland North China, 1853–1937* (Berkeley, CA: University of California Press, 1993).
The Great Divergence: China, Europe, and the Making of the Modern World Economy (Princeton, NJ: Princeton University Press, 2000).
"Political Economy and Ecology on the Eve of Industrialization: Europe, China, and the Global Conjuncture," *American Historical Review* 107 (2002), 425–446.
"Beyond the East–West Binary: Resituating Development Paths in the Eighteenth-Century World," *The Journal of Asian Studies* 61 (2002), 539–590.
Qian Yong, *Lüyuan conghua* (Taipei: Dali chubanshe, 1982).
Qingshilu (Beijing: Zhonghua shuju, 1985).
Ren Qiyun, "Jingyan jianyi wupian," in *Wangchao jingshi wenbian*, ed. by He Changling (accessed through http://hanji.sinica.edu.tw/).
Roncaglia, Alessandro, *A Brief History of Economic Thought* (Cambridge: Cambridge University Press, 2017).
Rostow, Walt Whitman, *The Stages of Economic Growth, a Non-Communist Manifesto* (Cambridge: Cambridge University Press, 1960).
Rothschild, Emma, *Economic Sentiments: Adam Smith, Condorcet, and the Enlightenment* (Cambridge, MA: Harvard University Press, 2001).
Rowe, William T., *Saving the World: Chen Hongmou and Elite Consciousness in Eighteenth-Century China* (Stanford, CA: Stanford University Press, 2002).

"Bao Shichen and Agrarian Reform in Early Nineteenth-Century China," *Frontiers of History in China* 9 (2014), 1–31.

Speaking of Profit: Bao Shichen and Reform in Nineteenth-Century China (Cambridge, MA: Harvard University Asia Center, 2018).

Rwaski, Evelyn S., "The Qing Formation and the Early-Modern Period," in *The Qing Formation in World-Historical Time*, ed. by Lynn A. Struve (Cambridge, MA: Harvard University Asia Center: Distributed by Harvard University Press, 2004), 207–241.

"Shengchan yu xiaofei xiangguan shuo," *Shenbao* (August 26, 1907), 2–3.

Schmitt, Carl, and Seitzer, Jeffrey *Legality and Legitimacy (1932)* (Durham, NC: Duke University Press, 2004).

Schneider, Helen M., *Keeping the Nation's House: Domestic Management and the Making of Modern China* (Vancouver: UBC Press, 2011).

Schwartz, Benjamin Isadore, *In Search of Wealth and Power: Yen Fu and the West* (Cambridge, MA: The Belknap Press of Harvard University Press, 1964).

Semmel, Bernard, *Rise of Free Trade Imperialism: Classical Political Economy, the Empire of Free Trade and Imperialism 1750–1850* (Cambridge: Cambridge University Press, 1970).

Sheehan, Brett, *Industrial Eden: A Chinese Capitalist Vision* (Cambridge, MA: Harvard University Press, 2015).

Shen Yu, "Zhizu zai jie shechi shu,'" *Dianzheng zhoukan* 31(March 1928), 1–3.

Shou Nan, "Xiaofei jieyue," *Qingnian yuekan* 2(1936), 2–3.

Smail, Daniel Lord, and Shryock, Andrew, "History and the 'Pre'," *The American Historical Review* 118 (2013), 709–737.

Smith, Adam, and Reich, Robert, *The Wealth of Nations* (New York, NY: Modern Library, 2000).

Smith, Paul Jakov, *Taxing Heaven's Storehouse: Horses, Bureaucrats, and the Destruction of the Sichuan Tea Industry, 1074–1224* (Cambridge, MA: Council on East Asian Studies, Harvard University, 1992).

"Shen-Tsung's Reign and the New Policies of Wang An-Shih, 1067–1085," in *The Cambridge History of China*, ed. by Denis Crispin Twitchett and Paul Jakov Smith (New York, NY: Cambridge University Press, 2008), 347–483.

Smith, Richard J., *China's Cultural Heritage: The Qing Dynasty, 1644–1912* (Boulder, CO: Westview Press, 1994).

Song, Jaeyoon, *Traces of Grand Peace: Classics and State Activism in Imperial China* (Cambridge, MA: Harvard University Asia Center, 2015).

Stearns, Peter N., *Consumerism in World History* (London: Routledge, 2006).

Sun E-tu Zen, "The Finance Ministry (Hubu) and Its Relationship to the Private Economy in Qing Times," in *To Achieve Security and Wealth: The Qing Imperial State and the Economy, 1644–1911*, ed. by Jane Kate Leonard and John R. Watt (Ithaca, NY: East Asia Program, Cornell University, 1992), 9–20.

Sun Yat-sen, *Sun Wen xuanji*. ed. by Yan Huang (Guangzhou Shi: Guangdong renmin chubanshe, [1924] 2006).

Suzuki, Chusei, *Shinchō Chūkishi Kenkyū* (Toyohashi-shi: Aichi Daigaku Kokusai Mondai Kenkyujo, 1952).

Tang Zhen, *Qian Shu* (Taipei: Heluo tushu chubanshe 1974).

Tawney, Richard Henry, *Land and Labor in China* (Boston, MA: Beacon Press, [1932] 1966).

The Acquisitive Society (Charleston, SC: BiblioBazaar, [1920] 2008).

Tawney, Richard Henry, and Wu Zhizhuang, *Jindai gongye shehui de binli* (Shanghai: Shangwu yinshuguan, 1928).

Taylor, Frederick Winslow, *The Principles of Scientific Management* (New York, NY: Productivity Press, 2017).

Taylor, Frederick Winslow, and Yokokawa, Tamisuke, *Kagakuteki keieihō genri* (Tokyo: Yokokawatamisuke, 1912).

Todeschini, Giacomo, "Theological Roots of the Medieval/Modern Merchants' Self-Representation," in *The Self-Perception of Early Modern Capitalists*, ed. by Margaret C. Jacob and Catherine Secretan (New York, NY: Palgrave Macmillan, 2008), 17–48.

Franciscan Wealth: From Voluntary Poverty to Market Society, ed. by Michael F. Cusato, Jean François Godet-Calogeras, and Daria Mitchell (Saint Bonaventure, NY: Franciscan Institute, Saint Bonaventure University, 2009).

Todeschini, Giacomo, Mitchell, Daria, Godet-Calogeras, Jean François, and Cusato, Michael F., *Franciscan Wealth from Voluntary Poverty to Market Society* (Saint Bonaventure, NY: Franciscan Institute, Saint Bonaventure University, 2009).

Trescott, Paul B., *Jingji Xue: The History of the Introduction of Western Economic Ideas into China, 1850–1950* (Hong Kong: Chinese University Press, 2007).

Tsai Weipin, *Reading Shenbao* (London: Palgrave Macmillan, 2010).

Tsai Weipin and Lin Pei-yin, *Print, Profit, and Perception* (Leiden: Brill, 2014).

Van de Ven, Hans J., *Breaking with the Past: The Maritime Customs Service and the Global Origins of Modernity in China* (New York, NY: Columbia University Press, 2014).

Veblen, Thorstein, *The Theory of the Leisure Class* (Oxford: Oxford University Press, [1920] 2008).

Veblen, Thorstein Bunde, and Ono, Shinzo, *Yukan kaikyuron* (Tokyo: Jiryusha, 1924).

Von Glahn, Richard, *Fountain of Fortune: Money and Monetary Policy in China, 1000–1700* (Berkeley, CA: University of California Press, 1996).

The Economic History of China: From Antiquity to the Nineteenth Century (Cambridge: Cambridge University Press, 2016).

Wang Fuzhi, and Nie Shiquan, *Huang shu* (Beijing: Beijing daxue chubanshe, 2014).

Wang Fuzhi, *Du tong jian lun*. 30 Vols., Vol. 24 (Taipei Shi: Shijie shuju, 1962).

Wang Fuzhi and Shiquan Nie, *Huang shu* (Beijing: Beijing daxue chubanshe, 2014).

Wang Shiying, "Xiaofeipai yu shengchanpai," *Jiangsu dangwu zhoukan* 24 (1930), 78–82.

"Xiaofeizhe de faxian," *Hezuo yuekan* 6(6) (1934), 3–5.

Wang Wensheng, *White Lotus Rebels and South China Pirates: Crisis and Reform in the Qing Empire* (Cambridge, MA: Harvard University Press, 2014).

Wang Xueping, "Rujia de jiejian zhizu xiaofeiguan ji qi xiandai jiazhi," *Shehui kexuejia* 2 (2010), 32–35.

Wei Yuan, *Wei Yuan ji* (Beijing: Zhonghua shuju, 1983).

Weibulin, T., and Yimo Hu, *Youxian jieji lun: Shehui zhidu zhi jingjixue de yanjiu* (Shanghai: Zhong huashuju, 1932).

Weston, Timothy B, *The Power of Position: Beijing University, Intellectuals, and Chinese Political Culture, 1898–1929* (Berkeley, CA: University of California Press, 2004).

Will, Pierre-Etienne, *Bureaucracy and Famine in Eighteenth-Century China* (Stanford, CA: Stanford University Press, 1990).

Will, Pierre-Etienne, and Wong, Roy Bin, *Nourish the People: The State Civilian Granary System in China, 1650–1850* (Ann Arbor, MI: Center for Chinese Studies, University of Michigan, 1991).

Wong, Roy Bin, "Chinese Traditions of Grain Storage," in *Nourish the People: The State Civilian Granary System in China, 1650–1850*, ed. by Pierre-Etienne Will, Roy Bin Wong, and James Z. Lee (Ann Arbor, MI: Center for Chinese Studies, University of Michigan, 1991), 1–16.

China Transformed: Historical Change and the Limits of European Experience (Ithaca, NY: Cornell University Press, 2014).

Wu Baosan and Li Puguo, *Zhongguo jingji sixiangshi zi liao xuanji, Ming Qing bufen* (Beijing: Zhongguo shehui kexue chubanshe, 1990).

Wu Jen-shu, *Pinwei shehua: wanMing de xiaofei shehui yu shidaifu* (Beijing: Zhonghua shuju, 2008).

Youyou fangxiang: MingQing jiangnan chengshi de xiuxian xiaofei yu kongjian bianqian (Beijing: Zhonghua shuju, 2017).

Wu Jen-shu and Wang Dagang, "A Preliminary Study of Local Consumption in the Qianlong Reign (1736–1796): The Case of Ba County in Sichuan Province," in *Living the Good Life: Consumption in the Qing and Ottoman Empires of the Eighteenth Century*, ed. by Elif Akçetin and Suraiya Faroqhi (Leiden: Brill, 2018), 187–212.

Xia Yande, *Zhongguo jinbainian jingji sixiang* (Shanghai: Shanghai shudian, 1989).

Xiao Gongquan, *A History of Chinese Political Thought* (Princeton, NJ: Princeton University Press, 1978).

Xie Peiqiong, "Jie shechi shuo," *Zhonghua funüjie* 2(5) (1916), 2–3.

Xu Youchun, *Minguo renwu dacidian* (Shijiazhuang: Hebei renmin chubanshe, 1991).

Xunzi and Hutton, Eric L., *Xunzi: The Complete Text* (Princeton, NJ: Princeton University Press, 2014).

Yang Lien-sheng, "Economic Justification for Spending–An Uncommon Idea in Traditional China," *Harvard Journal of Asiatic Studies* 20 (1957), 36–52.

Ye Shichang, "Wei Yuan yu 'Tui peng wu yu,'" in *Zhongguo jingji sixiangshi lunwen*, ed. by Shanghaishi jingji xuehui zhongguo jingji sixiangshi yanyouhui (Shanghai: Shanghai shehui kexueyuan chubanshe, 1986), 266–269.

Gudai zhongguo jingji sixiangshi (Shanghai: Fudan Daxue chubanshe, 2003).

Yeh Wen-Hsin, *Shanghai Splendor: Economic Sentiments and the Making of Modern China, 1843–1949* (Berkeley, CA: University of California Press, 2007).

"Yiban de hua: Shechi de zhongguoren," *Yiban* (September 1928), 148–151.

Yong, Qian, "Lüyuan cong hua," in *Xuxiu siku quanshu* (Shanghai: Shanghai guji chubanshe, 1997).

Yu Li, "Social Change during the Ming–Qing Transition and the Decline of Sichuan Classical Learning in the Early Qing," *Late Imperial China* 19 (1998), 26–55.

Yu Ziyi, "Shechi," *Shenghuo* 1 (1925), 79–78.

Yun Jing, *Dayun shanfang ji* (Taipei: Taiwan Zhonghua shu ju, 1965).

Zanasi, Margherita, "Far from the Treaty Ports: Fang Xianting and the Idea of Rural Modernity in 1930s China," *Modern China* 30 (2004), 113–146.

Saving the Nation: Economic Modernity in Republican China (Chicago, IL: University of Chicago Press, 2006).

"Fostering the People's Livelihood: Chinese Political Thought between Empire and Nation," *Twentieth-Century China* 30 (2013), 6–38.

"Western Utopias, Missionary Economics, and the Chinese Village," *Journal of World History* 24 (2013), 359–387.

"Frugality and Luxury: Morality, Market, and Consumption in Late Imperial China," *Frontiers of History China* 10 (2015), 457–485.

"Frugal Modernity: Livelihood and Consumption in Republican China," *The Journal of Asian Studies* 74 (2015), 391–409.

Zelin, Madeleine, *The Magistrate's Tael: Rationalizing Fiscal Reform in Eighteenth-Century Ching China* (Berkeley, CA: University of California Press, 1992).

The Merchants of Zigong: Industrial Entrepreneurship in Early Modern China (New York, NY: Columbia University Press, 2008).

Zhang Hao, *Liang Ch'i-ch'ao and Intellectual Transition in China, 1890–1907* (Cambridge, MA: Harvard University Press, 1971).

Zhang Li, "Jiangxi nongcun fuwu shiye 1934–1945," in *Kangzhan jianguoshi yanjiu taohui lunwen ji, 1937–1945* (Nangan: Zhongyang yanjiuyuan jindaishi yanjiusuo, 1985), 1035–1057.

Zhang Ning, "Cong paomating dao renmin guangchang: Shanghai paomating shouhui yundong, 1946–1951," *Zhongyang yanjiuyuan jindaishi yanjiusuo jikan* 48 (2005), 945–980.

"Pure Sport or a Gambling Disgrace? Greyhound Racing and the Formation of Modern Shanghai," in *Creating Chinese Modernity: Knowledge and Everyday Life, 1900–1940*, ed. by Peter Zarrow (New York, NY: Peter Lang, 2007).

Zhao Erxun, *Qing shi gao* (Beijing: Zhonghua shuju, 1977).

Zhao Fengtian, *WanQing wushinian jingji sixiangshi* (Shanghai: Shanghai shu dian, 1989).

Zhao Jing, *Zhongguo gudai jingji sixiangshi jianghua* (Beijing: Renmin chubanshe: Xinhua shudian faxing, 1986).

Zheng Guanying, *Shengshi weiyan* (Taipei: Taiwan xuesheng dushu, 1965).

"Shengshi weiyan," in *Zheng Guanying ji* (Shanghai: Shanghai renmin chubanshe, 1982).

Zhongguo jingji (Nanjing: Zhongguo jingji yanjiuhui, 1933–7).

Zhu Shikang, "Xiaofei yu minsheng," *Shenghuo* 2(3) (1933), 4–5.

Index